Gill Books
Hume Avenue, Park West, Dublin 12

www.gillbooks.ie

Gill Books is an imprint of M.H. Gill & Co.

Copyright © Teapot Press Ltd 2026

ISBN: 978-1-8045-8486-6

This book was created and produced by Teapot Press Ltd

Written & Edited by Fiona Biggs
Designed by Ben Potter & Tony Potter
Picture research and additional photography by Ben Potter
Home economics by Christine Potter, Imogen Tyler & Ben Potter

Printed in PRC

This book is typeset in Garamond and Dax

All rights reserved.

No part of this publication may be copied, reproduced or transmitted in any form or by any means, without permission of the publishers.

To the best of our knowledge, this book complies in full with the requirements of the General Product Safety Regulation (GPSR). For further information and help with any safety queries, please contact us at productsafety@gill.ie

A CIP catalogue record for this book is available from the British Library.

54321

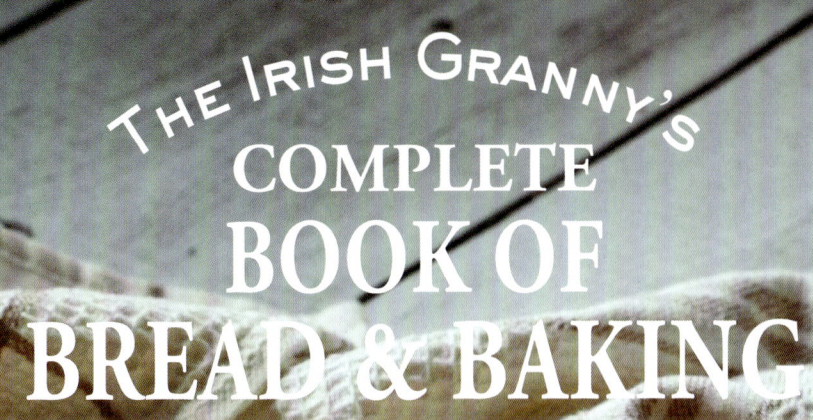

The Irish Granny's COMPLETE BOOK OF BREAD & BAKING

Fiona Biggs

OVER 200 HOMEMADE RECIPES

Gill Books

Contents

12 Introduction
14 **Bread & Scones**
16 White Soda Bread
18 Brown Soda Bread
20 Spotted Dog
22 Brown Bread
24 **Early Irish Baking Techniques**
26 Treacle Loaf
28 Oatmeal Bread
30 Seed Bread
32 Yogurt Soda Bread
34 Guinness Bread
36 Oven Boxty Bread
38 Cheese & Tomato Bread
40 Cheese & Onion Bread
42 Rye Bread
44 Cheesy Soda Bread
46 Hazelnut Bread
48 Wholemeal Walnut Bread
50 Oatmeal Soda Bread
52 Wheaten Bread
54 Kerry Treacle Bread
56 Guinness Seaweed Soda Bread
58 Wheaten Bread with Nuts, Seeds & Honey
60 Plain White Scones
62 Wholemeal Scones
64 Buttermilk Scones
66 Cheddar Cheese Scones
68 Oat Scones
70 Potato Scones
72 **Baking with Buttermilk**
74 Cinnamon Fruit Scones
76 Cherry Scones
78 Cornmeal Scones
80 Oat & Syrup Scones
82 Butter Cakes
84 Oven-baked Fadge
86 Waterford Blaa Buns
88 Belfast Baps

90 **Cakes**
92 Porter Cake
94 Banana & Walnut Loaf
96 Victoria Sponge
98 Lemon Cake
100 Seed Cake
102 Kerry Apple Cake
104 Upside-down Plum Cake
106 Fresh Plum Cake
108 Cherry Loaf
110 Ginger Cake
112 Rhubarb Cake
114 Irish Tea Cake
116 Whiskey Cake
118 Date Loaf
120 Apple & Blackberry Cake
122 Apple & Cider Cake
124 Rhubarb Streusel Cake
126 **Baking with Potatoes**
128 Spiced Potato Cake
130 Irish Mist Ring Cake
132 Cherry Cake
134 Coffee & Walnut Cake
136 Boiled Fruit Cake
138 Carrot Cake
140 Pineapple Upside-down Cake
142 Marmalade Cake
144 Buttermilk Cake
146 Orange Cake
148 Yogurt & Honey Cake
150 Gingerbread
152 Oaty Gingerbread
154 Light Cherry Cake
156 Dried Fruit Loaf
158 Date & Guinness Cake
160 Date & Walnut Loaf
162 Apple Cinnamon Cake
164 Very Easy Walnut Loaf
166 Slab Cake
168 Lemon Swiss Roll
170 Fresh Strawberry Swiss Roll
172 Magic Vanilla Custard Cake

Contents

- 174 Upside-down Pear Cake
- 176 Lemon & Raspberry Drizzle Cake
- 178 Almond & Coconut Cake
- 180 **Baking with Alcohol**
- 182 Madeira Cake
- 184 Marble Cake
- 186 Easy Fruit Loaf
- 188 Banana Fruit Loaf
- 190 Honey Cake
- 192 **Sweet Tarts, Crumbles & Pies**
- 194 Curd Tart
- 196 Jam Tart
- 198 Easy Lemon Tart
- 200 Open Apple Tart
- 202 Golden Syrup Tart
- 204 Walnut & Honey Tart
- 206 Apple Pie
- 208 Apple Charlotte
- 210 Apple Crumble
- 212 Apple Flan with Baileys
- 214 Nutty Treacle Tart
- 216 Lemon Curd & Almond Tart
- 218 Blueberry & Almond Tart
- 220 Orange & Lemon Star Tart
- 222 Apricot Tart
- 224 Banoffee Pie
- 226 Fruit Meringue Pie
- 228 Ginger & Honey Cheesecake
- 230 **Baking with Fruit**
- 232 Autumn Crumble
- 234 Rhubarb & Ginger Crumble
- 236 Vanilla Rhubarb Pie
- 238 Pear & Almond Tart
- 240 Strawberry Tart
- 242 Irish Cream Cheesecake
- 244 Gooseberry Tart
- 246 Gooseberry & Hazelnut Crumble
- 248 Apple & Almond Tart
- 250 Lemon Meringue Pie
- 252 Apple Amber
- 254 Bakewell Tart
- 256 Fruit Flan

258 Savoury Tarts & Pies
- 260 Donegal Pie
- 262 Dingle Pie
- 264 Bacon & Egg Flan
- 266 Steak & Kidney Pie with Guinness
- 268 Chicken Pie with Potato Pastry
- 270 Steak & Stout Pie
- 272 Caramelised Cherry Tomato & Goat's Cheese Tart
- 274 Shepherd's Pie
- 276 Smoked Salmon Tart
- 278 Luxury Fish Pie
- 280 Beef & Oyster Pie
- 282 Seaweed Flan
- 284 Individual Dingle Pies
- 286 Cheese & Spinach Pie
- 288 Roasted Vegetable Quiche
- 290 Salmon & Cream Cheese Tart

292 Biscuits & Buns
- 294 Crunchy Savoury Oatcakes
- 296 Ginger Nuts
- 298 Chocolate Biscuits
- 300 Dark Chocolate Oaties
- 302 Crunchy Oat Biscuits
- 304 Oaty Fruit & Nut Biscuits
- 306 Oat & Honey Crunch Biscuits
- 308 Portarlington Golden Biscuits
- 310 Porter Hope Biscuits
- 312 Coconut Biscuits
- 314 Lemon Biscuits
- 316 Hunting Nuts
- 318 Oaty Almond Biscuits
- 320 Iced Coffee Oat Biscuits
- 322 Orange Creams
- 324 Shah Biscuits
- 326 Almond Macaroons
- 328 Coffee Walnut Macaroons
- 330 Walnut Biscuits
- 332 Vanilla Biscuits
- 334 Shortbread Fingers

Contents

336 Almond Shortbread
338 Coconut Shortbread
340 Oat Shortbread
342 Coconut Biscuits
344 Sweet Oatcakes
346 Queen Cakes
348 **Baking with Oats & Other Grains**
350 Butterfly Cakes
352 Chocolate Butterfly Cakes
354 Jam Tarts
356 Meringues
358 Spiced Buns
360 Rock Buns
362 Vanilla Buns
364 Marmalade Buns
366 Cherry Buns
368 Orange & Almond Muffins
370 Buttermilk Berry Muffins
372 Lemon & Poppy Seed Muffins
374 Blackberry & Apple Muffins
376 Wholemeal Banana Muffins
378 Spiced Apple & Oat Muffins
380 **Traybakes**
382 Almond Fingers
384 Coconut Fingers
386 Apple Fingers
388 Flapjacks
390 Bakewell Flapjacks
392 Fruit Slices
394 Apricot Oat Fingers
396 Mincemeat Crumble Bars
398 Peanut Butter Bars
400 Fruity Flapjacks
402 Chocolate Chip Flapjacks
404 Hazelnut Squares
406 Gur Cake
408 Coconut & Walnut Bars
410 Currant Squares
412 Date Fingers
414 Nutty Fruit Slices

- 416 Coconut Flapjacks
- 418 Apple & Blackberry Crumble Squares
- 420 Raspberry & Coconut Squares
- 422 Apple & Walnut Squares
- 424 Cherry Bakewell Squares

426 Chocolate

- 428 Orange Chocolate Layer Cake
- 430 Chocolate Meringue Layer Cake
- 432 Chocolate Cheesecake
- 434 Chocolate Spice Cake
- 436 Chocolate Whiskey Mousse Tart
- 438 Chocolate Chiffon Pie
- 440 Chocolate Tart
- 442 Chocolate Swiss Roll
- 444 Chocolate Meringues
- 446 Chocolate Walnut Loaf
- 448 Chocolate Cherry Loaf
- 450 Chocolate & Raspberry Sandwich Cake
- 452 Chocolate Potato Cake
- 454 Chocolate & Pear Tart
- 456 Chocolate & Marmalade Bread Pudding
- 458 Sunken Chocolate Cake
- 460 Baileys Chocolate Cheesecake
- 462 Chocolate Rum Pie
- 464 Chocolate Marmalade Tart
- 466 Chocolate Pound Cake
- 468 Chocolate Banana Cake
- 470 Guinness Chocolate Cake

472 Celebration Bakes

- 474 Christmas Cake
- 476 Mince Pies
- 478 Baked Christmas Pudding
- 480 Yule Log
- 482 Christmas Stars
- 484 Mincemeat Bakewell Tart
- 486 Barmbrack with Whiskey-soaked Raisins
- 488 Barmbrack & Butter Pudding

Contents

490 Hot Cross Buns
492 Simple Simnel Cake
494 Easter Lemon Sponge
496 Easter Biscuits
498 Index
511 Conversion Charts
512 Picture Credits

Cast-iron stove at Carton House, County Kildare

INTRODUCTION

Introduction

The Irish baking tradition might seem to be confined to the delicious breads, bracks and oatcakes that could be made over an open fire using a bastible or griddle. Bread was hearty and substantial, biscuits were wholesome and sweet cakes were a very occasional treat. In the big houses, which had large range-type ovens, kitchens turned out bread, cakes and baked desserts that could rival those of any establishment in Britain or Europe.

The advent of domestic electrification in the 1950s and 1960s, coupled with a steady emigration from Ireland to the US, brought about a minor revolution in Irish kitchens. Recipes sent home from abroad for sweet bakes such as cheesecake, carrot cake and lemon meringue pie have been popular in Ireland for decades. People who had served in the kitchens of the big houses inherited recipes for British classics such as Victoria sponge, Bakewell tart and queen cakes,

and these also became part of the traditional Irish baking repertoire.

The home baker needs some basic equipment: some wooden spoons, a good rolling pin, a balloon whisk and a wire cooling rack. Use a kitchen scales or a measuring jug and spoons; you should always measure your baking ingredients. You'll need a few loaf tins in various sizes for bread, a baking sheet or tray for biscuits, a bun tin for small cakes and muffins, a medium-sized flan tin for tarts and flans and a traybake tin for bars and fingers. For larger cakes, you'll need several cake tins in a variety of shapes and sizes, some of which should be springform. When baking large cakes, always use the size and shape of tin specified in the recipe as this really does make the difference between success and failure. You don't need a lot of expensive kit, but if you're going to invest in a single piece of equipment, a good electric stand mixer will make light work of a lot of your baking tasks and will probably last a lifetime.

Once you get the baking bug, your delicious breads, scones, cakes, muffins and biscuits will make yours the most popular house in the neighbourhood.

BREAD & SCONES

Dingle seaport, County Kerry

INGREDIENTS

450 g/1 lb plain flour, plus extra for dusting
1 tsp salt
1 tsp bicarbonate of soda
400 ml/14 fl oz buttermilk

White Soda Bread

Soda bread is a distinctly Irish bread – unlike yeast bread it does not respond well to too much handling, so take care not to overwork the dough.

METHOD

Preheat the oven to 230°C/450°F/Gas Mark 8. Dust a baking sheet with flour.

Mix the dry ingredients in a large mixing bowl, then make a well in the centre and gradually add the buttermilk, drawing in the dry ingredients from the sides of the bowl. Mix until a soft dough forms.

Turn out onto a work surface lightly dusted with flour and shape into a round about 5 cm/2 inches in height. Place the round on the prepared baking sheet and use a floured knife to cut a deep cross in it.

Bake in the preheated oven for 30–45 minutes until the loaf sounds hollow when tapped on the base. Transfer to a wire rack and leave to cool completely.

MAKES 1 LOAF

INGREDIENTS

675 g/1 lb 8 oz wholemeal flour

450 g/1 lb strong white bread flour, plus extra for dusting

2 tsp bicarbonate of soda

2 tsp salt

750 m/1½ pints buttermilk, plus extra if needed

Brown Soda Bread

This is a lovely wholemeal alternative to traditional white soda bread. Wholemeal flour on its own makes a very heavy bread, so white flour is added to the mixture to lighten the texture.

METHOD

Preheat the oven to 230°C/450°F/Gas Mark 8. Dust a large baking sheet with flour.

Mix the dry ingredients in a large mixing bowl, then make a well in the centre and gradually add the buttermilk, drawing in the dry ingredients from the sides of the bowl. Mix until a soft dough forms, adding more buttermilk if necessary. The dough should not be too wet.

Turn out the dough onto a work surface lightly dusted with flour, divide into two pieces and shape both pieces into a round about 5 cm/2 inches in height. Place the rounds on the prepared baking sheet and use a floured knife to cut a deep cross in each loaf.

Bake in the preheated oven for 15–20 minutes, then reduce the oven temperature to 200°C/400°F/Gas Mark 6 and bake for a further 20–25 minutes until the loaves sound hollow when tapped on the base. Transfer them to a wire rack and leave to cool completely.

MAKES 2 LOAVES

INGREDIENTS

450 g/1 lb plain white flour, plus extra for dusting

1 tsp salt

1 tsp bicarbonate of soda

125 g/4½ oz currants, raisins or sultanas

400 ml/14 fl oz buttermilk

Spotted Dog

Currants or other dried fruit were often added to white soda bread to make the traditional 'sweet cake'.

METHOD

Preheat the oven to 230°C/450°F/Gas Mark 8. Dust a baking sheet with flour.

Mix the dry ingredients in a large mixing bowl, add the currants and stir until coated in the flour mixture, then make a well in the centre and gradually add the buttermilk, drawing in the dry ingredients from the sides of the bowl. Mix to a wet dough.

Turn out the dough onto a work surface lightly dusted with flour and shape it into a round about 5 cm/2 inches in height. Place the round on the prepared baking sheet and use a floured knife to cut a deep cross in it.

Bake in the preheated oven for 30–45 minutes until the loaf sounds hollow when tapped on the base. Transfer to a wire rack and leave to cool completely.

MAKES 1 LOAF

INGREDIENTS

vegetable oil, for greasing
1.3 kg/3 lb wholemeal flour
500 ml/18 fl oz milk, plus extra for brushing
500 ml/18 fl oz water
1 tbsp soft light brown sugar
55 g/2 oz fresh yeast
2 tsp salt

Brown Bread

A lovely nutty yeast bread with a slightly sweet flavour. It's well worth taking the time to make it with fresh yeast.

METHOD

Grease two 900-g/2-lb loaf tins and the inside of two large polythene bags.

Put half the flour into a large mixing bowl. Mix the milk and water together in a jug, then add the sugar and yeast. Add to the flour and beat well. Cover the bowl with a damp tea towel and leave to stand for 10–15 minutes, or until the mixture is frothy.

Add the remaining flour and the salt and mix until a soft dough forms. Knead for 10 minutes.

Divide the dough into two pieces and place one piece in each of the prepared tins. Put the tins into the prepared bags and leave to rise until the dough is level with the tops of the tins. Meanwhile, preheat the oven to 230°C/450°F/Gas Mark 8.

Brush the tops of the loaves with milk and bake in the preheated oven for 30–40 minutes until risen and golden brown and they sound hollow when tapped on the base. Transfer to a wire rack and leave to cool completely.

MAKES 2 LOAVES

BREAD & SCONES

Early Irish Baking Techniques

Baking without an oven might seem to be a contradiction in terms, but for the vast majority of the population of Ireland, that's just what home baking involved up to the middle of the 20th century.

In continental Europe, people baked in communal ovens. Fuel was scarce and expensive, so when the baking oven was fired up everyone took advantage of it. In Ireland, fuel was plentiful – every home had a hearth for a turf fire – so cooking could be carried out at home.

A bastible, or pot oven, was used for most forms of cooking in the Irish household. This three- or four-legged cast-iron pot was placed in the hot embers of the fire, and more embers were placed in the concave lid, thus surrounding the entire pot with heat. The even heat lent itself to all types of baking and roasting.

19th-century farmhouse, County Antrim

The bastible was an ideal vessel for baking traditional soda bread, which became popular in the early 19th century, but it could also be used for baking cakes, meat or fruit pies, scones, cobblers, fadge and even boxty.

The bakestone was introduced at a later stage. Rather like a pizza stone, this was preheated over the fire, then used to fry fish and to 'bake' oatcakes and potato cakes. It was easier to control the heat, as the bakestone was suspended over the fire by a chain on a hook and could be raised or lowered depending on the intensity of heat required for the recipe.

19th-century cooking forks and griddle, National Museum of Ireland

INGREDIENTS

butter, for greasing
900 g/2 lb wholemeal flour
450 g/1 lb strong white bread flour
55 g/2 oz caster sugar
2 tsp salt
3 sachets easy-blend dried yeast
2 tbsp black treacle
900 ml/1½ pints lukewarm water

Treacle Loaf

This quick bread is great for a baker who is new to yeast – the yeast is simply added with all the other ingredients.

METHOD

Grease a 900-g/2-lb loaf tin.

Put the wholemeal flour into a bowl and sift in the remaining dry ingredients. Mix the treacle with a little of the water, add to the bowl, then add the remaining water and mix well.

Put the dough into the prepared tin and leave to stand for about 40 minutes, or until doubled in volume. Meanwhile, preheat the oven to 220°C/425°F/Gas Mark 7.

Put the tin into the preheated oven and immediately reduce the oven temperature to 190°C/375°F/Gas Mark 5. Bake for 1 hour, or until the bread is shrinking from the side of the tin and it sounds hollow when tapped on the base.

Leave to cool in the tin for about 5 minutes, then turn out onto a wire rack and leave to cool completely.

MAKES 1 LOAF

INGREDIENTS

butter, for greasing
225 g/8 oz wholemeal flour
100 g/3½ oz strong white bread flour
100 g/3½ oz oatmeal
1 tsp salt
25 g/1 oz fresh yeast
600 ml/1 pint lukewarm water
2 tsp black treacle

Oatmeal Bread

This is a very quick-and-easy yeast bread – no kneading required!

METHOD

Grease a 450-g/1-lb loaf tin. Put the wholemeal flour, white flour, oatmeal and salt into a mixing bowl and stir to combine. Leave to stand in a warm place.

Put the yeast into a jug with the water and treacle and mix to combine, then leave to stand in a warm place until frothy.

Add the liquid to the dry ingredients and stir until well combined. Transfer the mixture to the prepared tin and leave to stand in a warm place until doubled in volume.

Meanwhile, preheat the oven to 230°C/450°F/Gas Mark 8. Place the tin in the preheated oven and bake for 10 minutes, then reduce the oven temperature to 180°C/350°F/Gas Mark 4 and bake for a further 40 minutes, or until the loaf is shrinking away from the side of the tin and it sounds hollow when tapped on the base.

Leave to cool in the tin for 5 minutes, then turn out onto a wire rack and leave to cool completely.

MAKES 1 LOAF

INGREDIENTS

350 g/12 oz wholemeal flour

350 g/12 oz plain white flour, plus extra for dusting

55 g/2 oz butter, plus extra for greasing

2 tbsp sunflower seeds, plus extra for sprinkling

2 tbsp sesame seeds

25 g/1 oz soft light brown sugar

1 tsp salt

1 tsp cream of tartar

1 tsp bicarbonate of soda

1 tsp baking powder

150 ml/5 fl oz buttermilk

300 ml/10 fl oz whole milk

Seed Bread

The seeds add lovely texture and crunch to this bread – you can experiment with different types of seeds.

METHOD

Preheat the oven to 220°C/425°F/Gas Mark 7. Grease two 450-g/1-lb loaf tins and dust with flour, shaking out any excess.

Put the wholemeal flour and white flour into a bowl, add the butter and rub in until the mixture has the texture of fine breadcrumbs. Add the sunflower seeds, sesame seeds, sugar, salt, cream of tartar, bicarbonate of soda and baking powder and mix well to combine.

Make a well in the centre of the dry mixture and pour in the buttermilk and enough whole milk to mix to a soft dough. Divide the dough into two pieces, knead lightly and place in the prepared tins, pushing it into the corners.

Sprinkle with sunflower seeds and bake in the preheated oven for 40 minutes, or until the loaves sound hollow when tapped on the base. Leave to cool in the tins for 5 minutes, then turn out onto a wire rack and leave to cool completely.

MAKES 2 LOAVES

Yogurt Soda Bread

This tasty soda bread uses yogurt instead of buttermilk and is enriched with egg.

INGREDIENTS

- butter, for greasing
- 175 g/6 oz plain white flour, plus extra for dusting
- 275 g/9¾ oz wholemeal flour
- 1¼ tsp bicarbonate of soda
- 3 tsp baking powder
- 2 tsp salt
- 1 egg
- 300 ml/10 fl oz natural yogurt
- 150 ml/5 fl oz water
- milk, for brushing

METHOD

Preheat the oven to 190°C/375°F/Gas Mark 5. Grease a baking tray.

Sift the white flour, wholemeal flour, bicarbonate of soda, baking powder and salt into a bowl, then beat in the egg, yogurt and water until a soft dough forms.

Shape the dough into a round, place on the prepared baking tray and cut a cross in the top using a floured knife. Bake in the preheated oven for 35 minutes, then brush the top with milk and bake for a further 10 minutes. Transfer to a wire rack and leave to cool completely.

MAKES 1 LOAF

INGREDIENTS

butter, for greasing

425 g/15 oz strong white bread flour

3½ tbsp baking powder

55 g/2 oz soft light brown sugar

1 egg, beaten

500 ml/18 fl oz Guinness

Guinness Bread

This unusual bread uses no yeast, relying on the Guinness to help with the rise.

METHOD

Preheat the oven to 200°C/400°F/Gas Mark 6. Grease a 450-g/1-lb loaf tin.

Put the flour, baking powder and sugar into a mixing bowl and stir to combine. Add the egg and Guinness and mix to a wet dough.

Place the dough in the prepared tin, levelling the top. Bake in the preheated oven for 45 minutes, or until the loaf is risen and browned and sounds hollow when tapped on the base.

Leave to cool in the tin for 5 minutes, then turn out onto a wire rack and leave to cool completely.

MAKES 1 LOAF

Oven Boxty Bread

INGREDIENTS

1.5 kg/3 lb 5 oz raw potatoes
750 g/1 lb 10 oz freshly cooked mashed potatoes
125 g/4½ oz plain flour
2 tbsp melted butter, plus extra for greasing
salt

Boxty is a traditional Irish food, made in different ways and named according to the cooking method used. This style of boxty is baked in the oven as a bread.

METHOD

Preheat the oven to 180°C/350°F/Gas Mark 4. Grease a 900-g/2-lb loaf tin.

Grate the raw potatoes and squeeze out as much liquid as possible by twisting them in a clean tea towel. Place in a bowl, add the mashed potatoes, flour, butter and a little salt and stir to combine.

Transfer the mixture to the prepared tin, press into the corners, level the top and bake in the preheated oven for 1 hour. Leave to cool in the tin for 5–10 minutes, then turn out onto a plate, slice and serve as a side dish.

MAKES 1 LOAF

INGREDIENTS

700 g/1 lb 9 oz strong white bread flour, plus extra for dusting

1½ tsp salt

1 sachet easy-blend dried yeast

150 g/5½ oz grated Cheddar cheese

150 ml/5 fl oz olive oil, plus extra for oiling

375 ml/13 fl oz warm water

3 tbsp tomato purée

3 garlic cloves, crushed

pinch of cayenne pepper

55 g/2 oz black olives, stoned and finely chopped

Cheese & Tomato Bread

This delicious Mediterranean-flavoured bread is kneaded only once and then left to rise for about four hours.

METHOD

Sift the flour into a bowl, mix in the salt and yeast and stir in the cheese.

Mix together the oil, water, tomato purée, garlic and cayenne pepper and add to the flour mixture. Mix well until a firm dough forms, then turn out the dough onto a work surface lightly dusted with flour. Knead for about 5 minutes until the dough is elastic.

Oil two 450-g/1-lb loaf tins and two plastic bags. Divide the dough between the prepared tins, then put the tins into the prepared bags and set aside to rise at room temperature for 4 hours, or until doubled in size.

Preheat the oven to 220°C/425°F/Gas Mark 7. Remove the tins from the plastic bags and gently press the chopped olives into the tops of the loaves. Bake in the preheated oven for 10 minutes, then reduce the temperature to 200°C/400°F/Gas Mark 6 and bake for a further 20 minutes. Remove from the oven and turn out onto a wire rack to cool.

MAKES 2 LOAVES

INGREDIENTS

25 g/1 oz fresh yeast
1 tsp sugar
300 ml/10 fl oz warm milk
300 ml/10 fl oz warm water
900 g/2 lb strong white bread flour, plus extra for dusting
¼ tsp salt
225 g/8 oz grated Cheddar cheese
4 garlic cloves, crushed
1 tbsp chopped parsley
25 g/1 oz butter, for greasing
4 large onions, sliced

MAKES 3 LOAVES

Cheese & Onion Bread

This bread has a lovely texture and is delicious served with cheese or cold meat or as an accompaniment to a hearty soup.

METHOD

Put the yeast and sugar into a bowl. Mix together the milk and water and add to the bowl, mixing until smooth. Cover with a cloth and leave to rise in a warm place.

Meanwhile, sift the flour and salt together into a large mixing bowl, then add the cheese, garlic and parsley.

Melt the butter in a frying pan over a medium heat, then add the onion slices and sauté until softened but not browned. Add to the dry ingredients together with the frothing yeast mixture. Mix well, then turn out onto a work surface lightly dusted with flour and knead until smooth. Return the dough to the bowl, cover with a cloth and set aside in a warm place to prove for 1–2 hours, or until doubled in size.

Turn out the dough onto the floured work surface and knock back. Knead the dough until smooth and elastic, then divide it into three pieces. Grease three 450-g/1-lb loaf tins with butter, then place a piece of dough in each, shaping it into a loaf. Set the tins aside in a warm place to rise.

Preheat the oven to 220°C/425°F/Gas Mark 7. When the dough has risen to the tops of the tins, bake in the preheated oven for 30 minutes, or until golden brown. Turn out onto a wire rack and leave to cool.

INGREDIENTS

55 g/2 oz butter, plus extra for greasing
55 g/2 oz treacle
350 ml/12 fl oz water
25 g/1 oz fresh yeast
450 g/1 lb rye flour
450 g/1 lb strong white bread flour, plus extra for dusting
1 tsp salt
55 g/2 oz sunflower seeds
125 g/4½ oz natural yogurt

Rye Bread

Rye flour makes a yeast bread with a chewy texture and a pleasantly sour flavour that is a good match with a variety of cheeses. This recipe includes treacle, which adds a little sweetness.

METHOD

Put the butter and treacle into a small saucepan with the water and heat over a low heat until the butter has melted. Add the yeast and leave to stand until it froths.

Mix together the rye flour, white flour, salt and sunflower seeds in a mixing bowl, then add the treacle/yeast mixture and yogurt and mix to a firm dough.

Cover the bowl with a tea towel and leave to rise at room temperature for 1 hour, or until the dough has doubled in size. Turn out onto a work surface lightly dusted with flour and knead until smooth. Grease a large baking sheet. Divide the dough in two, shape each piece into a round and place on the prepared baking sheet. Leave to rise for 1 hour.

Meanwhile preheat the oven to 230°C/450°F/Gas Mark 8. Place the loaves in the preheated oven and bake for 35 minutes. Transfer to a wire rack and leave to cool.

MAKES 2 LOAVES

Cheesy Soda Bread

This soda bread is delicious with cheese and can be successfully toasted. It's best eaten as soon as it has cooled.

INGREDIENTS

225 g/8 oz plain flour, plus extra for dusting
½ tsp bicarbonate of soda
1 tsp cream of tartar
1 tsp English mustard powder
pinch of salt
2 tbsp chilled butter, cubed
100g/3½ oz extra-mature Cheddar cheese, finely grated
2 tsp fresh herbs
150 ml/5 fl oz milk

METHOD

Preheat the oven to 200°C/400°F/Gas Mark 6. Sift together the flour, bicarbonate of soda, cream of tartar, mustard powder and salt into a bowl. Rub in the butter with your fingers until the mixture resembles breadcrumbs.

Add three-quarters of the cheese and the herbs and lightly stir in enough milk to make a soft dough.

Turn out the dough onto a work surface lightly dusted with flour, knead very lightly and shape into an 18-cm/7-inch round.

Place the round on a baking tray dusted with flour, brush with water and sprinkle the remaining cheese over the top.

Bake in the preheated oven for 20 minutes, or until the crust is golden brown and the base sounds hollow when tapped.

Leave to cool on a wire rack, then slice with a sharp knife.

MAKES 1 LOAF

INGREDIENTS

oil, for oiling

butter, for greasing

15 g/½ oz active dried yeast

600 g/1 lb 5 oz strong white bread flour, plus extra for dusting

1 tsp salt

115 g/4 oz hazelnuts, roughly chopped

375 ml/13 fl oz warm water

MAKES 2 SMALL LOAVES

Hazelnut Bread

Hazelnuts are native to Ireland and grow wild, so they were foraged to add some variety to a limited diet. They add a lovely texture to yeast bread.

METHOD

Oil a mixing bowl and grease a baking tray. Put the yeast into a small bowl and add a little warm water. Leave to stand in a warm place until frothy.

Mix together the flour and salt in a large bowl, then add the yeast, hazelnuts and enough warm water to knead to a smooth elastic dough. Add more water or flour if needed.

Place the dough in the prepared bowl, cover with clingfilm and leave to rise in a warm place until doubled in size (about 1–1½ hours).

Turn out the dough onto a work surface lightly dusted with flour, knock back and knead for several minutes. Divide into two pieces and shape each piece into a round. Place them on the prepared baking tray, cover with a damp cloth and leave in a warm place for about an hour, or until doubled in size.

Meanwhile, preheat the oven to 220°C/425°F/Gas Mark 7. Use a sharp knife to slash a cross in the top of each round, then bake in the preheated oven for 10 minutes. Reduce the heat to 190°C/375°F/Gas Mark 5 and bake for a further 25–30 minutes, until golden brown and the bases sound hollow when tapped. Leave to cool on a wire rack.

Wholemeal Walnut Bread

INGREDIENTS

butter, for greasing
1.1 kg/2 lb 8 oz wholemeal flour, plus extra for dusting
90 g/3¼ oz wheat germ
90 g/3¼ oz pinhead oatmeal
90 g/3¼ oz bran
90 g/3¼ oz oat flakes
90 g/3¼ oz chopped walnuts
2 tsp bicarbonate of soda
2 tsp salt
175 g/6 oz butter, melted
60 g/2¼ oz treacle
1.5 litres/2½ pints buttermilk

Sir Walter Raleigh is believed to have introduced the walnut tree to Ireland, allowing Irish cooks to add the delicious nut to a variety of recipes. This textured soda bread uses walnuts to good effect.

METHOD

Preheat the oven to 150°C/300°F/Gas Mark 2. Grease four 450-g/1-lb loaf tins and dust with flour.

Mix all the dry ingredients together in a large mixing bowl. Heat the butter with the treacle in a small saucepan and mix with the buttermilk.

Add the liquid to the dry ingredients and mix to a wet dough.

Put a quarter of the dough into each of the prepared tins and bake in the preheated oven for 3 hours. Turn out the loaves onto a wire rack and leave to cool before slicing. The bread can be frozen for up to a month.

MAKES 4 LOAVES

INGREDIENTS

475 ml/16 fl oz buttermilk

280 g/10 oz fine stoneground oatmeal

butter, for greasing

350 g/12 oz plain flour, plus extra for dustingr

1 tsp bicarbonate of soda

½ tsp salt

Oatmeal Soda Bread

This is a very early version of the ever-popular soda bread; the inclusion of oatmeal gives it a great texture, but it means you have to start the recipe the night before.

METHOD

Pour the buttermilk into a large bowl, add the oatmeal, cover with a cloth and leave to soak overnight.

Preheat the oven to 180°C/350°F/Gas Mark 4 and grease a baking tray.

Mix the flour, bicarbonate of soda and salt together and add to the oatmeal mixture, stirring until a dough forms. Add a little more buttermilk, if necessary. Shape the dough into a round and cut a cross in the top using a floured knife.

Place the dough on the prepared baking sheet and bake in the preheated oven for 1–1½ hours until the loaf sounds hollow when tapped on the base. Turn out onto a wire rack and leave to cool.

MAKES 1 LOAF

INGREDIENTS

900 g/2 lb plain wholemeal flour, plus extra for dusting
900 g/2 lb plain white flour
1 tsp salt
2 tbsp baking powder
water, for mixing

Wheaten Bread

This quick-and-easy bread uses baking powder as a raising agent instead of the traditional buttermilk and bicarbonate of soda mixture.

METHOD

Preheat the oven to 180°C/350°F/Gas Mark 4.

Place all the dry ingredients in a large mixing bowl and stir to combine. Add enough water to make a fairly wet dough.

Turn out the dough onto a work surface lightly dusted with flour and knead well. Shape into a round, transfer to a baking sheet and bake in the preheated oven for 1 hour until golden brown. Transfer to a wire rack to cool.

MAKES 1 LOAF

INGREDIENTS

1–2 tbsp treacle

1 egg, beaten

300 ml/10 fl oz buttermilk

450 g/1 lb plain flour, plus extra for dusting

1 tsp salt

1 tsp bicarbonate of soda

Kerry Treacle Bread

This is a rich and flavoursome soda bread. Treacle, which was cheaper than refined sugar, was a boon to the home baker in need of a little sweetness.

METHOD

Preheat the oven to 230°C/450°F/Gas Mark 8.

Put the treacle into a medium saucepan and heat over a low heat until runny. Remove from the heat, then add the egg and mix well. Add the buttermilk and mix again.

Sift the dry ingredients together into a large mixing bowl. Make a well in the centre and gradually pour in the treacle mixture, mixing in the flour from the sides of the bowl. When a reasonably firm dough has formed, turn it out onto a lightly floured work surface. Dust your hands with flour and shape the dough into a round about 2.5 cm/1 inch deep. Cut a cross in the top of the loaf, going from one side to the other.

Place the loaf on a baking tray and bake in the preheated oven for 15 minutes, then reduce the oven temperature to 200°C/400°F/Gas Mark 6 and bake for a further 30 minutes, or until the loaf sounds hollow when tapped on the base. Turn out onto a wire rack and leave to cool.

MAKES 1 LOAF

INGREDIENTS

butter, for greasing
250 g/9 oz plain wholemeal flour
250 g/9 oz plain white flour
55 g/2 oz porridge oats, plus extra for sprinkling
1 tsp salt
1 tsp bicarbonate of soda
1 tsp dillisk flakes
1 tbsp clear honey
1 tbsp treacle
200 ml/7 fl oz buttermilk
200 ml/7 fl oz Guinness

MAKES 1 LOAF

Guinness Seaweed Soda Bread

Seaweed is a great addition to a loaf of bread, providing a range of vitamins, minerals and omega-3 fatty acids.

METHOD

Preheat the oven to 200°C/400°F/Gas Mark 6. Grease a 450-g/1-lb loaf tin.

Put the wholemeal flour, white flour, oats, salt, bicarbonate of soda and dillisk into a large bowl and stir to combine.

Put the honey, treacle, buttermilk and Guinness into a jug and mix well. Pour the liquid onto the dry ingredients and mix to a soft, sticky dough.

Put the dough into the prepared tin and sprinkle with oats. Bake in the preheated oven for 30 minutes, or until the bread is golden and sounds hollow when tapped on the base.

Turn out onto a wire rack and leave to cool.

INGREDIENTS

butter, for greasing
325 g/11½ oz plain wholemeal flour
85 g/3 oz plain white flour
40 g/1½ oz rolled oats
1½ tsp bicarbonate of soda
1 tsp salt
2 tbsp sunflower seeds, plus extra for sprinkling
85 g/3 oz walnuts, chopped
325 g/11½ oz natural yogurt
1 tbsp clear honey
50 ml/1¼ fl oz milk

Wheaten Bread with Nuts, Seeds & Honey

The nuts and seeds give this bread a great texture, and there is a lovely hint of sweetness from the honey. Yogurt is used instead of buttermilk.

METHOD

Preheat the oven to 230°C/450°F/Gas Mark 8. Grease a 900-g/2-lb loaf tin.

Put the wholemeal flour, white flour, oats, bicarbonate of soda, salt, sunflower seeds and walnuts into a large bowl. Put the yogurt and honey into a separate bowl, stir to combine, then add to the dry ingredients with the milk. Mix gently until a soft dough forms.

Shape the dough into a loaf shape and place in the prepared tin. Bake in the preheated oven for 10 minutes, then reduce the oven temperature to 200°C/400°F/Gas Mark 6 and bake for a further 20–30 minutes, until golden and firm and the base sounds hollow when tapped.

Turn out onto a wire rack and leave to cool.

MAKES 1 LOAF

INGREDIENTS

225 g/8 oz plain flour, plus extra for dusting

pinch of salt

1 heaped tsp baking powder

55 g/2 oz butter

150 ml/5 fl oz milk, plus extra for brushing

MAKES 8

Plain White Scones

Scones are a basic recipe and take no time at all to prepare. Don't overhandle the dough and get the scones into the oven as quickly as possible.

METHOD

Preheat the oven to 230°C/450°F/Gas Mark 8. Dust a baking sheet with flour.

Sift the flour, salt and baking powder into a mixing bowl. Add the butter and rub it in until fine crumbs form.

Make a well in the centre and add enough milk to mix to a soft but firm dough. Turn out the dough onto a work surface lightly dusted with flour and very lightly roll it out to a thickness of 2.5 cm/1 inch. Stamp out 8 rounds, or cut the dough into squares using a sharp knife.

Place the scones on the prepared baking sheet, brush with a little milk and bake in the preheated oven for 8–10 minutes until browned on top and well-risen. Transfer to a wire rack and leave to cool slightly. Serve warm.

INGREDIENTS

175 g/6 oz plain wholemeal flour, plus extra for dusting

175 g/6 oz plain white flour

1 tsp bicarbonate of soda

½ tsp salt

55 g/2 oz butter

1 tbsp soft light brown sugar

200 ml/7 fl oz buttermilk

1 egg, beaten, for glazing

Wholemeal Scones

These are a great accompaniment to a hearty winter soup, or could be served with butter and home-made jam.

METHOD

Preheat the oven to 200°C/400°F/Gas Mark 6. Dust a baking sheet with flour.

Put the wholemeal flour, white flour, bicarbonate of soda and salt into a bowl and mix to combine. Add the butter and rub it in with your fingertips until fine crumbs form. Add the sugar and mix to combine.

Gradually add enough buttermilk to mix to a soft dough. Turn out the dough onto a work surface lightly dusted with flour and knead for a few seconds.

Press out the dough to a thickness of 4 cm/1½ inches, then use a 6-cm/2½-inch round biscuit cutter to cut out 8–10 rounds, reshaping the trimmings as necessary.

Place the scones on the prepared baking sheet, then brush with the beaten egg and bake in the preheated oven for 15 minutes, or until risen and golden. Transfer to a wire rack and leave to cool slightly. Serve warm.

MAKES 8–10

INGREDIENTS

450 g/1 lb self-raising flour, plus extra for dusting

pinch of salt

100 g/3½ oz chilled butter, diced

85 g/3 oz caster sugar

300 m/10 fl oz buttermilk

whole milk, for brushing

Buttermilk Scones

These lovely scones are perfect for serving at afternoon tea, with lashings of butter and home-made jam.

METHOD

Preheat the oven to 220°C/425°F/Gas Mark 7. Dust a baking sheet with flour.

Put the flour and salt into a bowl. Add the butter and rub it in with your fingertips until fine crumbs form. Add the sugar and mix to combine.

Heat the buttermilk over a low heat until lukewarm. Gradually add to the flour mixture, cutting it in with a knife until just combined.

Turn out the dough onto a work surface lightly dusted with flour and bring it together with your hands. Press it out to a thickness of 4 cm/1½ inches, then use a 6-cm/2½-inch round biscuit cutter to cut out 12 rounds, reshaping the trimmings as necessary.

Place the scones on the prepared baking sheet, then brush with a little milk and bake in the preheated oven for 10–12 minutes until golden. Remove from the oven, transfer to a wire rack and leave to cool slightly. Serve warm.

MAKES 12

INGREDIENTS

225 g/8 oz plain flour, plus extra for dusting

1 heaped tsp baking powder

55 g/2 oz butter, plus extra for greasing

100 g/3½ oz extra-mature Cheddar cheese, grated

1 tsp English mustard powder

100 ml/3½ fl oz milk, plus extra for brushing

salt and freshly ground black pepper

Cheddar Cheese Scones

These make a good lunchtime scone, and are delicious served with soup. Use a really mature Cheddar for the best flavour.

METHOD

Preheat the oven to 230°C/450°F/Gas Mark 8. Grease a large baking sheet.

Sift the flour and baking powder into a mixing bowl, then cut in the butter and rub it in with your fingertips until fine crumbs form. Mix in the cheese and mustard powder, adding salt and pepper to taste.

Make a well in the centre of the dry ingredients and add the milk, mixing to a soft dough. Turn out the dough onto a work surface lightly dusted with flour and roll out to a thickness of 2 cm/¾ inch.

Using a lightly floured cutter, cut out 10 scones and place them on the prepared baking sheet. Brush with milk and bake in the preheated oven for 10–15 minutes, or until well risen and golden. Transfer to a wire rack and leave to cool. Eat on the day of baking.

MAKES 10

INGREDIENTS

butter, for greasing

175 g/6 oz wholemeal flour, plus extra for dusting

55 g/2 oz porridge oats, plus extra for sprinkling

1 heaped tsp bicarbonate of soda

large pinch of salt

55 g/2 oz white vegetable fat

150 ml/5 fl oz buttermilk

beaten egg, for brushing

Oat Scones

A great breakfast scone, made with standard porridge oats.

METHOD

Preheat the oven to 230°C/450°F/Gas Mark 8. Grease a baking sheet.

Put the flour, oats, bicarbonate of soda, salt and vegetable fat into a mixing bowl and mix well to combine. Make a well in the centre and add enough buttermilk to mix to a fairly soft dough.

Turn out the dough onto a work surface lightly dusted with flour, knead lightly, then roll out to a thickness of 2 cm/¾ inch. Using a sharp knife, cut the dough into 8 triangles.

Place the triangles on the prepared baking sheet, brush with beaten egg and sprinkle with oats. Bake in the preheated oven for 8–10 minutes until risen and browned. Transfer to a wire rack and leave to cool. Eat the scones on the day of baking.

MAKES 8

Ingredients

100 g/3½ oz plain flour, plus extra for dusting
1 tsp baking powder
large pinch of salt
55 g/2 oz butter, plus extra for greasing
4 tbsp mashed potatoes
milk, for mixing and brushing
butter, to serve

Potato Scones

Just a small amount of leftover mashed potatoes gives these scones a light texture and hearty flavour.

Method

Preheat the oven to 180°C/350°F/Gas Mark 4. Grease a baking sheet.

Sift the flour, baking powder and salt together into a bowl, then rub in the butter. Add the potatoes and a little milk and mix to a soft dough.

Turn out the dough onto a work surface lightly dusted with flour and roll out to a thickness of 2 cm/¾ inch. Use a floured cutter to cut out rounds, then place them on the prepared baking sheet.

Brush the tops with milk and bake in the preheated oven for about 15 minutes until golden brown. Transfer to a wire rack and leave to cool slightly. Serve warm with butter.

MAKES ABOUT 6

Baking with Buttermilk

Buttermilk is used to add lightness and softness to breads, scones and cakes. When combined with bicarbonate of soda or baking powder the buttermilk begins to fizz, and this chemical reaction also cancels out the sour taste of the buttermilk.

Buttermilk is an essential ingredient in soda bread. It lends itself particularly well to the soft wheat flour traditionally used in Ireland, which didn't have the structure to support the use of yeast as a raising agent.

Buttermilk itself is a by-product of butter churning – it's the thin liquid left behind. Many families had a milk cow and the butter they made was sold to provide a small income. When butter making became a commercial concern, dairies sold off the buttermilk cheaply at the end of the day, profiting from selling what would otherwise be discarded. People no longer queue outside dairies for the leavings of the butter churning – commercial buttermilk is produced by adding a bacterial culture to skimmed milk.

Buttermilk in a bottle

IF YOU CAN'T GET BUTTERMILK, THERE ARE SEVERAL EASY SUBSTITUTES:

Natural yogurt – make up a 3:1 mixture of yogurt and water.

Soured cream – make up a 3:1 mixture of soured cream and water.

Kefir – thin the kefir with water or milk until it has the consistency of buttermilk.

You can also use cream of tartar to make buttermilk. Mix 225 ml/8 fl oz whole milk with 1¾ teaspoons cream of tartar. Stir and leave to stand for 5–10 minutes until thick and curdled.

Use a liquid acid such as lemon juice or vinegar for a handy buttermilk substitute made with everyday storecupboard ingredients. Mix 225 ml/8 fl oz whole milk or cream with 1 tablespoon of lemon juice or white vinegar. Leave to stand for 5–10 minutes until slightly curdled.

The chemistry that enables buttermilk to be used in baking was identified in France in 1791. Alkaline bicarbonate of soda produced a 'raising' action when combined with the acid in buttermilk. Bicarbonate of soda was inexpensive, so bread could be produced easily and cheaply with limited cooking facilities. Yeast bread needs a temperature-regulated oven, and most Irish homes were limited to using a cast-iron pot over the fire.

The simple ingredients for soda bread – flour, buttermilk, bicarbonate of soda and salt – are mixed together quickly (no need for proving) to make a simple and wholesome bread, as delicious as any yeast bread, and now celebrated worldwide. It can be savoury or sweet, white or wholemeal, and dried fruit was sometimes added as a sweetener for special occasions – perhaps this is why soda bread is always referred to as a 'cake' rather than a 'loaf'?

INGREDIENTS

450 g/1 lb plain flour, plus extra for dusting

175 g/6 oz butter

1 heaped tsp baking powder

85 g/3 oz sugar

1 tsp cinnamon

100 g/3½ oz mixed currants, raisins and sultanas

2 eggs, beaten

milk, for mixing and brushing

Cinnamon Fruit Scones

These traditional fruit scones are given a little added spice with the addition of cinnamon. You could ring the changes by substituting the currants with chopped dried dates or figs.

METHOD

Preheat the oven to 180°C/350°F/Gas Mark 4. Dust a baking sheet with flour.

Sift the flour into a mixing bowl. Cut in the butter and rub it in with your fingertips until fine crumbs form. Add the baking powder and mix well to combine. Add the sugar, cinnamon and dried fruit and stir.

Make a well in the centre and add the eggs and enough milk to mix to a soft dough. Turn out the dough onto a work surface lightly dusted with flour and roll it out very lightly to a thickness of 2.5 cm/1 inch. Stamp out 16 rounds, or cut the dough into squares using a sharp knife.

Place the scones on the prepared baking sheet, brush with a little milk and bake in the preheated oven for 25–35 minutes until well risen and golden. Transfer to a wire rack and leave to cool slightly. Serve warm.

MAKES 16

INGREDIENTS

250 g/9 oz self-raising flour, plus extra for dusting
½ tsp salt
55 g/3 oz frozen butter, plus extra for greasing
55 g/3 oz caster sugar, plus extra for dusting
85 g/3 oz glacé cherries
150 ml/5 fl oz milk, plus extra for glazing

Cherry Scones

These attractive scones make the most of a classic store-cupboard ingredient and will enhance any tea table.

METHOD

Preheat the oven to 220°C/425°F/Gas Mark 7. Grease a baking tray.

Put the flour and salt into a mixing bowl and stir to combine. Grate the butter into the mixture and rub in lightly using your fingertips.

Add the sugar and cherries, stir to combine, then add the milk and mix to a soft dough.

Turn out the dough onto a work surface lightly dusted with flour, and flatten to a thickness of 2 cm/¾ inch.

Using a plain round cutter, cut out 6 rounds, place on the prepared baking sheet, brush with milk and dust with caster sugar.

Bake in the preheated oven for 12–15 minutes until golden. Serve warm or cold, with lots of butter.

MAKES 6

Cornmeal Scones

These were originally made with cornmeal, which was readily available but had to be soaked before using. Using quick-cook polenta reduces the preparation time significantly.

INGREDIENTS

butter, for greasing
225 g/8 oz quick-cook polenta
225 g/8 oz plain white flour, plus extra for dusting
½ tsp bicarbonate of soda
½ tsp cream of tartar
½ tsp salt
1 tbsp sugar
55 g/2 oz lard or vegetable shortening
buttermilk, for mixing

METHOD

Preheat the oven to 200°C/400°F/Gas Mark 6. Grease a large baking sheet.

Put the polenta into a mixing bowl and sift in the flour, bicarbonate of soda, cream of tartar, salt and sugar. Rub in the lard, then add enough buttermilk to mix to a soft dough.

Turn out the dough onto a work surface lightly dusted with flour and roll out to a thickness of 2 cm/¾ inch. Cut into 16 squares, place on the prepared baking sheet and bake in the preheated oven for 15–20 minutes. Transfer to a wire rack and leave to cool slightly. Serve warm or cold.

MAKES 16

INGREDIENTS

250 g/9 oz plain flour, plus extra for dusting
1 tsp baking powder
½ tsp salt
55 g/2 oz butter, plus extra for greasing
55 g/2 oz rolled oats
85 g/3 oz caster sugar
6–7 tbsp milk

Topping
2 tbsp golden syrup
15 g/½ oz butter
25 g/1 oz rolled oats

Oat & Syrup Scones

A textured sweet scone with a luscious syrupy crunch topping.

METHOD

Preheat the oven to 220°C/425°F/Gas Mark 7. Grease a baking sheet.

Sift the flour, baking powder and salt into a bowl. Rub in the butter with your fingertips until the mixture resembles breadcrumbs. Add the oats, sugar and milk and stir until a soft dough forms.

Knead the dough briefly, then turn it out onto a work surface lightly dusted with flour and roll out to a thickness of 3 cm/1¼ inches. Use a floured cutter to cut out rounds, then place them on the prepared baking sheet.

To make the topping, heat the golden syrup and butter together in a small saucepan until the butter is melted, then remove from the heat and add the oats. Spoon some of the mixture onto each scone, then bake in the preheated oven for 12–15 minutes. Transfer to a wire rack and leave to cool slightly.

MAKES 8

INGREDIENTS

450 g/1 lb plain flour, plus extra for dusting
large pinch of salt
1 tsp baking powder
175 g/6 oz butter, plus extra for greasing
55 g/2 oz caster sugar
300 ml/10 fl oz buttermilk

Butter Cakes

These are very popular in the northern counties of Ireland. They get their name from the generous quantity of butter used.

METHOD

Preheat the oven to 220°C/425°F/Gas Mark 7. Grease a large baking sheet.

Sift the flour, salt and baking powder into a mixing bowl. Cut in the butter and rub it in with your fingertips until fine crumbs form. Add the sugar and mix well. Add enough buttermilk to mix to a soft but not wet dough.

Turn out onto a work surface lightly dusted with flour and knead very lightly. Roll out to a thickness of 2 cm/¾ inch and cut into 16 rounds.

Place the rounds on the prepared baking sheet and bake in the preheated oven for 15–20 minutes until well risen and golden. Transfer to a wire rack and leave to cool slightly. Serve warm with butter and jam.

MAKES 16

Oven-baked Fadge

INGREDIENTS

225 g/8 oz self-raising flour, plus extra for dusting
½ tsp baking powder
large pinch of salt
55 g/2 oz butter, plus extra for greasing
175 g/6 oz mashed potatoes
buttermilk, for mixing

Potato cakes are traditionally 'baked' on a griddle, but this oven method is just as good. You can use leftover mashed potatoes if you like, but these will taste better if the potatoes are freshly cooked.

METHOD

Preheat the oven to 220°C/425°F/Gas Mark 7. Grease a large baking tray.

Sift the flour into a mixing bowl with the baking powder and salt and rub in the butter. Add the potatoes and mix well to combine.

Add enough buttermilk to mix to a soft dough, then turn out onto a work surface lightly dusted with flour and knead lightly. Roll out the dough to a thickness of 2 cm/¾ inch and cut into 12 squares with a sharp knife.

Place the squares on the prepared tray and bake in the preheated oven for 20–25 minutes until risen, golden and crisp. Serve hot.

MAKES 12

Waterford Blaa Buns

These soft, pillowy yeast buns are traditional in County Waterford. They are usually eaten with lots of butter and some fried bacon.

INGREDIENTS

- sunflower oil, for oiling
- 150 ml/5 fl oz lukewarm water
- 15 g/½ oz active dried yeast
- 1 tsp sugar
- 780 g/1 lb 11 oz strong white bread flour, plus extra for dusting
- 1 tsp salt
- 300 ml/10 fl oz water

METHOD

Oil a large bowl and a baking tray.

Put the lukewarm water, yeast and sugar into a small bowl and stir to dissolve.

Put the flour into a mixing bowl with the salt and stir to combine. Gradually whisk in the yeast mixture and enough cold water to form a ball.

Knead the dough for about 5 minutes until smooth and elastic. Place in the prepared bowl and leave in a warm place for about 1 hour to prove, or until doubled in size. Turn out onto a work surface lightly dusted with flour, knock back and return to the bowl for a second proving for 30 minutes.

Turn out the dough onto the worktop and divide into 12 equal-sized pieces. Roll each piece into a ball and place on the prepared tray about 2.5 cm/1 inch apart. Cover with clingfilm and prove for a further 45 minutes.

Meanwhile, preheat the oven to 220°C/425°F/Gas Mark 7. Dust the rolls with flour and bake in the preheated oven for 35 minutes, until the bases are crisp but the tops are still pale.

Transfer to a wire rack and leave to cool.

MAKES 12

INGREDIENTS

sunflower oil, for oiling

500 g/1 lb 2 oz strong white bread flour, plus extra for dusting

300 ml/10 fl oz lukewarm milk

100 ml/3½ fl oz lukewarm water

1 sachet easy-blend dried yeast

2 tsp crushed sea salt

2 tsp softened butter

2 tsp sugar

Belfast Baps

This large white crusty roll originated in Belfast, and was designed to sandwich an entire 'Ulster fry'.

METHOD

Oil a large bowl and a baking tray.

Put all the ingredients into a large bowl and mix until a soft, silky dough forms. Put the dough into the prepared bowl, cover with clingfilm and leave in a warm place to prove until it has doubled in size.

Preheat the oven to 200°C/400°F/Gas Mark 6. Line a baking tray with baking paper.

Turn out the dough onto a work surface lightly dusted with flour, knock back and divide into 6 pieces. Shape each piece into a bun and place on the prepared tray. Dust with a little flour and bake in the preheated oven for 30 minutes until golden. Transfer to a wire rack and leave to cool.

MAKES 6

CAKES

Lighthouse at The Old Head Of Kinsale, County Cork

INGREDIENTS

225 g/8 oz butter, plus extra for greasing

225 g/8 oz soft light brown sugar

300 ml/10 fl oz Irish stout

225 g/8 oz raisins

225 g/8 oz sultanas

115 g/4 oz chopped mixed peel

450 g/1 lb plain flour

½ tsp bicarbonate of soda

½ tsp allspice

½ tsp ground nutmeg

115 g/4 oz glacé cherries, halved

finely grated rind of 1 lemon

3 eggs, beaten

Porter Cake

A rich fruit cake, steeped in stout for extra depth of flavour.

METHOD

Preheat the oven to 180°C/350°F/Gas Mark 4. Grease a 25-cm/10-inch round cake tin and line with baking paper.

Put the butter, sugar and stout into a saucepan and heat over a low heat until the butter is melted. Add the raisins, sultanas and mixed peel, bring to the boil, then simmer for 10 minutes.

Leave to cool, then add the flour, bicarbonate of soda, allspice, nutmeg, cherries and lemon rind. Gradually add the eggs and mix well to combine.

Pour the batter into the prepared tin and bake in the preheated oven for about 1½ hours, or until a skewer inserted into the centre comes out clean. Leave to cool in the tin, then turn out onto a plate. This cake can be stored in an airtight tin for up to 1 week.

SERVES 12

INGREDIENTS

85 g/3 oz butter, plus extra for greasing

150 g/5½ oz caster sugar

2 eggs, beaten

4 very ripe bananas, mashed well

225 g/8 oz self-raising flour

1 tsp mixed spice

1 tsp salt

100 g/3½ oz chopped walnuts

Banana & Walnut Loaf

Make this nutty loaf with very ripe bananas for delicious sweetness and texture.

METHOD

Preheat the oven to 180°C/350°F/Gas Mark 4. Grease a 900-g/2-lb loaf tin.

Put the butter into a bowl and cream until soft, then add the sugar and eggs beat until smooth.

Add the bananas and stir to combine. Sift in the flour, mixed spice and salt and mix well. Add the walnuts and stir until evenly distributed.

Pour the batter into the prepared tin and bake in the preheated oven for 1 hour–1 hour 10 minutes until golden brown. Cover with a piece of foil if the top is browning too quickly. Leave to cool in the tin for 10 minutes, then turn out onto a wire rack and leave to cool completely.

MAKES 1 LOAF

INGREDIENTS

150 g/5½ oz butter, plus extra for greasing
150 g/5½ oz caster sugar
3 eggs, lightly beaten
150 g/5½ oz self-raising flour
1½ tsp baking powder
½ tsp vanilla extract
icing sugar, for dusting

Filling
4 tbsp raspberry jam
250 ml/9 fl oz double cream, whipped

Victoria Sponge

This traditional afternoon tea sponge is even more delicious when home-made jam is used for the filling.

METHOD

Preheat the oven to 160°C/325°F/Gas Mark 3. Grease two 20-cm/8-inch sandwich tins and line the bases with baking paper.

Put the butter and sugar into a bowl and cream together until pale and fluffy. Gradually add the eggs, alternating with two-thirds of the flour. Fold in the baking powder with the remaining flour and the vanilla extract.

Divide the batter between the prepared tins and bake in the preheated oven for 30 minutes. Leave to cool in the tins for 10 minutes, then turn out onto a wire rack and leave to cool completely.

For the filling, spread the jam on the base of one of the cakes. Spread the cream on the jam and place the other cake on top to make a sandwich. Dust with icing sugar and serve.

SERVES 8

INGREDIENTS

175 g/6 oz butter, softened, plus extra for greasing

175 g/6 oz caster sugar

175 g/6 oz self-raising flour, sifted

4 eggs, beaten

finely grated zest of 3 lemons

3 tsp lemon extract

icing sugar, for dusting

Lemon Cake

This tangy lemon cake is delicious served with coffee or tea, or with whipped cream or ice cream as a dessert.

METHOD

Preheat the oven to 180°C/350°F/Gas Mark 4. Grease a 23-cm/9-inch round springform cake tin and line with baking paper.

Cream the butter and sugar together until pale and fluffy. Gradually add the flour and the eggs alternately, beating after each addition until incorporated.

Add the lemon zest and lemon extract, stirring well to combine. The batter will be quite stiff.

Transfer the batter to the prepared tin and bake in the preheated oven for 20 minutes. Reduce the oven temperature to 160°C/300°F/Gas Mark 2 and bake for a further 20–30 minutes until a skewer inserted into the centre of the cake comes out clean.

Leave to cool in the tin for 10 minutes, then unclip and remove the springform and leave to cool completely. Transfer to a plate, dust with icing sugar and serve.

SERVES 8

INGREDIENTS

240 g/8½ oz butter, softened, plus extra for greasing
240 g/8½ oz caster sugar
4 large eggs, beaten
25 g/1 oz caraway seeds
½ tsp ground mace
½ tsp freshly ground nutmeg
325 g/11½ oz self-raising flour
3 tbsp brandy
4–6 tbsp milk
soft light brown sugar, for sprinkling

Seed Cake

This classic cake has a surprisingly sophisticated flavour. Don't be too heavy-handed with the caraway seeds!

METHOD

Preheat the oven to 180°C/350°F/Gas Mark 4. Grease an 18-cm/7-inch round cake tin and line the base with baking paper.

Cream the butter and caster sugar together in a large bowl until pale and fluffy, then gradually add the eggs, beating after each addition until incorporated.

Add the caraway seeds, mace and nutmeg, then sift in the flour and fold it in. Stir in the brandy.

Add enough milk to loosen the batter to a good dropping consistency. Spoon the batter into the prepared tin, smoothing the surface with the back of a spoon. Sprinkle with brown sugar and bake in the middle of the preheated oven for 40–50 minutes, or until a skewer inserted into the centre of the cake comes out clean.

Leave to cool in the tin for 10 minutes, then turn out onto a wire rack and leave to cool completely.

SERVES 6–8

INGREDIENTS

500 g/1 lb 2 oz Bramley apples, peeled, cored and cut into chunks

2 tbsp soft light brown sugar

250 g/9 oz plain flour, plus extra if needed

½ tsp baking powder

100 g/3½ oz chilled butter, plus extra for greasing

100 g/3½ oz caster sugar

1 large egg, beaten

100 ml/3½ fl oz milk

Kerry Apple Cake

This cake is a cross between an apple tart and an apple pie. The texture of the pastry – a bit like a soft shortbread – is key.

METHOD

Preheat the oven to 180°C/350°F/Gas Mark 4. Grease a 20-cm/8-inch round loose-based cake tin and line the base with baking paper.

Toss the apples with the brown sugar. Sift the flour and baking powder together into a bowl and rub in the butter with your fingertips until fine crumbs form.

Add the caster sugar, mixing it in with a blunt knife, then add the egg. Add the milk very gradually and mix until a soft dough forms. Add a little more flour if the mixture becomes too wet to handle.

Spread half the dough in the base of the prepared tin. Tip in the apples, then spread the remaining dough on top. Bake in the preheated oven for 40 minutes, or until the dough is golden and the apples are tender. Leave to cool in the tin for about 10 minutes, then turn out and serve.

SERVES 8

INGREDIENTS

25 g/1 oz flaked almonds

400 g/14 oz plums, stoned and halved

175 g/6 oz softened butter, plus extra for greasing

175 g/6 oz caster sugar

3 eggs, beaten

1 tsp almond extract

175 g/6 oz self-raising flour

Upside-down Plum Cake

This deliciously moist cake can be served with morning coffee or as a dessert with a dollop of cream, ice cream or mascarpone.

METHOD

Preheat the oven to 190°C/375°F/Gas Mark 5. Grease a 20-cm/8-inch loose-based cake tin.

Toast the almonds in a dry frying pan, taking care that they don't burn. Arrange the plum halves in the base of the prepared tin, round sides facing upwards, and sprinkle over the toasted almonds.

Put the butter into a mixing bowl with the sugar and cream together until light and fluffy. Add the eggs and beat until they are fully incorporated, then stir in the almond extract.

Sift in the flour, folding it in with a metal spoon. Spoon the batter over the plums and bake in the preheated oven for 40 minutes. The cake should spring back when pressed lightly in the centre.

Leave to cool in the tin for 15 minutes, then invert the cake onto a plate.

SERVES 8

INGREDIENTS

350 g/12 oz self-raising flour

½ tsp salt

2 tsp ground cinnamon

175 g/6 oz chilled butter, cubed, plus extra for greasing

85 g/3 oz sultanas

100 g/3½ oz soft brown sugar

450 g/1 lb fresh plums, stoned and halved

6 tbsp golden syrup

3 eggs

Fresh Plum Cake

This cake needs to mature for a couple of days after baking, but it will keep for at least a week.

METHOD

Preheat the oven to 180°C/350°F/Gas Mark 4. Grease a 20-cm/8-inch round cake tin and line it with baking paper.

Sift the flour, salt and 1 teaspoon of cinnamon into a large mixing bowl. Add the butter and rub it in with your fingertips until the mixture resembles breadcrumbs. Stir in the sultanas and all but 2 tablespoons of the sugar.

Reserving 10 plum halves, finely chop the remainder. Put the golden syrup into a bowl with the eggs and beat until combined. Add to the dry ingredients, mix to combine and fold in the chopped plums. Spoon the batter into the prepared tin and level with the back of a spoon. Arrange the reserved plum halves on top.

Mix the reserved sugar with the remaining cinnamon and sprinkle over the top of the cake. Bake in the preheated oven for 2 hours; the centre of the cake should spring back when lightly pressed. Leave to cool completely in the tin, then turn out, wrap in foil and leave for at least 2 days before eating.

SERVES 8

INGREDIENTS

125 g/4½ oz white self-raising flour

pinch of salt

125 g/4½ oz ground almonds

125 g/4½ oz softened butter, plus extra for greasing

125 g/4½ oz caster sugar

2 eggs, beaten

225 g/8 oz glacé cherries, halved

Cherry Loaf

This satisfying fruit loaf is a good teatime treat, and is best served spread with a little butter.

METHOD

Preheat the oven to 190°C/375°F/Gas Mark 5. Grease a 900-g/2-lb loaf tin with butter.

Mix together the flour, salt and almonds in a bowl.

In a separate large bowl, cream together the butter and sugar, add the eggs and beat well. Add the flour mixture, folding it in with a metal spoon. Stir in the glacé cherries.

Spoon the batter into the prepared tin and bake in the preheated oven for 55 minutes. Leave to cool in the tin for at least 10 minutes before turning out onto a wire rack to cool completely.

MAKES 1 LOAF

Ingredients

175 g/6 oz black treacle
55 g/2 oz golden syrup
100 g/3½ oz butter, plus extra for greasing
150 ml/5 fl oz milk
2 eggs, beaten
225 g/8 oz plain flour
55 g/2 oz caster sugar
2 tsp mixed spice
2 tsp ground ginger
1 tsp bicarbonate of soda

Ginger Cake

This is a traditional cut-and-come-again cake. The treacle and golden syrup keep it moist and the mixed spice and ginger add a warm depth of flavour.

METHOD

Preheat the oven to 150°C/300°F/Gas Mark 2. Grease a 450-g/1-lb loaf tin and line it with baking paper.

Put the treacle, golden syrup and butter into a saucepan and heat over a medium heat until the butter is melted. Add the milk and eggs.

Sift the flour, sugar, mixed spice, ginger and bicarbonate of soda together into a bowl. Add the treacle mixture and beat until smooth.

Pour the batter into the prepared tin and bake in the preheated oven for 1¼–1½ hours, or until a skewer inserted into the centre of the cake comes out clean.

Leave to cool in the tin for 10 minutes, then turn out onto a wire rack and leave to cool completely. Slice and serve.

SERVES 8

Rhubarb Cake

This is a cross between a pie and a cake. The 'pastry' is a scone dough, and the thick syrup from the fruit soaks into it while cooking, resulting in a very moist cake.

INGREDIENTS

340 g/11¾ oz plain flour, plus extra for dusting
½ tsp bicarbonate of soda
pinch of salt
55 g/2 oz caster sugar, plus extra for sprinkling
85 g/3 oz butter, plus extra for greasing
1 egg
175 ml/6 fl oz buttermilk
700 g/1 lb 9 oz rhubarb, trimmed and cut into chunks
200 g/7 oz demerara sugar
milk, for brushing
whipped cream, to serve

METHOD

Preheat the oven to 180°C/350°F/Gas Mark 4. Grease a 25-cm/10-inch pie dish.

Sift the flour, bicarbonate of soda and salt into a large bowl. Add the caster sugar and rub in the butter until fine crumbs form.

Put the egg into a separate bowl, add the buttermilk and beat well, then gradually add to the flour mixture, mixing to a firm but soft dough.

Turn out the dough onto a work surface lightly dusted with flour, knead lightly, divide into two pieces and roll out both pieces. Use one piece to line the prepared dish.

Add the rhubarb to the dish, sprinkle over the demerara sugar, then brush the rim of the base with a little water and cover with the second piece of dough. Crimp the edges together, brush with milk and sprinkle over some caster sugar. Pierce with a fork several times.

Bake in the preheated oven for 50–55 minutes, or until the top is golden. Leave to cool for 10–15 minutes, then serve warm with whipped cream.

SERVES 6–8

Irish Tea Cake

The unusual flavour and texture of this popular cake is produced by soaking the dried fruit in tea.

INGREDIENTS

- 225 ml/8 fl oz cold tea
- 200 g/7 oz sugar
- 175 g/6 oz mixed sultanas and raisins
- 1 tsp mixed spice
- 1 tsp ground cinnamon
- 25 g/1 oz butter, plus extra for greasing and serving
- 250 g/9 oz self-raising flour
- 1 egg, beaten

METHOD

Put the tea, sugar, dried fruit, mixed spice, cinnamon and butter into a saucepan and bring to the boil over a low heat, stirring constantly. Remove from the heat and leave to cool.

Meanwhile, preheat the oven to 180°C/350°F/Gas Mark 4. Grease a 900-g/2-lb loaf tin and line the base and sides with baking paper.

Add the flour and the egg to the cooled mixture and beat until well combined.

Pour the batter into the prepared tin and bake in the preheated oven for about 1 hour, or until a skewer inserted into the centre of the cake comes out clean. Cover with foil if the top is browning too quickly.

Leave to cool in the tin for 10 minutes, then turn out onto a wire rack and leave to cool completely. Peel off the baking paper, slice thickly and serve with butter.

SERVES 8

INGREDIENTS

225 g/8 oz sultanas
grated zest of 1 lemon
150 ml/5 fl oz whiskey
175 g/6 oz butter, softened, plus extra for greasing
175 g/6 oz soft light brown sugar
175 g/6 oz self-raising flour
pinch of salt
pinch of ground nutmeg
4 eggs, separated

Whiskey Cake

The sultanas absorb the whiskey really well, so this cake is very moist and full of warm whiskey flavour.

METHOD

Put the sultanas in a bowl with the lemon zest and pour over the whiskey. Cover and leave to soak overnight.

Preheat the oven to 180°C/350°F/Gas Mark 4. Grease an 18-cm/7-inch round loose-based cake tin and line with baking paper.

Put the butter and sugar into a bowl and cream until pale and fluffy. Sift the flour, salt and nutmeg into a separate bowl. Beat the egg yolks and gradually add to the butter and sugar mixture with a little of the flour mixture, beating well after each addition.

Gradually add the sultana and whiskey mixture, alternating with the remaining flour mixture, stirring lightly to combine.

Whisk the egg whites until they hold stiff peaks, then fold into the mixture with a metal spoon. Do not overmix.

Transfer the batter to the prepared tin and bake in the preheated oven for 1½ hours, until the cake is well risen and a skewer inserted into the centre comes out clean. Leave to cool in the tin for 10 minutes, then turn out onto a wire rack and leave to cool completely.

SERVES 8

INGREDIENTS

225 g/8 oz self-raising flour

pinch of salt

pinch of mixed spice

100 g/3½ oz butter, plus extra for greasing

100 g/3½ oz demerara sugar, plus extra for sprinkling

100 g/3½ oz dried stoned dates, roughly chopped

1 egg, beaten

4 tbsp milk

Date Loaf

This is lovely served warm, with butter. It's best eaten on the day of baking, but any leftovers are delicious toasted.

METHOD

Preheat the oven to 180°C/350°F/Gas Mark 4. Grease a 450-g/1-lb loaf tin with butter and line with baking paper.

Sift the flour, salt and mixed spice into a mixing bowl. Add the butter and rub it in with your fingertips until fine crumbs form.

Stir in the sugar and dates, then add the egg and milk and mix well to combine – the batter should have a good dropping consistency. Transfer the batter to the prepared tin, levelling the top. Sprinkle with a little sugar and bake in the preheated oven for 1½ hours until golden and a skewer inserted into the centre of the cake comes out clean.

Leave to cool in the tin for 10 minutes, then turn out onto a wire rack and leave to cool completely.

MAKES 1 LOAF

INGREDIENTS

250 g/9 oz plain flour
2 tsp baking powder
1 tsp ground cinnamon
100 g/3½ oz soft light brown sugar
85 g/3 oz butter, melted, plus extra for greasing
150 ml/5 fl oz milk
2 large eggs, beaten
4 Granny Smith apples, cored
250 g/9 oz fresh blackberries
icing sugar, for dusting

Apple & Blackberry Cake

This deliciously moist dessert cake makes the most of the autumn fruit harvest – apples straight from the orchard and blackberries foraged along country lanes.

METHOD

Preheat the oven to 190°C/375°F/Gas Mark 5. Grease a 23-cm/9-inch springform cake tin and line the base with baking paper.

Sift the flour, baking powder and cinnamon together into a mixing bowl. Add the brown sugar, butter, milk and eggs and beat with a hand-held electric mixer until creamy. Spoon the batter into the prepared tin.

Cut each apple into eight wedges and arrange the wedges on top of the cake. Add the blackberries, pushing them down into the batter slightly.

Bake in the preheated oven for 45–50 minutes, or until a skewer inserted into the centre of the cake comes out clean. Leave to cool in the tin, then unclip and remove the springform and transfer the cake to a serving plate. Dust with icing sugar just before serving.

SERVES 6–8

Apple & Cider Cake

The flavour of the apples in this lovely autumn cake is enhanced by the addition of cider.

INGREDIENTS

- 300 g/10½ oz self-raising flour
- 2 tsp ground cinnamon
- pinch of salt
- 175 g/6 oz soft brown sugar
- 175 g/6 oz sultanas
- 175 g/6 oz softened butter, plus extra for greasing
- 2 large eggs, beaten
- 175 ml/6 fl oz cider
- 225 g/8 oz Bramley apples, peeled, cored and chopped
- 25 g/1 oz flaked almonds

METHOD

Preheat the oven to 180°C/350°F/Gas Mark 4. Grease a 23-cm/9-inch round cake tin and line with baking paper.

Sift the flour, cinnamon and salt into a mixing bowl, then add the sugar and sultanas.

Add the butter, eggs, cider and apples and beat well until smooth. Spoon the batter into the prepared tin, level with the back of a spoon and sprinkle the almonds over the top.

Bake in the preheated oven for 1 hour 15 minutes, or until a skewer inserted into the centre of the cake comes out clean. Leave to cool in the tin for 15 minutes, then turn out onto a wire rack to cool completely.

SERVES 8–10

Rhubarb Streusel Cake

Rhubarb is the first edible fruit to appear each year in Ireland, and its arrival is always greeted enthusiastically. This cake with a crunchy topping showcases its unique flavour.

INGREDIENTS

175 g/6 oz self-raising flour
pinch of salt
100 g/3½ oz softened butter, plus extra for greasing
1–2 tbsp milk
450 g/1 lb rhubarb, trimmed and cut into 2.5-cm/1-inch pieces
caster sugar and flaked almonds, to decorate
icing sugar, for dusting

Streusel topping
100 g/3½ oz caster sugar
85 g/3 oz softened butter
2 eggs, beaten
100 g/3½ oz self-raising flour
1–2 tbsp milk

METHOD

Preheat the oven to 180°C/350°F/Gas Mark 4. Grease a 23-cm/9-inch loose-based cake tin.

Sift the flour and salt into a bowl, rub in the butter and gradually add a little milk, mixing until it comes together. Spoon the mixture into the prepared tin, level the surface with the back of a spoon and distribute the rhubarb evenly over the top.

To make the streusel topping, put the sugar and butter into a mixing bowl and cream together until light and fluffy. Gradually add the eggs with a little flour, beating well after each addition. Gently fold in half of the remaining flour with a metal spoon, then add the rest of the flour with the milk and mix well.

Spread the streusel topping over the cake, and sprinkle with flaked almonds and some sugar.

Bake in the preheated oven for 1 hour, or until a skewer inserted into the centre of the cake comes out clean. Leave to cool in the tin, then release and remove the springform, dust with icing sugar and serve.

SERVES 8–10

CAKES

Baking with Potatoes

Potatoes, the staple diet of the Irish for centuries, have uses that extend far beyond simple boiling, baking and frying. Mixing cooked potatoes with flour produces delicious bread and cakes with an unexpectedly moist texture.

Boxty is usually made with grated raw potatoes and a little flour, shaped into a flat cake and fried in a pan, but a variation of the traditional recipe is a combination of raw and cooked potatoes, baked in the oven.

The simple savoury potato cake, traditionally fried in a pan or on a griddle (but just as good baked), is a great way to use up leftover mashed potatoes and is still a popular Sunday evening snack after the filling Sunday roast. To keep them as light as possible, use about 75 per cent mashed potatoes to 25 per cent plain flour, mix well with salt, black pepper, chives and a little melted butter and shape into patties. Bake on a lined baking sheet in a hot oven for 10 minutes.

You can bring them right up to date by sprinkling them with a little Parmesan cheese before putting them in the oven.

Beyond savoury baking, potatoes have been an unexpectedly useful ingredient in Irish sweet baking. Apple potato cake is a type of farl made with mashed potatoes, apples and a little flour. It's usually cooked on the griddle, but a different version, using the same combination of ingredients, is a delicious apple pie made with a potato pastry – the moist pastry is wonderfully crisp on the outside. Spiced potato cake, made with raisins, made a frequent appearance on the tea table, and potatoes are now being used in ingenious and unlikely ways – they are even combined with chocolate to make deliciously light, moist cakes.

Using potatoes for baking is nothing new, but for those with wheat or gluten sensitivities this uninspiring white tuber has almost magical properties. Potato starch flour is, as its name suggests, a flour made from potato starch. It is an excellent substitute for wheat flour and gives a light and airy result to all baked goods. It shouldn't, however, be confused with the stodgier potato flour, which should be used sparingly and always in conjunction with wheat flour.

Spiced Potato Cake

The main ingredient in this delicious cake is potatoes. It is best prepared with freshly cooked mashed potatoes rather than leftovers.

INGREDIENTS

250 g/9 oz self-raising flour, plus extra for dusting
pinch of salt
6 tsp mixed spice
150 g/5½ oz butter, softened, plus extra for greasing
400 g/14 oz caster sugar
2 eggs, beaten
175 ml/6 fl oz milk
425 g/15 oz mashed potatoes
150 g/5 oz raisins or sultanas

METHOD

Preheat the oven to 160°C/325°F/Gas Mark 3. Grease a 25-cm/10-inch round cake tin and dust with flour, shaking out any excess.

Sift the flour, salt and mixed spice into a bowl. Put the butter and sugar into a separate bowl and cream together until pale and fluffy. Beat in the eggs, then gradually add the flour mixture, alternating with the milk and potatoes.

Stir in the raisins, then pour the batter into the prepared tin and bake in the preheated oven for 1½–2 hours, or until a skewer inserted into the centre of the cake comes out clean. Leave to cool in the tin for 10 minutes, then turn out onto a wire rack and leave to cool completely.

SERVES 8–10

INGREDIENTS

100 g/3½ oz butter, softened, plus extra for greasing

100 g/3½ oz caster sugar

2 tsp clear honey

150 g/5½ oz self-raising flour, plus extra for dusting

½ tsp baking powder

2 tbsp milk

2 eggs

3 tbsp Irish Mist liqueur

Glaze

175 g/6 oz plain chocolate, broken into pieces

300 ml/10 fl oz water

100 g/3½ oz granulated sugar

Irish Mist Ring Cake

This is very simple to make but looks impressive – it's a bit sticky, so it's best eaten with a fork!

METHOD

Preheat the oven to 190°C/375°F/Gas Mark 5. Grease a 20-cm/8-inch ring tin and dust with flour, shaking out any excess.

Put all the cake ingredients, except the liqueur, into a mixing bowl and beat well until smooth. Add 1 tablespoon of the liqueur and beat to combine. Pour the batter into the prepared tin and bake in the preheated oven for 35–40 minutes.

Leave to cool in the tin for 10 minutes, then turn out onto a serving plate and slowly pour over the remaining liqueur. Leave to cool completely before glazing.

To make the glaze, put the chocolate into a saucepan with the water and heat gently, stirring until melted. Add the sugar and simmer, uncovered, for 15 minutes until thick and shiny.

Pour the glaze over the cake, allowing it to dribble down the sides. Leave to cool and set before serving.

SERVES 6–8

INGREDIENTS

225 g/8 oz self-raising flour

pinch of salt

225 g/8 oz glacé cherries, quartered, plus a few whole cherries to decorate

175 g/6 oz butter, plus extra for greasing

175 g/6 oz caster sugar

3 eggs, beaten

4 tbsp milk

¼ tsp vanilla extract

demerara sugar, for sprinkling

SERVES 6–8

Cherry Cake

Glacé cherries are a great storecupboard standby, and they add an old-fashioned touch to this afternoon tea cake.

METHOD

Preheat the oven to 180°C/350°F/Gas Mark 4. Grease a 20-cm/8-inch round loose-based cake tin and line with baking paper.

Sift the flour and salt into a mixing bowl. Add the quartered cherries and mix until coated with the flour.

Put the butter and caster sugar into a separate bowl and cream together until light and fluffy. Beat in the eggs, one at a time, adding a little of the flour mixture with each addition. Mix well, then stir in the remaining flour mixture, milk and vanilla extract and mix until quite stiff.

Put the batter into the prepared tin and level the top. Halve some whole glacé cherries and press them into the top of the cake. Sprinkle with demerara sugar and bake in the preheated oven for 1½ hours until golden and a skewer inserted into the centre of the cake comes out clean.

Leave to cool in the tin for 10–15 minutes, then turn out onto a wire rack and leave to cool completely before peeling off the baking paper.

INGREDIENTS

150 g/5½ oz caster sugar

150 g/5½ oz butter, plus extra for greasing

3 eggs, lightly beaten

150 g/5½ oz self-raising flour

1½ tsp baking powder

4 tbsp coffee essence or cold espresso coffee

walnut halves, to decorate

Buttercream

100 g/3½ oz butter

225 g/8 oz icing sugar

2 tbsp coffee essence or cold espresso coffee

Coffee & Walnut Cake

Before coffee became a popular drink in Ireland, most storecupboards contained a bottle of concentrated coffee essence for use in baking.

METHOD

Preheat the oven to 160°C/325°F/Gas Mark 3. Grease two 20-cm/8-inch sandwich tins and line the bases with baking paper.

Beat the sugar and butter together until light and fluffy. Gradually add the eggs, alternating with two-thirds of the flour. Fold in the baking powder with the remaining flour. Add the coffee essence and fold in carefully.

Divide the batter between the prepared tins and bake in the preheated oven for 30 minutes. Leave to cool in the tins for 10 minutes, then turn out onto a wire rack and leave to cool completely.

Meanwhile, to make the buttercream, cream the butter and sugar until light and fluffy. Gradually add the coffee essence, mixing after each addition until incorporated. Chill in the refrigerator until needed.

Spread half the buttercream on the base of one of the cakes and top with the other cake. Spread the remaining icing on top, decorate with walnut halves and serve.

SERVES 8

INGREDIENTS

225 g/8 oz butter, plus extra for greasing
300 ml/10 fl oz water
225 g/8 oz soft light brown sugar
450 g/1 lb raisins
450 g/1 lb currants
275 g/10 oz plain flour
1 tsp baking powder
1 tsp mixed spice
4 eggs
150 ml/5 fl oz milk

Boiled Fruit Cake

This is probably the most popular of the traditional Irish fruit cakes. It keeps well and tastes best the day after baking.

METHOD

Preheat the oven to 190°C/375°F/Gas Mark 5. Grease a 20-cm/8-inch round cake tin and line the base with baking paper.

Put the butter, water, sugar, raisins and currants into a medium-sized saucepan over a low heat and bring to the boil, stirring to dissolve the sugar. Boil for 10 minutes, then pour into a mixing bowl and leave to cool slightly.

Sift the flour, baking powder and mixed spice into a separate bowl. Beat the eggs with a little milk, then slowly add the egg mixture to the cooled fruit mixture. Add the flour mixture with as much milk as is needed to make a fairly stiff mixture.

Transfer the batter to the prepared tin and bake in the preheated oven for 30 minutes. Reduce the oven temperature to 160°C/325°F/Gas Mark 3 and bake for a further 30 minutes, then reduce the oven temperature to 140°C/275°F/Gas Mark 1 and bake for a further 1 hour, until the cake is springy to the touch and shrinking away from the side of the tin.

Leave to cool in the tin, then turn out and wrap in greaseproof paper or foil and store in an airtight tin.

SERVES 8–10

INGREDIENTS

butter, for greasing
175 g/6 oz soft light brown sugar
3 eggs
175 ml/6 fl oz sunflower oil
175 g/6 oz carrots, coarsely grated
2 very ripe bananas, mashed
55 g/2 oz chopped walnuts, plus extra to decorate
280 g/10 oz plain flour
1 tsp ground cinnamon
½ tsp salt
1 tsp bicarbonate of soda
2 tsp baking powder

Frosting
200 g/7 oz full-fat cream cheese
115 g/4 oz icing sugar

Carrot Cake

This is not a traditional Irish bake, but it has become very popular in the last 40 years or so. It can be made with butter, but the texture is better when sunflower oil is used.

METHOD

Preheat the oven to 180°C/350°F/Gas Mark 4. Grease a 23-cm/9-inch round springform cake tin and line the base with baking paper.

Put the sugar, eggs, oil, carrots, bananas and walnuts into a mixing bowl. Sift in the flour, cinnamon, salt, bicarbonate of soda and baking powder and beat until smooth.

Pour the batter into the prepared tin and bake in the preheated oven for 1 hour 5 minutes until well risen and golden and a skewer inserted into the centre of the cake comes out clean. Leave to cool in the tin for 10 minutes, then unclip and release the springform, peel off the lining paper, transfer the cake to a wire rack and leave to cool completely.

To make the frosting, put the cheese into a mixing bowl and gradually add the icing sugar, beating well after each addition, until smooth. Spread the icing over the top of the cooled cake, decorate with chopped walnuts and leave in a cool place until the frosting has set slightly.

SERVES 8

INGREDIENTS

100 g/3½ oz butter, softened
100 g/3½ oz caster sugar
100 g/3½ oz self-raising flour
1 tsp baking powder
2 eggs

Base/topping
55 g/2 oz butter, softened
55 g/2 oz soft light brown sugar
7 canned pineapple rings, drained, 2 tbsp syrup reserved
7 whole glacé cherries

Pineapple Upside-down Cake

This colourful cake is usually served at afternoon tea, but it also makes a good dessert, served warm with whipped cream or ice cream.

METHOD

Preheat the oven to 180°C/350°F/Gas Mark 4. Grease a 23-cm/9-inch round cake tin.

To make the base/topping, put the butter and sugar into a bowl and cream together until pale and fluffy. Spread over the base and a little way up the side of the prepared tin. Place a pineapple ring in the centre, then arrange the remaining six rings in a circle around it. Place a cherry in each ring.

Put the butter, sugar, flour, baking powder, eggs and reserved pineapple syrup into a mixing bowl and beat well until the mixture has a soft dropping consistency.

Spoon the mixture into the tin, levelling the top. Bake in the preheated oven for 35 minutes, then leave to cool in the tin for 5 minutes. Invert the tin over a serving plate and turn out the cake. Leave to cool or serve warm.

SERVES 6–8

INGREDIENTS

125 g/4½ oz butter, plus extra for greasing

125 g/4½ oz caster sugar

125 g/4½ oz marmalade

225 g/8 oz self-raising flour

2 eggs, beaten

2 tbsp milk

icing sugar, for dusting

Marmalade Cake

This delicious cut-and-come-again cake has a distinctly breakfasty flavour and is good toasted and spread with butter.

METHOD

Preheat the oven to 190°C/375°F/Gas Mark 5. Grease a 20-cm/8-inch round cake tin and line with baking paper.

Cream the butter and sugar together until pale and fluffy. Add the marmalade and beat in well. Gradually add the flour, eggs and milk and spread the mixture in the prepared tin, levelling the top.

Bake in the preheated oven for 1 hour, then leave to cool in the tin. Dust with icing sugar just before serving.

SERVES 6–8

INGREDIENTS

350 g/12 oz plain flour
100 g/3½ oz chilled butter, cubed, plus extra for greasing
100 g/3½ oz soft dark brown sugar
85 g/3 oz raisins
85 g/3 oz currants
pinch of mixed spice
1 heaped tsp baking powder
1 egg, beaten
300 ml/10 fl oz buttermilk

Buttermilk Cake

This easy tea cake should be served thickly sliced and buttered.

METHOD

Preheat the oven to 180°C/350°F/Gas Mark 4. Grease a 20-cm/8-inch round cake tin and line the base with baking paper.

Sift the flour into a mixing bowl and rub in the butter until the mixture resembles fine breadcrumbs. Add the remaining dry ingredients and mix well to combine.

Add the egg and enough buttermilk to achieve a dropping consistency. Spoon the mixture into the prepared tin and bake in the preheated oven for 1 hour 30 minutes, or until a skewer inserted into the centre of the cake comes out clean.

Leave to cool in the tin for 15 minutes, then turn out onto a wire rack and leave to cool completely.

SERVES 8

INGREDIENTS

115 g/4 oz softened butter, plus extra for greasing
115 g/4 oz caster sugar
3 eggs
115 g/4 oz white self-raising flour
zest of 1 orange

Orange syrup
115 g/4 oz caster sugar
2 tbsp boiling water
juice of 1 orange

Icing
225 g/8 oz icing sugar
zest of 1 orange
3 tbsp orange juice

Orange Cake

This zesty cake is a nice alternative to the ever-popular lemon drizzle cake.

METHOD

Preheat the oven to 180°C/350°F/Gas Mark 4. Grease a 20-cm/8-inch round cake tin and line with baking paper.

Cream the butter and sugar together in a mixing bowl. Add the eggs, one at a time, beating after each addition, and adding a little flour to prevent curdling. Stir in the orange zest.

Fold in the flour with a metal spoon, then spoon the batter into the prepared tin and bake in the preheated oven for 20–25 minutes, or until a skewer inserted into the centre of the cake comes out clean.

Meanwhile, to make the syrup, put all the ingredients in a bowl and stir until the sugar has dissolved.

Make holes in the warm cake with a skewer and pour the syrup over the top. Leave in the tin overnight, then turn it out onto a plate.

To make the icing, put the icing sugar and orange rind into a bowl and add enough orange juice to make a stiff mixture. Spread the icing evenly over the top of the cake before serving.

SERVES 6–8

INGREDIENTS

juice and zest of 2 oranges

juice and zest of 2 lemons

175 g/6 oz caster sugar, plus extra for sprinkling

125 g/4½ oz natural yogurt

3 eggs

125 ml/4 fl oz olive oil

1 tbsp clear honey

175 g/6 oz self-raising flour

75 g/2¾ oz ground almonds

juice and zest of 1 lemon

pinch of salt

Yogurt & Honey Cake

The fat used in this luscious cake is olive oil. Sunflower oil is a good substitute.

METHOD

Preheat the oven to 180°C/350°F/Gas Mark 4. Line a 23-cm/9-inch round cake tin with baking paper.

Put the orange juice, half the lemon juice and 1 tablespoon of the sugar into a small saucepan and set aside.

Put the yogurt into a large bowl and beat in the eggs, one at a time. Add the oil and honey and beat well. Sift the flour into the bowl, add the ground almonds, the remaining sugar and lemon juice, the lemon zest and orange zest and salt, and mix well to combine.

Pour the batter into the prepared tin and bake in the preheated oven for 30 minutes or until a skewer inserted into the centre of the cake comes out clean.

Bring the saucepan of orange and lemon juice and sugar to the boil and boil for 1 minute, then spoon over the cake. Sprinkle the cake with sugar and leave to cool in the tin for several hours or overnight.

SERVES 8

INGREDIENTS

450 g/1 lb plain white flour
½ tsp salt
2 tsp ground ginger, or to taste
2 tsp baking powder
½ tsp bicarbonate of soda
225 g/8 oz demerara sugar
175 g/6 oz butter, plus extra for greasing
350 g/12 oz treacle
300 ml/10 fl oz milk
1 large egg, beaten

Gingerbread

When domestic chores were very labour intensive, fixed days were allocated to particular household tasks, with the week's baking for the family done in a single day. This sticky cake will last for at least a week.

METHOD

Preheat the oven to 180°C/350°F/Gas Mark 4. Grease a 26-cm/10-inch x 20-cm/8-inch rectangular cake tin and line the base with baking paper.

Sift the flour, salt, ginger, baking powder and bicarbonate of soda into a bowl. Put the sugar, butter and treacle into a saucepan and heat over a low heat until the butter has just melted. Make a well in the flour mixture and add the melted treacle mixture, stirring it in with the milk and egg.

Pour the mixture into the prepared tin and bake in the preheated oven for 1 hour 30 minutes, until the cake is well-risen and firm to the touch. Leave to cool in the tin for 15 minutes, then turn out onto a wire rack (do not remove the lining paper) and leave to cool completely. Wrap in foil and leave to mature for a few days, then cut into squares to serve.

SERVES 12

INGREDIENTS

175 g/6 oz plain flour
55 g/2 oz chilled butter, diced, plus extra for greasing
55 g/2 oz fine oatmeal
55 g/2 oz soft dark brown sugar
1 tsp ground ginger, or to taste
¾ tsp bicarbonate of soda
1 tbsp treacle
1 tbsp golden syrup
1 egg, beaten
buttermilk, for mixing

Oaty Gingerbread

This is similar to the parkin baked in the north of England. The oatmeal gives it a pleasantly nutty texture.

METHOD

Preheat the oven to 180°C/350°F/Gas Mark 4. Grease a 20-cm/8-inch square tin.

Sift the flour into a mixing bowl, then rub in the butter with your fingertips. Add the oatmeal, sugar, ginger and bicarbonate of soda and mix to combine.

Heat the treacle and golden syrup over a low heat, then add to the flour mixture and mix well. Add the egg with enough buttermilk to achieve a dropping consistency.

Pour the batter into the prepared tin and bake in the preheated oven for 1 hour, or until a skewer inserted into the centre of the cake comes out clean. Leave to cool in the tin for 15 minutes, then turn out onto a wire rack and leave to cool completely. Wrap in foil and store in a tin for several days before serving.

SERVES 6–8

INGREDIENTS

225 g/8 oz white self-raising flour

pinch of salt

100 g/3½ oz chilled butter, diced, plus extra for greasing

100 g/3½ oz sugar, plus extra for sprinkling

100 g/3½ oz chopped glacé cherries

1 egg, beaten

milk, for mixing

Light Cherry Cake

This simple cake can be served in wedges, or sliced and toasted and spread with lots of butter.

METHOD

Preheat the oven to 180°C/350°F/Gas Mark 4. Grease a 20-cm/8-inch round springform cake tin.

Sift the flour and salt into a mixing bowl. Rub in the butter until the mixture resembles fine breadcrumbs. Add the sugar and cherries, then mix in the egg and enough milk to achieve a dropping consistency.

Spoon the batter into the prepared tin, levelling the top with the back of the spoon. Sprinkle with sugar and bake in the preheated oven for 1 hour 30 minutes, or until a skewer inserted into the centre of the cake comes out clean. Leave to cool in the tin for 15 minutes, then unclip and release the springform and transfer the cake to a wire rack to cool completely.

SERVES 8

Ingredients

- 225 g/8 oz plain wholemeal flour
- 175 g/6 oz plain white flour
- 3 tsp baking powder
- ½ tsp bicarbonate of soda
- ½ tsp grated nutmeg
- ½ tsp ground cloves
- ½ tsp ground ginger
- ½ tsp ground cinnamon
- grated zest of 2 oranges
- 250 g/9 oz dried dates, stoned and chopped
- 100 g/3½ oz almonds, chopped
- 200 g/7 oz candied mixed peel
- 275 g/9¾ oz butter
- 200 g/7 oz soft dark brown sugar
- 2 tsp grated fresh ginger
- 4 eggs
- 5 ripe bananas, mashed

Dried Fruit Loaf

This traditional fruit cake includes mashed bananas, so it's a good way to use up those bananas that have softened and blackened.

Method

Preheat the oven to 150°C/300°F/Gas Mark 2. Line two 900-g/2-lb loaf tins with baking paper.

Put the wholemeal flour, white flour, baking powder, bicarbonate of soda and dried spices into a bowl. Combine the orange zest, dates, almonds and mixed peel in a separate bowl. Add the butter, sugar and fresh ginger to a large mixing bowl and cream together until light and fluffy. Add the flour mixture in batches, alternating with the bananas. Fold in the fruit and nut mixture and mix well to combine.

Divide the batter between the prepared tins and level with the back of a spoon. Bake in the preheated oven for 1 hour–1 hour 15 minutes, until brown on top and the cakes spring back when pressed in the middle. Leave to cool in the tins, then turn out (do not remove the lining paper), wrap in tin foil and store for a few days before serving.

MAKES 2 LOAVES

INGREDIENTS

350 g/12 oz stoned dried dates, chopped

175 ml/6 fl oz Guinness

175 g/6 oz white self-raising flour

100 g/3½ oz porridge oats

pinch of salt

175 g/6 oz soft dark brown sugar

150 g/5½ oz butter, melted, plus extra for greasing

Date & Guinness Cake

Guinness is the Irish cook's secret weapon, frequently used in savoury stews and casseroles and, more unexpectedly, in a variety of cakes.

METHOD

Preheat the oven to 190°C/375°F/Gas Mark 5. Grease a 25-cm/10-inch x 20-cm/8-inch rectangular cake tin.

Put the dates into a saucepan with the Guinness and bring to the boil over a high heat. Reduce the heat to simmering and stir the mixture constantly until it is thick and jammy.

Put the dry ingredients into a large bowl and mix to combine. Add the butter, stirring until it is incorporated. Spoon half of the mixture into the prepared tin and flatten with a palette knife. Spread the date and Guinness mixture evenly over the base, then cover with the remaining oat mixture, smoothing it with a palette knife.

Bake in the preheated oven for 1 hour, or until crisp and golden. Leave to cool in the tin for 15 minutes, then loosen the edges with a knife and turn out onto a wire rack to cool completely.

SERVES 12

Date & Walnut Loaf

This quick and easy cut-and-come-again loaf will keep in an airtight tin for several days.

INGREDIENTS

- 225 g/8 oz stoned dried dates, chopped
- 200 ml/7 fl oz boiling water
- 125 g/4½ oz butter, plus extra for greasing
- 55 g/2 oz chopped walnuts
- 200 g/7 oz caster sugar
- 275 g/9¾ oz plain white flour
- 1 egg, beaten
- 1 tsp bicarbonate of soda, mixed with a little milk

METHOD

Put the dates into a large bowl, cover with the boiling water and leave to soak for 15 minutes. Add the butter and stir until melted. Leave to cool for about 10 minutes, then add the walnuts, sugar, flour, egg and bicarbonate of soda mixture. Mix thoroughly to combine.

Meanwhile, preheat the oven to 180°C/350°F/Gas Mark 4. Grease two 450-g/1-lb loaf tins and line the bases with baking paper. Divide the mixture between the prepared tins and bake in the preheated oven for 1 hour 10 minutes. Leave to cool in the tins for 10 minutes, then turn out onto a wire rack and leave to cool completely.

MAKES 2 LOAVES

Ingredients

- 200 g/7 oz white self-raising flour
- 125 g/4½ oz butter, plus extra for greasing
- 85 g/3 oz sugar
- 1 tsp ground coriander
- 2 tsp ground cinnamon
- 55 g/2 oz mixed peel
- 1 Bramley apple, peeled, cored and thinly sliced
- 1 egg, beaten
- 2 tbsp milk

Apple Cinnamon Cake

This spiced cake has the unusual addition of ground coriander, which complements the pairing of apple and cinnamon.

METHOD

Preheat the oven to 200°C/400°F/Gas Mark 6. Grease a 20-cm/8-inch round cake tin.

Sift the flour into a mixing bowl, cut in the butter and rub into the flour. Stir in the sugar, coriander, cinnamon and mixed peel, then add the apple slices and mix to combine. Stir in the egg and milk. Knead lightly until the dough is smooth and elastic.

Place the dough in the prepared tin and bake in the preheated oven for 35 minutes, covering the top with tin foil if it begins to brown too quickly.

Leave to cool in the tin for 10 minutes, then turn out onto a wire cooling rack and leave to cool completely.

SERVES 8

INGREDIENTS

280 g/10 oz self-raising flour

225 g/8 oz caster sugar

175 ml/6 fl oz milk

115 g/4 oz softened butter, plus extra for greasing

3 eggs

1 tsp almond extract

55 g/2 oz chopped walnuts

Very Easy Walnut Loaf

This is a very quick method of making a cake – preparation and cooking will take just over an hour, from start to finish.

METHOD

Preheat the oven to 180°C/350°F/Gas Mark 4. Grease two 450-g/1-lb loaf tins.

Put all of the ingredients except the walnuts into a large mixing bowl and mix with a hand-held mixer on low speed for 2–3 minutes, then increase the speed to high and mix for a further 2 minutes.

Stir in the walnuts, then divide the batter between the prepared tins and bake in the preheated oven for 50 minutes. Leave to cool in the tin for 10 minutes, then turn out onto a wire rack and leave to cool completely.

MAKES 2 LOAVES

Slab Cake

This is a more refined version of the traditional gur cake, which was sold in groceries and frequently contained leftover plain cakes and bread, mixed with a handful of dried fruit and some fat and sugar.

INGREDIENTS

- 350 g/12 oz sultanas
- 115 g/4 oz glacé cherries
- 140 g/5 oz candied peel
- 115 g/4 oz chopped almonds
- grated rind of 1 lemon
- grated rind of 1 orange
- 500 g/1 lb 2 oz softened butter
- 500 g/1 lb 2 oz caster sugar
- 9 eggs, beaten
- 850 g/1 lb 14 oz white self-raising flour
- a little milk, if needed

METHOD

Preheat the oven to 160°C/325°F/Gas Mark 3. Line a 25 x 35-cm/10 x 14-inch deep rectangular baking tin with baking paper.

Mix together the sultanas, cherries, candied peel, almonds and lemon and orange rind in a large bowl. Put the butter and sugar into another large bowl and cream together until light and fluffy. Gradually add the eggs, beating after each addition, adding a little flour if the mixture begins to curdle.

Stir in the flour, then add the fruit and nut mixture. If the mixture seems too stiff, add a little milk and stir.

Spoon the mixture into the prepared tin and bake in the preheated oven for 1 hour 30 minutes–1 hour 45 minutes. Leave to cool in the tin, then turn out and store in an airtight tin.

SERVES 12

INGREDIENTS

4 eggs

150 g/5½ oz caster sugar, plus extra for dusting

130 g/4¾ oz plain flour

50 g/1¾ oz butter, melted

250 g/8 oz lemon curd

200 ml/7 fl oz double cream, whipped

icing sugar, for dusting

SERVES 6

Lemon Swiss Roll

The zesty citrus flavour is an interesting twist on the standard jam or chocolate Swiss roll. It's important to let the cake cool for a while before attempting to roll it up.

METHOD

Preheat the oven to 180°C/350°F/Gas Mark 4. Line a 30 x 20-cm/12 x 8-inch Swiss roll tin with baking paper.

Put the eggs and sugar into a mixing bowl and beat with a hand-held mixer on a medium speed for 4–5 minutes until thick and fluffy.

Fold in the flour with a metal spoon, then stir in the butter.

Transfer the batter to the prepared tin, gently levelling the top and making sure it gets into the corners (you want a completely rectangular cake). Bake in the preheated oven for 12–15 minutes until golden.

Leave to cool in the tin for several minutes, then carefully turn out onto a sheet of baking paper lightly dusted with caster sugar. Peel away the paper used to line the tin, then, starting at a short side, carefully roll up the sugared paper and the cake and leave to cool.

Unroll the cake, spread with lemon curd and cover with cream. Carefully roll it up from one of the short sides and transfer to a serving plate. Dust with icing sugar and serve.

INGREDIENTS

3 large eggs

125 g/4½ oz caster sugar, plus extra for dusting

125 g/4½ oz plain white flour

1 tbsp hot water

200 g/7 oz fromage frais

1 tsp almond extract

225 g/8 oz strawberries

toasted flaked almonds and icing sugar, to decorate

SERVES 8

Fresh Strawberry Swiss Roll

This Swiss roll is unusual in that it is filled with fresh strawberries rather than jam and fromage frais instead of cream. Use small strawberries, as these will make it easier to roll the cake.

METHOD

Preheat the oven to 220°C/425°F/Gas Mark 7. Line a 35 x 25-cm/14 x 10-inch Swiss roll tin with baking paper.

Put the eggs and sugar into a heatproof mixing bowl and place over a saucepan of hot but not boiling water. Whisk with a hand-held electric mixer until pale and thick.

Remove the bowl from the pan, sift in the flour and fold into the egg mixture with the hot water. Pour the batter into the prepared tin and bake in the preheated oven for 8–10 minutes until golden. Leave to cool in the tin for 15 minutes, then turn out onto a sheet of baking paper dusted with caster sugar. Carefully peel away the paper used to line the tin. Starting at a short side, roll up the sugared paper and the cake. Set aside to cool.

Meanwhile mix the fromage frais with the almond extract. Reserve a few strawberries to decorate and hull and slice the remainder.

Unroll the sponge, spread with fromage frais and sliced strawberries and roll up again. Transfer to a serving plate, sprinkle with flaked almonds, dust with icing sugar and serve.

INGREDIENTS

500 ml/17 fl oz milk
1 tsp vanilla bean paste
4 eggs, separated
130 g/4¾ oz icing sugar, plus extra for dusting
125 g/4½ oz butter, melted and cooled, plus extra for greasing
115 g/4 oz plain flour
pinch of salt
1 tbsp caster sugar

Magic Vanilla Custard Cake

This cake, seemingly magically, forms three distinct layers – sponge, custard, fudgy – while baking. The batter is more liquid than a standard cake batter.

METHOD

Preheat the oven to 160°C/325°F/Gas Mark 3. Grease a 20-cm/8-inch square cake tin and line with baking paper.

Put the milk into a saucepan with the vanilla bean paste and heat over a low heat until lukewarm.

Meanwhile, put the eggs yolks into a bowl with the icing sugar and whisk with a hand-held electric mixer until light and fluffy. Add the butter and stir to combine.

Fold the flour into the batter and gradually add the milk. Put the egg whites into a clean, grease-free bowl with the salt and whisk until foamy, then add the caster sugar and whisk until the mixture has thickened.

Gradually add the egg whites to the batter, folding them in gently with a whisk until there are no large chunks.

Pour the batter into the prepared tin and bake in the preheated oven for 45–60 minutes until the cake jiggles when shaken. If it is still a bit runny, bake for a further 5 minutes. Leave to cool in the tin, then turn out onto a plate and serve.

SERVES 6

INGREDIENTS

125 g/4½ oz softened butter, plus extra for greasing
2 large eggs
125 g/4½ oz caster sugar
125 g/4½ oz self-raising flour
1 tsp ground ginger
½ tsp ground allspice

Topping
55 g/2 oz caster sugar
55 g/2 oz butter
1 tbsp ginger syrup (from a jar of preserved ginger)
2 large pears, peeled, cored and quartered

Upside-down Pear Cake

A lovely moist teatime cake in which the flavour of the pears is perfectly complemented by zingy ginger.

METHOD

Grease a 20-cm/8-inch round springform cake tin and line the base with baking paper.

To make the topping, put the sugar into a deep saucepan over a low heat and stir until the sugar has melted and is golden brown in colour. Add the butter, stirring until melted. Remove from the heat, stir in the ginger syrup and leave to cool for about 20 minutes.

Slice the pear quarters in three lengthways and place them in the caramel, turning to coat. Arrange the slices in the base of the prepared tin, fanning them out from the centre.

Meanwhile, preheat the oven to 180°C/350°F/Gas Mark 4. Put all of the cake ingredients into a mixing bowl and beat with a wooden spoon until smooth. Spoon the mixture over the pears, smoothing the surface with the back of a spoon. Bake in the preheated oven for 35–40 minutes, until well risen and a skewer inserted into the centre of the cake comes out clean. Leave to cool slightly, then release and remove the springform. Place a plate over the cake and invert the cake onto it. Remove the base and baking paper while the cake is still warm and the caramel is soft.

SERVES 8

INGREDIENTS

225 g/8 oz softened butter, plus extra for greasing
225 g/8 oz caster sugar
4 eggs, beaten
250 g/9 oz white self-raising flour
finely grated rind and juice of 1 lemon
25 g/1 oz ground almonds
200 g/7 oz fresh raspberries

Topping
juice of 2 lemons
115 g/4 oz caster sugar

Lemon & Raspberry Drizzle Cake

You could use any sweet berries in season for this deliciously tart cake, an adaptation of the traditional lemon drizzle cake.

METHOD

Preheat the oven to 180°C/350°F/Gas Mark 4. Grease a 20-cm/8-inch square cake tin and line the base with baking paper.

Put the butter and sugar into a mixing bowl and beat until light and fluffy. Gradually beat in the eggs, adding a little of the flour to prevent curdling. Beat in the lemon rind and fold in the flour and ground almonds, adding enough lemon juice to achieve a good dropping consistency.

Fold in three-quarters of the raspberries and transfer the batter to the prepared tin. Level the surface with a palette knife, then scatter the remaining berries on top. Bake in the preheated oven for 1 hour, or until firm to the touch and a skewer inserted into the centre of the cake comes out clean.

Meanwhile, to make the topping, put the lemon juice and sugar into a small bowl and mix together. Prick the surface of the hot cake all over with a skewer and pour over the topping. Leave to cool completely in the tin, then cut into squares to serve.

SERVES 8

Almond & Coconut Cake

INGREDIENTS

180 g/6½ oz ground almonds
60 g/2¼ oz desiccated coconut
pinch of salt
240 g/8½ oz caster sugar
4 eggs
1 tsp vanilla extract
200 g/7 oz butter, melted and cooled, plus extra for greasing
2 tbsp flaked almonds
icing sugar, for dusting

This light and delicious cake is made without any flour. It's great with a cup of coffee but also makes a lovely dessert when served with whipped cream.

METHOD

Preheat the oven to 180°C/350°F/Gas Mark 4. Grease a 20-cm/8-inch round springform cake tin and line with baking paper.

Put the ground almonds, coconut, salt and caster sugar into a bowl and mix to combine. Put the eggs and vanilla extract into a separate bowl and beat well. Stir in the butter and add to the flour mixture, mixing well.

Pour the batter into the prepared tin, sprinkle with the flaked almonds and bake in the preheated oven for 45–50 minutes. Leave to cool in the tin, then release and remove the springform, dust the top of the cake with icing sugar and serve.

SERVES 6–8

Baking with Alcohol

Wine and spirits have been used in baking for centuries as a way of adding flavour and preserving cakes. Alcohol keeps baked goods moist and the addition of a healthy dose of spirits will preserve them for a relatively long time. It was an old Irish wedding tradition to keep the top tier of the wedding cake for the christening of the first child of the marriage, so the cake had to last for at least nine months! Injecting them with spirits extended their shelf life.

While spirits – brandy or whiskey – are the most common alcoholic additions, stout (which is cheaper) is a time-honoured Irish tradition. Porter cake and Guinness chocolate cake are two perennial favourites. Stout is even added to the traditional Christmas pudding, giving a rich, dark flavour and colour to the festive dessert.

Most people believe that the alcohol burns off during cooking. However, while this may be true in the case of pan-fried recipes, cakes, especially those that continue to be injected with spirits during storage, retain some of their alcohol content, although not enough that an elegant slice will make you tipsy!

Liqueurs are also used to add interesting flavour. Irish Mist is a long-time favourite, while fruit-flavoured brandies and liqueurs, such as triple sec and Tia Maria, have all been given a successful whirl in Irish kitchens.

In 1974 there was an alcoholic sea change with the advent of the first of the Irish cream liqueurs, innovative emulsifications of whiskey and cream that have increased in popularity since they burst upon the drinking scene. They have been utilised to great effect in baking, used as one of the main components in delicious cheesecakes, as a substitute for cream in luxury versions of bread and butter pudding, and in fillings for macarons and frosting for cupcakes.

INGREDIENTS

175 g/6 oz self-raising flour
165 g/5¾ oz caster sugar
1 tsp baking powder
125 g/4½ oz butter
3 eggs, beaten
2 tbsp milk

Madeira Cake

Despite its name, this plain cake contains no alcohol – it was intended to be eaten with a glass of Madeira wine or sherry.

METHOD

Preheat the oven to 200°C/400°F/Gas Mark 6. Grease a 450-g/1-lb loaf tin and line with baking paper.

Sift the flour and sugar into a mixing bowl and add the baking powder. Put the butter into a separate bowl and cream until light and fluffy.

Add the flour mixture to the butter, then add the eggs and milk and beat well for 3 minutes.

Put the batter into the prepared tin, levelling the top, and bake in the preheated oven for 1 hour, or until golden and a skewer inserted into the centre comes out clean. Leave to cool in the tin for 5–10 minutes, then turn out onto a wire rack and leave to cool completely.

SERVES 6–8

INGREDIENTS

250 g/9 oz plain flour, plus extra for dusting
2 tsp baking powder
½ tsp salt
200 g/7 oz caster sugar
125 g/4½ oz butter, softened, plus extra for greasing
2 eggs
1 tsp vanilla extract
250 ml/9 fl oz milk
2 tbsp cocoa powder

Marble Cake

This is a variation on plain Madeira cake – don't mix in the dark batter too vigorously, or you'll spoil the effect.

METHOD

Preheat the oven to 180°C/325°F/Gas Mark 4. Grease a 23-cm/9-inch cake tin and dust with flour, shaking out any excess.

Put all the ingredients, except the cocoa powder, into a mixing bowl and beat with a hand-held electric mixer until smooth. Pour all but 175 g/6 oz of the batter into the prepared tin.

Stir the cocoa powder into the remaining batter, then use a dessert spoon to drop it onto the batter in the tin. Use a knife to swirl the two batters together very lightly, so that you get a marbled effect.

Bake in the preheated oven for 30–35 minutes, or until a skewer inserted into the centre of the cake comes out clean. Leave to cool in the tin for 10 minutes, then turn out onto a wire rack and leave to cool completely.

SERVES 8–10

INGREDIENTS

225 g/8 oz plain flour
225 g/8 oz dried fruit (raisins, sultanas, currants, glacé cherries)
85 g/3 oz caster sugar
1 tsp mixed spice
1 tsp ground cinnamon
85 g/3 oz butter, plus extra for greasing
1 tbsp golden syrup
175 ml/6 fl oz milk
1 tsp baking powder

Easy Fruit Loaf

This very easy cut-and-come-again cake is made with any dried fruit you might have to hand.

METHOD

Preheat the oven to 180°C/350°F/Gas Mark 4. Grease a 450-g/1-lb loaf tin.

Put the flour, dried fruit, sugar, mixed spice and cinnamon into a mixing bowl and stir to combine.

Put the butter and golden syrup into a small saucepan and heat over a low heat until the butter has melted. Stir to combine, then pour into the flour mixture and mix well. Add the milk and mix to incorporate, then add the baking powder and fold in gently.

Spoon the batter into the prepared tin and bake in the preheated oven for 1 hour 20 minutes. Leave to cool in the tin for 15 minutes, then turn out onto a wire rack and leave to cool completely.

MAKES 1 LOAF

INGREDIENTS

butter, for greasing
175 g/6 oz self-raising flour
85 g/3 oz soft light brown sugar
125 g/4½ oz mixed dried fruit
1 egg, beaten
2 ripe bananas, mashed

Banana Fruit Loaf

Ripe bananas add sweetness and moistness to this easy cut-and-come-again cake.

METHOD

Preheat the oven to 190°C/375°F/Gas Mark 5. Grease a 450-g/1-lb loaf tin and line the base with baking paper.

Put the flour, sugar and dried fruit into a mixing bowl and stir to combine. Add the egg and mix, then add the bananas and mix until the mixture is very soft.

Transfer the batter to the prepared tin and bake in the preheated oven for 45 minutes, or until a skewer inserted into the centre of the cake comes out clean. Leave to cool in the tin for 15 minutes, then turn out onto a wire rack and leave to cool completely.

MAKES 1 LOAF

Honey Cake

The sweetness in this delicious cake comes mainly from honey, which complements the warm spices and tangy citrus.

INGREDIENTS

- 85 g/3 oz clear honey
- 225 g/8 oz self-raising flour
- 1 tsp ground ginger
- 1 tsp ground cinnamon
- ¼ tsp ground cloves
- 85 g/3 oz caster sugar
- grated zest of 1 orange
- grated zest of 1 lemon
- 115 g/4 oz chilled butter, cubed, plus extra for greasing
- 1 large egg, beaten
- 1 tsp bicarbonate of soda, dissolved in 3 tbsp cold water
- 55 g/2 oz candied peel

Icing
- 175 g/6 oz icing sugar
- 2 tbsp lukewarm water
- 1 tbsp lemon juice

METHOD

Preheat the oven to 160°C/325°F/Gas Mark 3. Grease a 20-cm/8-inch round cake tin.

Put the honey into a bowl set over a saucepan of gently simmering water and heat until warm.

Sift the flour into a mixing bowl with the spices, then add the sugar, orange zest and lemon zest. Gradually add the butter, rubbing it in with your fingertips, until the mixture resembles breadcrumbs. Add the egg and mix, then add the honey and mix to incorporate. Add the bicarbonate of soda and beat well until the mixture is soft and smooth. Stir in the candied peel and spoon the mixture into the prepared tin, levelling it with a palette knife. Bake in the preheated oven for 50 minutes, or until well risen. Leave to cool in the tin for 10 minutes, then turn out onto a wire rack and leave to cool completely.

To make the icing, sift the icing sugar into a bowl, then add the water and lemon juice and mix to a thin consistency that just coats the back of a spoon. Pour the icing over the cake so that it runs down the sides a bit. Store in an airtight tin until needed.

SERVES 8

Sweet Tarts, Crumbles & Pies

Deck of cards houses and St Colman's Cathedral, Cobh, County Cork

INGREDIENTS

225 g/8 oz ready-made shortcrust pastry

3 eggs

450 g/1 lb curd cheese or cottage cheese

4 tbsp caster sugar

25 g/1 oz butter, softened, plus extra for greasing

finely grated zest and juice of 1 small lemon

1 tsp vanilla extract

1 tbsp plain flour, plus extra for dusting

Curd Tart

Curd cheese gives this baked cheesecake a lovely texture. Cottage cheese makes a good substitute.

METHOD

Preheat the oven to 180°C/350°F/Gas Mark 4 and grease a 20-cm/8-inch round loose-based tart tin. Roll out the pastry on a work surface lightly dusted with flour, then use to line the prepared tin.

Separate 2 of the eggs and beat the yolks, then whisk the whites until they hold stiff peaks. Put the cheese, 3 tablespoons of the sugar, half the butter and the egg yolks into a bowl and mix to combine.

Stir in the lemon zest and juice and the vanilla extract. Beat well, then gradually fold in the egg whites.

Spread the filling evenly in the pastry case. Melt the remaining butter and mix with the remaining egg and sugar and the flour. Spread the mixture evenly over the filling.

Bake in the preheated oven for 35–40 minutes, or until golden brown. Leave to cool in the tin, then turn out, cut into wedges and serve.

SERVES 6–8

INGREDIENTS

butter, for greasing
plain flour, for dusting
250 g/9 oz ready-made shortcrust pastry
450 g/1 lb jam
milk, for brushing
whipped cream or custard, to serve

Jam Tart

This is a great standby dessert for unexpected guests. You can use any jam, but one that provides a good colour contrast with the pastry is best.

METHOD

Preheat the oven to 200°C/400°F/Gas Mark 6 and grease a 20-cm/8-inch tart tin.

Roll out the pastry on a work surface lightly dusted with flour and use to line the prepared tin. Chill in the fridge until needed. Re-roll the pastry trimmings and cut out 8 strips, each slightly longer than the diameter of the tin.

Heat the jam over a low heat until warm, then spread over the pastry case. Weave the pastry strips in a lattice pattern over the top, pressing the ends into the edge of the pastry case. Brush with a little milk.

Bake in the preheated oven for about 30 minutes until the pastry is golden. Leave to cool in the tin for 30 minutes, then cut into wedges and serve with whipped cream or custard.

SERVES 6–8

INGREDIENTS

butter, for greasing
flour, for dusting
250 g/9 oz ready-made shortcrust pastry
1 large egg
4 large egg yolks
150 g/5½ oz caster sugar
finely grated zest and juice of 4 lemons
150 ml/5 fl oz double cream

Easy Lemon Tart

This popular tart has been borrowed from the French tradition and simplified.

METHOD

Grease a 23-cm/9-inch loose-based tart tin. Roll out the pastry on a work surface lightly dusted with flour and use to line the tin. Chill for 30 minutes.

Meanwhile, preheat the oven to 190°C/375°F/Gas Mark 5. Prick the base of the pastry case, line with baking paper and fill with baking beans, then bake in the preheated oven for 10 minutes. Remove the paper and beans, return to the oven and bake for a further 8–10 minutes. Reduce the oven temperature to 160°C/325°F/Gas Mark 3.

Put the egg, egg yolks and sugar into a jug and beat until smooth. Stir in the lemon zest and juice and the cream and mix to combine.

Return the tin to the oven, carefully pour in the filling and bake for 25–30 minutes. Leave to cool for 15 minutes, then serve warm, or leave to cool completely and chill until ready to serve.

SERVES 8

INGREDIENTS

flour, for dusting

375 g/13 oz ready-made puff pastry

5 Bramley apples, peeled, cored and thinly sliced

juice of 1 lemon

25 g/1 oz butter, diced

2 tbsp caster sugar

3 tbsp apricot jam, for glazing

Open Apple Tart

A rustic-looking apple tart that's quick and easy to prepare.

METHOD

Preheat the oven to 220°C/425°F/Gas Mark 7. Line a baking sheet with baking paper.

Roll out the pastry to a 35-cm/14-inch round on a work surface lightly dusted with flour and place on the prepared baking sheet.

Toss the apple slices in the lemon juice and arrange them over the pastry to within 2 cm/¾ inch of the edge. Raise the edge of the pastry and fold it over the outer ring of apples to make a rim. Dot with butter, sprinkle with sugar and bake in the preheated oven for 20–25 minutes until the apples are tender and the pastry is golden.

Heat the jam in a small saucepan over a medium heat and pass through a small sieve to remove the fruit pieces. Brush the apples and pastry rim with the glaze and serve the tart hot.

SERVES 6–8

INGREDIENTS

butter, for greasing
plain flour, for dusting
250 g/9 oz ready-made shortcrust pastry
150 g/5 oz fresh white breadcrumbs
225 ml/8 fl oz golden syrup
beaten egg, for brushing
golden caster sugar, for sprinkling
whipped cream or vanilla ice cream, to serve

Golden Syrup Tart

Golden syrup has so many uses in home baking that many people keep a tin on standby in the storecupboard.

METHOD

Preheat the oven to 180°C/350°F/Gas Mark 4. Grease a 20-cm/8-inch round loose-based tart tin.

Roll out the pastry on a work surface lightly dusted with flour and use to line the prepared tin.

Mix the breadcrumbs and golden syrup together and spread evenly in the pastry case.

Bake in the preheated oven for 20 minutes. Brush the pastry edges with beaten egg and sprinkle the tart with sugar, then return to the oven for a further 15 minutes, or until the pastry is golden.

Leave to cool for 15–20 minutes, then cut into wedges and serve with cream.

SERVES 6–8

INGREDIENTS

butter, for greasing
250 g/9 oz ready-made shortcrust pastry
3 large eggs
3 medium egg yolks
200 g/7 oz soft light brown sugar
350 g/12 oz clear honey
2 tbsp double cream
1 tbsp plain flour
1 tsp vanilla extract
200 g/7 oz toasted walnuts, roughly chopped

Walnut & Honey Tart

This very sweet and sticky tart is delicious served with vanilla ice cream.

METHOD

Preheat the oven to 200°C/400°F/Gas Mark 6. Grease a 23-cm/9-inch fluted tart tin. Roll out the pastry and use to line the tin, trimming off any excess. Chill for 15 minutes, then prick the base with a fork, line with baking paper, fill with baking beans and bake blind for 20 minutes. Remove the paper and beans, return to the oven and bake for a further 5 minutes until golden.

Meanwhile, put all of the ingredients except the walnuts into a mixing bowl and beat until smooth. Spread the walnuts evenly over the pastry case, then pour in the filling. Bake in the preheated oven for 45–50 minutes until just set (there should be a slight wobble). Leave to cool in the tin until warm, then serve.

SERVES 8–10

INGREDIENTS

plain flour, for dusting

300 g/10½ oz ready-made shortcrust pastry

150 g/5½ oz golden caster sugar, plus extra for dusting

½ tsp cinnamon

1 kg/2 lb 4 oz Bramley apples, cored, peeled and thickly sliced

beaten egg white, for brushing

vanilla ice cream, to serve

Apple Pie

Apple pie is the ultimate comfort food dessert. This one is full of succulent Bramley apples and is delicious served with vanilla ice cream.

METHOD

Preheat the oven to 190°C/375°F/Gas Mark 5. Cut off a third of the pastry and set aside until needed. Roll out the remaining pastry on a work surface lightly dusted with flour and use to line a 20-cm/8-inch deep pie tin, leaving an overhang.

Mix the sugar and cinnamon together in a large bowl, then toss the apples in the mixture. Put the apples into the tin.

Roll out the reserved pastry to a round about 2.5 cm/1 inch larger than the diameter of the top of the tin. Brush some cold water around the pastry rim, then lay the pastry round on top, crimping the edges to seal. Pierce the pastry about five times to allow the steam to escape during baking.

Brush the pie with the egg white and dust with sugar. Bake in the preheated oven for 40–45 minutes until golden. Dust with sugar, then serve with ice cream.

SERVES 6

Apple Charlotte

INGREDIENTS

butter, for greasing and to butter the bread

10–12 thin slices white bread

900 g/2 lb Bramley apples

140 g/5 oz caster sugar, plus extra for sprinkling

This is a lovely winter dessert, which is simplicity itself to prepare. This easy version is baked in a tart tin rather than a moulded baking tin.

METHOD

Preheat the oven to 160°C/325°F/Gas Mark 3. Grease a 23-cm/9-inch tart tin.

Generously butter the bread slices. Peel, core and finely slice the apples.

Arrange a layer of apples, sugar and bread slices in the prepared tin, repeating until the tin is full.

Cover the tin with greased baking paper and bake in the preheated oven for 45 minutes. Serve hot.

SERVES 4–6

Apple Crumble

A crumble is one of the easiest desserts to make and is prepared in a flash.

INGREDIENTS

butter, for greasing
450 g/1 lb Bramley apples, peeled, cored and roughly chopped
55 g/2 oz soft light brown sugar
1 tbsp plain flour
¼ tsp ground cinnamon

Crumble

300 g/10½ oz plain flour
pinch of salt
175 g/6 oz demerara sugar
200 g/7 oz butter, cubed, plus extra for greasing

METHOD

Preheat the oven to 180°C/350°F/Gas Mark 4. Grease a 24-cm/9-inch baking dish.

To make the crumble, put the flour, salt and demerara sugar into a mixing bowl and stir to combine. Gradually add the butter, rubbing it into the mixture until crumbs form.

Put the apples into a separate bowl and add the brown sugar, flour and cinnamon. Stir to combine.

Spoon the fruit mixture into the prepared dish and sprinkle the crumble on top. Bake in the preheated oven for 40–55 minutes until bubbling and browned. Serve hot.

SERVES 6

Ingredients

Pastry
- 225 g/8 oz plain flour
- 5 g/2 oz caster sugar
- 2 tsp cinnamon
- pinch of salt
- 175 g/6 oz chilled butter, cubed
- 2 egg yolks

Filling
- butter, for greasing
- 4 eating apples
- 2–3 tbsp Baileys Irish Cream liqueur, or to taste
- demerara sugar, for sprinkling

Apple Flan with Baileys

This is a luxurious take on a plain apple tart. It's well worth your while making the sugar-crust pastry.

METHOD

Preheat the oven to 190°C/375°F/Gas Mark 6. Grease a 20-cm/8-inch loose-based tart tin.

To make the pastry, sift the flour, caster sugar, cinnamon and salt into a mixing bowl. Rub in the butter until the mixture resembles fine breadcrumbs, then add the egg yolks and mix to a dough. Set aside to rest.

Meanwhile, peel and core the apples and slice fairly thinly. Put the apple slices into a saucepan, add the cream liqueur and cook over a low heat for 5 minutes.

Roll out the pastry and use to line the prepared tin. Spread the apple mixture over the base, adding more liqueur if it seems too dry. Sprinkle with demerara sugar and bake in the preheated oven until the pastry is golden and the sugar has caramelised. Serve warm or cold.

SERVES 6

INGREDIENTS

butter, for greasing
250 g/9 oz ready-made shortcrust pastry
550 g/1 lb 4 oz golden syrup
225 g/8 oz breadcrumbs
85 g/3 oz roasted nuts, roughly chopped
juice and zest of 1 lemon

Nutty Treacle Tart

This is a step up from the conventional treacle tart; lemon is added to cut through the sweetness and the nuts give it a lovely texture.

METHOD

Preheat the oven to 190°C/375°F/Gas Mark 5. Grease a 23-cm/9-inch loose-based tart tin.

Roll out the pastry and use to line the prepared tin.

Put all of the remaining ingredients into a bowl, mix thoroughly and spoon into the pastry case, spreading the mixture evenly.

Bake in the preheated oven for 30 minutes, then leave to cool. Serve cold or at room temperature, with ice cream or cream.

SERVES 12

INGREDIENTS

250 g/8 oz ready-made shortcrust pastry
3 heaped tbsp lemon curd
55 g/2 oz butter, plus extra for greasing
150 g/5½ oz semolina
150 g/5½ oz sugar
1 tsp baking powder
1 tsp almond extract
40 g/1½ oz finely chopped almonds
1 egg, beaten

Lemon Curd & Almond Tart

Lemon curd has long had pride of place as a standby ingredient in the Irish larder. It's a great substitute for jam in a variety of cakes and buns, and even as a spread on fresh soda bread.

METHOD

Preheat the oven to 180°C/350°F/Gas Mark 4. Grease a 28 x 18-cm/11 x 7-inch rectangular tart tin.

Roll out the pastry and use to line the prepared tin. Spread the lemon curd over the base and leave to chill in the refrigerator while you make the topping.

Melt the butter in a medium saucepan over a low heat, then remove from the heat and add the semolina, sugar, baking powder, almond extract and almonds. Stir in the egg, then spread the mixture over the lemon curd.

Bake in the preheated oven for 25–30 minutes. Serve warm.

SERVES 6–8

INGREDIENTS

250 g/8 oz ready-made shortcrust pastry

100 g/3½ oz softened butter, plus extra for greasing

100 g/3½ oz caster sugar

1 egg, beaten

1 egg yolk

115 g/4 oz ground almonds

25 g/1 oz plain flour

300 g/10½ oz fresh blueberries

2 tbsp redcurrant jelly, warmed

SERVES 8

Blueberry & Almond Tart

Blueberries don't grow wild in Ireland but are very successfully cultivated in the country's acidic peaty boglands. You could use any other berry for this tart.

METHOD

Preheat the oven to 180°C/350°F/Gas Mark 4. Grease a 23-cm/9-inch loose-based tart tin.

Roll out the pastry and use to line the prepared tin. Prick the base and chill in the refrigerator until firm. Line with baking paper, fill with baking beans and bake blind in the preheated oven for 15 minutes. Remove the paper and beans and bake for a further 5 minutes until golden. Leave to cool and increase the oven temperature to 200°C/400°F/Gas Mark 6.

Meanwhile, put the butter into a mixing bowl with the sugar and cream until light and fluffy. Gradually beat in the egg and egg yolk. Stir in the almonds and flour, then add the blueberries and stir them in gently. Spoon the mixture into the pastry case, levelling the top with a palette knife.

Bake the tart for 10–15 minutes until the pastry is beginning to brown, then reduce the oven temperature to 180°C/350°F/Gas Mark 4 and bake for a further 15–20 minutes until the fruit is tender and the tart is golden and set.

Leave to cool slightly, then spread the redcurrant jelly over the top.

INGREDIENTS

300 g/10½ oz ready-made shortcrust pastry
4 eggs
25 g/1 oz softened butter, plus extra for greasing
200 g/7 oz sugar
1 tbsp finely chopped orange zest
1½ tsp finely chopped lemon zest
125 ml/4 fl oz freshly squeezed orange juice
125 ml/4 fl oz freshly squeezed lemon juice
2 tbsp double cream
1½ tbsp icing sugar
1 lemon peeled and cut into segments
whipped cream, to serve

SERVES 10

Orange & Lemon Star Tart

This is a really zesty tart, perfect for serving at the end of a dinner party. It needs a little attention just before serving, but the effort is worth it.

METHOD

Preheat the oven to 190°C/375°F/Gas Mark 5. Grease a 28-cm/11-inch loose-based tart tin.

Roll out the pastry and use to line the prepared tin. Chill in the refrigerator until firm, then line with baking paper, fill with baking beans and bake blind in the preheated oven for 15 minutes. Remove the paper and beans and bake for a further 5 minutes until light brown in colour. Leave to cool.

Meanwhile, put the eggs into a mixing bowl and beat until frothy. Add the butter and sugar and beat until thick. Add the orange and lemon zest and juice and the cream and mix well (the mixture will be quite liquid).

Pour the filling into the pastry case and bake for 10 minutes, then reduce the oven temperature to 180°C/350°F/Gas Mark 4 and bake for a further 15 minutes, until the filling is just set in the centre. Remove from the oven.

Preheat the grill and sift the icing sugar evenly over the top of the tart. Arrange the lemon segments in the centre of the tart in a star pattern and place the tart under the grill for 1–1½ minutes until the area around the lemon segments has browned. Serve at room temperature with whipped cream.

INGREDIENTS

butter, for greasing
100 g/3½ oz ready-made shortcrust pastry
800 g/1 lb 12 oz ripe apricots
55 g/2 oz sponge cake crumbs
25 g/1 oz caster sugar
1 egg yolk
125 ml/4 fl oz double cream

Glaze
1 tbsp apricot jam
1 tbsp caster sugar
1 tbsp water

Apricot Tart

Fresh fruit makes a delicious tart, but the fruit juices can make the pastry soggy. Adding a layer of cake crumbs prevents this, and gives this tart an interesting texture.

METHOD

Preheat the oven to 200°C/400°F/Gas Mark 6. Grease a 20-cm/8-inch loose-based tart tin. Roll out the pastry and use to line the prepared tin. Prick the base, line with baking paper and fill with baking beans. Chill in the refrigerator until firm. Bake in the preheated oven for 15 minutes, then remove the paper and beans and bake for a further 5 minutes until the pastry is crisp and golden.

Halve and stone the apricots. Sprinkle the breadcrumbs over the base of the pastry case in an even layer. Arrange the apricot halves, rounded sides facing upwards, to fill the case.

Put the sugar, egg yolk and cream into a bowl and mix well. Pour the liquid over the fruit and return the tart to the oven to bake for 15 minutes until set.

Meanwhile, to make the glaze, put the ingredients into a small saucepan and bring to the boil. Leave to simmer for a few minutes, then brush the glaze over the warm tart. Serve warm or cold.

SERVES 6

Banoffee Pie

This popular dessert uses a traditional larder ingredient – sweetened condensed milk. The bananas used should be ripe but firm.

INGREDIENTS

- 2 x 400-ml/14-fl oz cans sweetened condensed milk
- 6 tbsp melted butter, plus extra for greasing
- 150 g/5½ oz digestive biscuits, crushed into crumbs
- 50 g/1¾ oz ground almonds
- 50 g/1¾ oz ground hazelnuts
- 4 ripe bananas
- 1 tbsp lemon juice
- 1 tsp vanilla extract
- 85 g/3 oz grated chocolate
- 450 ml/16 fl oz double cream, whipped

METHOD

Place the unopened cans of condensed milk in a large saucepan and cover with water. Bring to the boil, then simmer for 2 hours, topping up the water to keep the cans covered. Remove the cans from the saucepan and leave to cool.

Preheat the oven to 180°C350°F/Gas Mark 4. Grease a 23-cm/9-inch flan tin.

Put the butter into a bowl with the biscuit crumbs, almonds and hazelnuts. Mix together, then press into the base and sides of the prepared tin. Bake in the preheated oven for 10–12 minutes, then leave to cool.

Meanwhile, peel the bananas and slice them into a bowl. Sprinkle with the lemon juice and vanilla extract and mix gently. Spread this mixture over the biscuit crust, then open the cans of condensed milk and spoon the milk over the bananas. Sprinkle with half the chocolate, then top with cream. Scatter over the remaining chocolate and serve.

SERVES 6

INGREDIENTS

butter, for greasing
250 g/8 oz ready-made shortcrust pastry
225 g/8 oz granulated sugar
2 tbsp water
½ tsp cream of tartar
⅛ tsp salt
2 egg whites
450 g/1 lb fresh berries
55 g/2 oz caster sugar

Fruit Meringue Pie

This was part of the Irish cook's repertoire long before pavlova made its appearance. You could use any soft fruit in season.

METHOD

Preheat the oven to 180°C/350°F/Gas Mark 4. Grease a 23-xm/9-ich tart tin.

Roll out the pastry and use to line the prepared tin. Chill in the refrigerator until firm, then line with baking paper, fill with baking beans and bake blind in the preheated oven for 15 minutes. Remove the beans, prick the base with a fork and bake for a further 5 minutes until light brown in colour. Leave to cool.

Put the granulated sugar, water, cream of tartar, salt and egg whites into a bowl, place over a saucepan of rapidly boiling water and beat steadily with a wire whisk until soft peaks hold (about 7 minutes). Remove from the heat and continue to beat for 3 minutes.

Mix the fruit with the caster sugar and distribute evenly in the pastry case. Cover with the meringue and place under a hot grill for 2 minutes to colour the meringue. Serve cold.

SERVES 6

Ginger & Honey Cheesecake

With no base and a streusel topping, this cake looks a bit like an upside-down cheesecake.

INGREDIENTS

butter, for greasing
600 g/1 lb 5 oz cream cheese
40 g/1½ oz plain flour
2 tsp ground ginger
250 g/9 oz clear honey
200 ml/7 fl oz double cream
4 large eggs, beaten

Topping
100g/3½ oz plain flour
55 g/2 oz chilled butter, cubed
100 g/3½ oz demerara sugar
½ tsp ground ginger
25 g/1 oz crystallised ginger, cubed

METHOD

Preheat the oven to 220°C/425°F/Gas Mark 7. Grease a 20-cm/8-inch round cake tin and line with baking paper.

Put the cream cheese into a large mixing bowl and beat until smooth, then stir in the flour and ginger, add the honey, cream and eggs and mix well. Pour the mixture into the prepared tin and bake in the preheated oven for 30 minutes. Turn the tin and bake for a further 15 minutes, until the surface is brown but the cake is still a bit wobbly in the middle. Leave to cool, then chill for 4 hours.

Reduce the oven temperature to 200°C/400°F/Gas Mark 6. To make the topping, put the flour, butter, sugar and ground ginger into the bowl of a food processor and pulse until crumbs form. Spread out on a baking tray and chill in the freezer for 10 minutes, then bake for 15 minutes.

Just before serving, scatter the streusel over the top of the cake, and sprinkle with the crystallised ginger.

SERVES 10

Baking with Fruit

One of the best ways to give sweetness to your bakes if you prefer not to use a lot of sugar is to incorporate fruit.

Dried fruit

Dried fruit plays a vital role in traditional Irish recipes – it's used in porter cake, Christmas cake, Christmas pudding, Simnel cake and gur cake. It's also an important ingredient in the richest fruit cake of all, the traditional Irish wedding cake.

Fresh fruit and berries

Fresh fruit also has an important part to play in home baking. There was a time when fresh fruit could be had only when it was in season – apples were about the only fruit that could be stored and used through the year. Berries were bottled or made into jam.

Summer fruit

Tangy rhubarb, available in spring for a very short space of time, is used mainly in crumbles and pies. Strawberries appear in early summer – perfect for pavlovas, open fruit tarts and for jam making. Raspberries, loganberries, cherries and blueberries appear in the early summer. Tart, juicy gooseberries are also plentiful, and are perfect for crumbles and tarts. Delicious wild fraughans (bilberries) can be foraged in the countryside in July and August – they are smaller and sweeter than their close relative, the blueberry, and are a great addition to muffins and buns.

Late summer is pear season – you don't have to add too much sugar when baking with them, and their flavour is a perfect complement to chocolate and almonds. They look decorative when sliced vertically and arranged artistically, making them ideal for open tarts served as desserts or for afternoon tea.

Autumn fruit

Autumn brings crisp apples and blackberries foraged from the hedgerows, a fruity match made in heaven. The best cooking apple is one that breaks down when heated – Bramleys are the perfect 'cookers'. Eating apples are not recommended as they are often mealy and bland when cooked.

INGREDIENTS

225 g/8 oz blackberries, picked over

450 g/1 lb Bramley apples, peeled, cored and sliced

100 g/3½ oz granulated sugar

100 g/3½ oz plain flour

55 g/2 oz porridge oats

85 g/3 oz butter, plus extra for greasing

100 g/3½ oz demerara sugar

ice cream, to serve

SERVES 6

Autumn Crumble

This mellow crumble makes the most of two of autumn's most plentiful fruity offerings – apples and blackberries.

METHOD

Preheat the oven to 180°C/350°F/Gas Mark 4. Grease a 1.2-litre/2-pint baking dish.

Put the blackberries, apples and granulated sugar into the prepared dish and stir to combine.

Put the flour, oats, butter and demerara sugar into a mixing bowl and rub together until coarse crumbs form. Spread evenly over the fruit mixture, pressing down slightly, then bake in the preheated oven for 40 minutes until the topping is browned and the fruit juices are bubbling up at the sides.

Serve hot, with ice cream.

Rhubarb & Ginger Crumble

The rhubarb season is very short, so make sure you take advantage of it with this delicious crumble.

INGREDIENTS

450 g/1 lb trimmed rhubarb, cut into 2.5-cm/1-inch lengths
100 g/3½ oz caster sugar
150 g/5½ oz plain flour
85 g/3 oz butter, at room temperature, plus extra for greasing.
55 g/2 oz demerara sugar
5-cm/2-inch piece fresh ginger, grated
55 g/2 oz hazelnuts, finely chopped
custard, to serve

METHOD

Grease a 1.2-litre/2 pint baking dish.

Put the rhubarb into a saucepan with the caster sugar and a little water and cook over a low heat for about 15 minutes, until soft but not disintegrating. Transfer to the prepared baking dish.

Meanwhile, preheat the oven to 200°C/400°F/Gas Mark 6. Sift the flour into a bowl, cut in the butter and rub it in with your fingertips until coarse crumbs form.

Add the demerara sugar, ginger and nuts and mix to combine, then sprinkle the crumble over the rhubarb.

Bake in the preheated oven for 30 minutes and serve hot, with custard.

SERVES 6

Vanilla Rhubarb Pie

The warm sweetness of vanilla is a perfect complement to the sharp flavour of rhubarb.

INGREDIENTS

- 450 g/1 lb ready-made shortcrust pastry
- 250 g/9 oz caster sugar, plus extra for sprinkling
- 6 tbsp plain flour, plus extra for dusting
- 500 g/1 lb 2 oz trimmed rhubarb, chopped
- ½ tsp vanilla bean paste

METHOD

Preheat the oven to 230°C/450°F/Gas Mark 8. Divide the pastry into two pieces. Roll out one piece on a work surface lightly dusted with flour and use to line a 23-cm/9-inch pie dish.

Combine the sugar and flour in a bowl and spread a quarter of the mixture over the pastry in the pie dish. Pile in the rhubarb, dot with the vanilla bean paste and cover with the remaining flour mixture.

Roll out the second piece of pastry and place on top of the pie dish, trimming the edge and crimping it to seal. Use a sharp knife to cut a few slits in the pastry to allow the steam to escape during cooking.

Sprinkle with sugar and bake on the bottom shelf of the preheated oven for 15 minutes, then reduce the oven temperature to 180°C/350°F/Gas Mark 4 and cook for a further 40–45 minutes. Serve warm or cold.

SERVES 6–8

Pear & Almond Tart

This luscious tart has a sweet pastry and is particularly good when made with firm pears. The almonds give it a lovely texture.

INGREDIENTS

85 g/3 oz chilled butter, diced, plus extra for greasing
175 g/6 oz plain flour, plus extra for dusting
25 g/1 oz caster sugar
1 egg

Filling
2 eggs
100 g/3½ oz caster sugar
100 g/3½ oz ground almonds
25 g/1 oz butter, melted
55 g/2 oz self-raising flour
3 firm pears, peeled and halved

METHOD

To make the pastry, rub the butter into the flour until fine crumbs form. Add the sugar and mix to combine, then add the egg and mix until the dough comes together. Add a little water if necessary. Leave to stand for at least 1 hour.

Preheat the oven to 180°C/325°F/Gas Mark 4. Grease a 20-cm/8-inch round loose-based tart tin. Roll out the pastry on a work surface lightly dusted with flour and use to line the prepared tin. Prick the base with a fork and chill in the fridge until needed.

Meanwhile, to make the filling, put the eggs and sugar into a bowl and whisk with a hand-held electric mixer until pale and creamy. Fold in the almonds, then mix in the butter. Add the flour and mix to combine.

Spread some of the almond mixture in the pastry case, then arrange the pears on top. Top with the remaining almond mixture and bake in the preheated oven for about 40 minutes. Serve warm.

SERVES 6

INGREDIENTS

butter, for greasing
250 g/9 oz ready-made shortcrust pastry
350 ml/12 fl oz milk
4 large egg yolks
100 g/3½ oz caster sugar
1 tbsp plain flour, plus extra for dusting
1 tbsp cornflour
½ tsp vanilla extract
3 tbsp apricot jam
1 tsp water
600 g/1 lb 5 oz strawberries, hulled and sliced

SERVES 6–8

Strawberry Tart

Custard provides a creamy base for strawberries in this classic summer tart.

METHOD

Preheat the oven to 190°C/375°F/Gas Mark 5. Grease a 23-cm/9-inch round loose-based tart tin. Roll out the pastry on a work surface lightly dusted with flour and use to line the prepared tin. Prick the pastry case all over with a fork, line with baking paper and fill with baking beans, then bake in the preheated oven for 15 minutes. Remove the paper and beans and bake for a further 5 minutes. Leave to cool.

Heat the milk to just below boiling point, then leave to cool slightly. Put the egg yolks into a bowl with the sugar and whisk until thick and pale. Add the flour and cornflour and whisk until smooth, then gradually add the milk, whisking constantly.

Pour into a clean saucepan and heat over a medium heat, stirring constantly until beginning to thicken, then reduce the heat to low and simmer, stirring constantly until thick. Stir in the vanilla extract, spread the custard in the pastry case and chill for 5 hours, or until set.

Heat the jam in a small saucepan with the water, then pass through a sieve to remove the fruit. Arrange the strawberry slices on the custard, brush with the apricot glaze and serve.

Irish Cream Cheesecake

This plain cheesecake is given a luxurious touch with the addition of a healthy glug of Irish cream liqueur.

INGREDIENTS

- 85 g/3 oz butter, melted
- 225 g/8 oz digestive biscuit crumbs
- 700 g/1 lb 9 oz cream cheese, softened
- 115 g/4 oz sugar
- 3 eggs, beaten
- 2 tbsp plain flour
- 225 ml/8 fl oz Irish cream liqueur
- 1 tsp vanilla extract

METHOD

Preheat the oven to 180°C/350°F/Gas Mark 4. Mix the butter and biscuit crumbs together and press into the base of a 20-cm/8-inch round springform cake tin. Bake in the preheated oven for 5 minutes. Remove from the oven (do not switch off the oven).

Meanwhile, put the cheese and sugar into a bowl and mix to combine, then add the eggs, flour, liqueur and vanilla extract and beat until smooth.

Pour the mixture onto the crumb base, return to the oven and bake for 40 minutes. Leave to cool, then chill overnight.

SERVES 6–8

Gooseberry Tart

This easy tart is a luscious way of using up some of the summer glut of gooseberries.

INGREDIENTS

- butter, for greasing
- flour, for dusting
- 250 g/9 oz ready-made shortcrust pastry
- 2 large eggs
- 200 ml/7 fl oz double cream
- 85 g/3 oz caster sugar
- 1 tsp vanilla extract
- 300 g/10½ oz gooseberries, topped and tailed

METHOD

Preheat the oven to 190°C/375°F/Gas Mark 5. Grease a 23-cm/9-inch round loose-based tart tin. Roll out the pastry on a work surface lightly dusted with flour and use to line the prepared tin. Prick the pastry case all over with a fork.

Line the pastry case with baking paper and baking beans and bake blind in the preheated oven for 15 minutes. Remove the paper and beans and return to the oven for a further 5 minutes. Leave to cool (do not switch off the oven).

Meanwhile, put the eggs, cream, sugar and vanilla extract into a large jug and beat well together.

Arrange the gooseberries on the pastry case and pour over the egg mixture. Bake in the preheated oven for 35–40 minutes until the custard is set. Serve warm or cold.

SERVES 6–8

INGREDIENTS

1 kg/2 lb 4 oz gooseberries, topped and tailed

2 tbsp water

55 g/2 oz caster sugar

55 g/2 oz plain white flour

25 g/1 oz plain wholemeal flour

55 g/2 oz chilled butter, diced

55 g/2 oz soft light brown sugar

25 g/1 oz porridge oats

25 g/1 oz chopped hazelnuts

Gooseberry & Hazelnut Crumble

A delicious combination of contrasts – tart and sweet, soft and crunchy – this is a great summer dessert.

METHOD

Preheat the oven to 200°C/400°F/Gas Mark 6. Put the gooseberries into a large saucepan with the water and heat gently until they are beginning to release their juices. Add the caster sugar, stirring to dissolve, then pour into a large baking dish.

Sift the white flour and wholemeal flour into a mixing bowl. Rub in the butter until coarse crumbs form. Add the brown sugar, oats and nuts and stir to combine.

Spoon the crumble mixture over the gooseberries and bake in the preheated oven for 20–25 minutes. Serve hot or warm.

SERVES 6

INGREDIENTS

Pastry

85 g/3 oz chilled butter, diced, plus extra for greasing

175 g/6 oz plain flour, plus extra for dusting

25 g/1 oz caster sugar

1 egg

Filling

2 eggs

100 g/3½ oz caster sugar

100 g/3½ oz ground almonds

25 g/1 oz butter, melted

55 g/2 oz self-raising flour

3 large apples, peeled, cored and halved

SERVES 6

Apple & Almond Tart

This delicious tart is crisp outside with a soft and fruity filling.

METHOD

To make the pastry, rub the butter into the flour until fine crumbs form. Add the sugar and mix to combine, then add the egg and mix until the dough comes together, adding a little water if necessary. Leave to stand for at least 1 hour.

Preheat the oven to 180°C/325°F/Gas Mark 4. Grease a 20-cm/ 8-inch round loose-based tart tin. Roll out the pastry on a work surface lightly dusted with flour and use to line the prepared tin. Prick the pastry case all over with a fork and chill until needed.

To make the filling, put the eggs and sugar into a bowl and whisk with a hand-held electric mixer until pale and creamy. Fold in the almonds, then mix in the butter. Add the flour and mix to combine.

Spread some of the almond mixture in the pastry case, then arrange the apple halves on top. Top with the remaining almond mixture and bake in the preheated oven for about 40 minutes. Serve warm.

INGREDIENTS

butter, for greasing
flour, for dusting
250 g/9 oz ready-made shortcrust pastry
300 ml/10 fl oz milk
1 tbsp cornflour
1 tbsp caster sugar
2 egg yolks
juice and grated zest of 1 large lemon

Meringue
2 egg whites
115 g/4 oz caster sugar

Lemon Meringue Pie

This classic dessert is very simple to make. The meringue should be soft and a bit chewy, not so hard that it turns to dust when you bite into it.

METHOD

Preheat the oven to 190°C/375°F/Gas Mark 5. Grease a 20-cm/8-inch cake tin. Roll out the pastry on a work surface lightly dusted with flour and use to line the prepared tin. Prick with a fork several times, line with baking paper and fill with baking beans, then bake in the preheated oven for 15 minutes. Remove the paper and beans (do not switch off the oven).

Meanwhile, mix a little of the milk with the cornflour in a mixing bowl. Heat the remaining milk in a saucepan and pour it into the cornflour mixture, then return to the pan, bring to the boil and cook for 3–4 minutes, stirring constantly. Remove from the heat and add the sugar. Leave to cool slightly, then beat in the egg yolks and the lemon juice and zest. Pour the filling into the pastry case and bake for 5 minutes until set. Reduce the oven temperature to 150°C/300°F/Gas Mark 2.

To make the meringue, whisk the egg whites until they hold stiff peaks, then whisk in 2 teaspoons of the sugar. Fold in the remaining sugar very carefully. Pile on top of the filling, covering it completely, and bake in the oven for 30 minutes until browned. Serve warm or chilled.

SERVES 6

INGREDIENTS

flour, for dusting
250 g/9 oz ready-made shortcrust pastry
4 large apples, peeled, cored and cut into chunks
2 tbsp water
3 large eggs, separated
juice of 1 lemon
85 g/3 oz caster sugar

Apple Amber

The meringue is very sweet, so use a tart apple, such as Bramley.

METHOD

Preheat the oven to 190°C/375°F/Gas Mark 5. Roll out the pastry on a work surface lightly dusted with flour and use to line a 20-cm/8-inch pie tin. Prick a few times with a fork, line with baking paper and fill with baking beans, then bake in the preheated oven for 15 minutes. Remove from the oven and take out the paper and beans. Reduce the oven temperature to 180°C/350°F/Gas Mark 4.

Put the apples and water into a large saucepan and heat over a medium heat until the apples have broken down (do not be tempted to add more water). Remove from the heat.

Beat the egg yolks. Add the lemon and three-quarters of the sugar to the apple, then add the egg yolks and stir. Spoon the mixture into the pastry case and bake for 20 minutes.

Meanwhile, whisk the egg whites until they hold stiff peaks, then gradually whisk in the remaining sugar. Pile on top of the filling, covering it completely, and bake in the oven for 10 minutes, or until the meringue is browned. Serve warm or chilled.

SERVES 6

INGREDIENTS

Pastry

175 g/6 oz plain flour, plus extra for dusting
85 g/3 oz icing sugar
100 g/3½ oz chilled butter, diced, plus extra for greasing
1 large egg yolk

Filling

100 g/3½ oz butter, softened
100 g/3½ oz caster sugar
3 eggs, beaten
100 g/3½ oz ground almonds
55 g/2 oz plain flour
¼ tsp almond extract
250 g/9 oz raspberry jam
25 g/1 oz flaked almonds

SERVES 6–8

Bakewell Tart

This jam tart is an old favourite – it makes a great standby dessert or a classic afternoon tea cake.

METHOD

To make the pastry, put the flour and icing sugar into a food processor and pulse to combine. Add the butter and pulse until fine crumbs form. Add the egg yolk and pulse until the pastry comes together. Shape into a ball, wrap in clingfilm and chill for up to 1 hour.

Preheat the oven to 180°C/350°F/Gas Mark 4 and preheat a baking sheet. Grease a 20-cm/8-inch loose-based tart tin.

To make the filling, cream the butter and caster sugar until pale and fluffy, then beat in the eggs until smooth. Add the ground almonds, flour and almond extract and stir until combined.

Roll out the pastry on a work surface lightly dusted with flour and use to line the prepared tin. Spread the jam over the base of the pastry case, then cover with the batter, distributing it evenly and levelling until smooth. Sprinkle over the flaked almonds and bake in the preheated oven for 30–35 minutes until golden brown. Serve warm or cold.

INGREDIENTS

butter, for greasing
85 g/3 oz caster sugar
3 eggs, beaten
85 g/3 oz plain flour, plus extra for dusting
1 tbsp raspberry jam
400 g/14 oz fresh sliced fruit, such as peaches, kiwis and strawberries
whipped cream, to serve

Fruit Flan

In the 1960s and 1970s fruit flan was usually made with a ready-made flan case and canned fruit. It's easy to make the flan case from scratch, and using fresh fruit makes it even more delicious.

METHOD

Preheat the oven to 200°C/400°F/Gas Mark 6. Grease a 20-cm/8-inch flan tin and dust it with flour, shaking out any excess.

Put the sugar and eggs into a bowl set over a saucepan of gently simmering water and whisk until pale and creamy.

Remove from the heat and gradually sift in the flour, folding it in with a metal spoon.

Pour the batter into the prepared tin and bake in the preheated oven for 10–15 minutes until golden.

Leave to cool in the tin for 10 minutes, then turn out onto a wire rack and leave to cool completely. Spread the jam on the base of the sponge, then fill with the fruit and serve immediately with whipped cream.

SERVES 6–8

Savoury Tarts & Pies

Blackrock Castle Observatory, Cork, County Cork

INGREDIENTS

Pastry

225 g/8 oz plain white flour, plus extra for dusting
pinch of salt
150 g/5 oz chilled butter, cubed
1 egg yolk, beaten

Filling

450 g/1 lb potatoes
2 tbsp chopped fresh parsley
2 tbsp snipped fresh chives
3 hard-boiled eggs, sliced
4 bacon rashers, fried
salt

Donegal Pie

A filling savoury pie that makes good use of everyday ingredients. It tastes great cold, so it's a good choice for a packed lunch or picnic.

METHOD

To make the pastry, put the flour and salt into a bowl and rub in the butter until coarse crumbs form. Add the egg yolk and as much water as is needed to mix to a soft but firm dough. Turn out onto a work surface lightly dusted with flour and knead for 1–2 minutes. Set aside until ready to assemble the pie.

To make the filling, steam the potatoes and mash well. Mix in the parsley and chives and add salt to taste. Line the base of a 23-cm/9-inch pie dish with half the potatoes and place a layer of egg slices on top. Cut the bacon into small pieces and scatter it over the egg with any of the fat from frying. Spread the remaining potato mixture over the bacon.

Meanwhile, preheat the oven to 200°C/400°F/Gas Mark 6. Roll out the pastry with a floured rolling pin and use to cover the pie. Bake in the preheated oven for 25–30 minutes, covering with foil after 10 minutes. Serve hot or cold.

SERVES 6–8

INGREDIENTS

Pastry

350 g/12 oz plain flour, plus extra for dusting
pinch of salt
25 g/1 oz butter, plus extra for greasing
2 egg yolks, beaten
water, for mixing
milk, for brushing

Filling

350 g/12 oz lamb shoulder, trimmed and cubed
2 tbsp chopped fresh marjoram
2 tbsp snipped fresh chives
4 tbsp lamb stock
salt

SERVES 6–8

Dingle Pie

A tasty and very filling lamb pie that is great for picnics.

METHOD

Preheat the oven to 200°C/400°F/Gas Mark 6. Grease a 20-cm/8-inch pie dish.

To make the pastry, put the flour and salt into a mixing bowl and rub in the butter until coarse crumbs form. Add the egg yolks and as much water as is needed to mix to a soft but firm dough. Turn out onto a work surface lightly dusted with flour and knead for 1–2 minutes.

Divide the dough into two pieces and roll out each piece to a round with a diameter of about 20 cm/8 inches. Use one round to line the prepared pie dish, then add the lamb, season to taste with salt and scatter over the marjoram and chives. Sprinkle over the stock, then place the second pastry round on top and crimp the edges to seal. Brush with milk and slash the pastry lid a few times to allow the steam to escape during cooking.

Bake in the preheated oven for 20 minutes, then cover the pie with foil, reduce the oven temperature to 180°C/350°F/Gas Mark 4 and bake for a further 45 minutes. Serve hot or cold.

INGREDIENTS

butter, for greasing
plain flour, for dusting
250 g/9 oz ready-made shortcrust pastry
6 streaky bacon rashers, chopped
4 large eggs
½ tsp salt
¼ tsp freshly ground black pepper
1 onion, roughly chopped
100 g/3½ oz mature Cheddar cheese, coarsely grated

Bacon & Egg Flan

You can make a subtle alteration to the flavour by using smoked bacon rashers.

METHOD

Preheat the oven to 220°C/425°F/Gas Mark 7. Grease a 23-cm/9-inch flan tin.

Roll out the pastry on a work surface lightly dusted with flour and use to line the prepared tin, trimming the pastry 2.5 cm/1 inch above the top of the tin. Line with baking paper, fill with baking beans and bake in the preheated oven for 10 minutes. Remove the paper and beans and return to the oven for a further 2 minutes.

Meanwhile, add the bacon to a hot frying pan and fry until cooked to your liking. Beat the eggs with the salt and pepper.

Remove the pastry case from the oven and reduce the oven temperature to 150°C/325°F/Gas Mark 3. Sprinkle the bacon, onion and most of the cheese over the base of the pastry case. Pour in the egg mixture and sprinkle with the remaining cheese.

Return the flan to the oven and bake for 45–50 minutes. Serve warm or cold.

SERVES 6–8

INGREDIENTS

675 g/1 lb 8 oz stewing steak, trimmed and cubed
225 g/8 oz beef kidneys, chopped
flour, for dusting
2 tbsp chopped fresh thyme
2 tbsp chopped fresh marjoram
125 ml/4 fl oz Guinness
salt and freshly ground black pepper

Pastry
275 g/9¾ oz plain flour, plus extra for dusting
pinch of salt
175 g/6 oz butter
2 egg yolks, beaten
milk, for brushing

SERVES 6–8

Steak & Kidney Pie with Guinness

This hearty, rib-sticking pie will warm you up on the coldest day. The Guinness loses its bitterness in the cooking and adds a subtle depth of flavour.

METHOD

Preheat the oven to 200°C/400°F/Gas Mark 6.

Put the steak and kidneys into a large bowl, add some flour and toss to coat. Arrange in a pie dish, add the thyme, marjoram and salt and pepper to taste and pour in the Guinness. Set aside while you prepare the pastry.

Put the flour and salt into a mixing bowl and rub in the butter until coarse crumbs form. Add the egg yolks and as much water as is needed to mix to a soft but firm dough. Turn out the pastry onto a work surface lightly dusted with flour and knead for 1–2 minutes. Roll out and place over the meat, with an upturned egg cup placed in the centre of the dish to support the weight of the pastry. Trim the edges.

Reroll the pastry trimmings and cut out leaves to decorate the top of the pie. Brush with milk and bake in the preheated oven for 15–20 minutes. Reduce the oven temperature to 150°C/300°F/Gas Mark 2 and bake for a further 2 hours, covering with foil to prevent the pastry drying out.

Chicken Pie with Potato Pastry

The soft potato pastry is great for mopping up the lovely cooking juices.

INGREDIENTS

1 chicken, boned and cut into pieces
flour, for dusting
vegetable oil and butter, for frying
3 tomatoes, peeled and chopped
1 tbsp chopped fresh parsley
1 tbsp snipped fresh chives
4 tbsp Guinness
4 lean bacon rashers, cut into strips

Pastry

300 g/10½ oz self-raising flour, plus extra for dusting
125 g/4½ oz butter
85 g/3 oz mashed potatoes
pinch of salt
1 egg, beaten
milk, for brushing

METHOD

Preheat the oven to 200°C/400°F/Gas Mark 6.

Dust the chicken pieces with flour. Heat some oil and butter in a frying pan, add the chicken and fry, turning occasionally, until golden brown. Transfer to a shallow casserole dish, add the tomatoes, parsley and chives and pour in the Guinness. Cover with a layer of bacon and set aside while you make the pastry.

Put the flour into a mixing bowl and rub in the butter. Add the potatoes and salt and mix. Add the egg and mix well.

Turn out onto a work surface lightly dusted with flour and knead until soft and elastic. Roll out the dough to a thickness of 2.5 cm/1 inch and place on top of the bacon.

Brush with milk and bake in the preheated oven for 20 minutes. Reduce the oven temperature to 180°C/350°F/Gas Mark 4 and cook for a further 30 minutes, or until the chicken is cooked through. Serve hot.

SERVES 6

INGREDIENTS

1 tbsp seasoned flour
900 g/2 lb best quality beef steak, cut into small pieces
85 g/3 oz butter
8 streaky bacon rashers, chopped
5 onions, chopped
1 tbsp raisins
1 tsp soft light brown sugar
300 ml/10 fl oz Irish stout
450 g/1 lb ready-rolled shortcrust pastry
beaten egg, for glazing

Steak & Stout Pie

Beef and stout blend perfectly in this delicious pie. The crust is broken open to reveal a rich, dark interior.

METHOD

Put the seasoned flour in a large bowl, add the beef and toss to coat. Melt the butter in a frying pan, then add the beef and the bacon and cook, stirring occasionally, until browned.

Transfer the meat to a casserole dish. Add the onions to the pan and fry until golden. Add to the casserole with the raisins, sugar and stout.

Cover tightly, bring to the boil over a medium heat, then reduce the heat and simmer for about 2 hours until the meat is tender, adding more liquid if needed.

Meanwhile, preheat the oven to 200°C/400°F/Gas Mark 6. Transfer the contents of the casserole dish to a deep pie dish and cover with the pastry, trimming and sealing the edges. Brush with the beaten egg and cook in the preheated oven for 30–35 minutes, until golden brown.

Serve hot.

SERVES 6

Caramelised Cherry Tomato & Goat's Cheese Tart

This is a good option for lunch and is delicious served hot or cold.

INGREDIENTS

butter, for greasing
flour, for dusting
250 g/9 oz ready-made shortcrust pastry
1 tbsp olive oil
1 onion, roughly chopped
200 g/7 oz cherry tomatoes, halved
1 tsp sugar
5 large eggs
1 tsp chopped fresh sage
200 g/7 oz soft goat's cheese, roughly chopped
chopped fresh parsley
salt and freshly ground black pepper

METHOD

Preheat the oven to 220°C/425°F/Gas Mark 7. Grease a 23-cm/9-inch round flan tin.

Roll out the pastry on a work surface lightly dusted with flour to a round 5 cm/2 inches larger than the diameter of the tin. Use to line the tin, prick with a fork, then line with baking paper and baking beans and bake in the preheated oven for 10 minutes. Remove the paper and beans and return to the oven for a further 2 minutes.

Meanwhile, heat the oil in a frying pan over a medium heat, then add the onion and cook until softened. Add the tomatoes and cook until soft and beginning to burst, then stir in the sugar and cook for a further 5 minutes, until the tomatoes are lightly caramelised. Meanwhile, beat the eggs with the sage and some salt and pepper.

Remove the pastry case from the oven and reduce the oven temperature to 160°C/325°F/Gas Mark 3. Carefully pour the tomato mixture over the base of the pastry case and scatter over the cheese, making sure that the cheese and tomatoes are evenly distributed. Pour in the egg mixture and scatter the parsley on top. Return to the oven and bake for 30–35 minutes until the egg is set. Leave to cool for 5 minutes.

SERVES 6–8

INGREDIENTS

3 tbsp rapeseed oil
1 onion, chopped,
900 g/2 lb minced lamb
2 carrots, chopped
2 tbsp finely chopped fresh parsley
1 tsp finely chopped fresh thyme
1½ tbsp plain flour
700 ml/1¼ pints lamb or beef stock
900 g/2 lb potatoes, peeled and cut into chunks
125 ml/4 fl oz milk
salt and freshly ground black pepper

SERVES 6

Shepherd's Pie

Less common than cottage pie, which is made with beef, this is a delicious way of using up the leftover Sunday lamb roast. It can also be prepared with uncooked lamb mince.

METHOD

Heat 2 tablespoons of the oil in a large frying pan over a medium heat. Add the onion and fry for 5 minutes until translucent. Add the lamb and cook, stirring, for 5 minutes until browned. Add the carrots, parsley and thyme and season with salt and pepper. Cook, stirring, for 2–3 minutes until the carrots are coated in oil.

Stir in the flour, then slowly pour in the stock and bring to the boil, scraping up any sediment from the base of the pan. Reduce the heat to low and simmer for 20–25 minutes until the sauce has thickened.

Meanwhile, preheat the oven to 200°C/400°F/Gas Mark 6. Put the potatoes into a large saucepan of lightly salted water, bring to the boil and cook for 10–12 minutes until tender. Drain and mash well with the milk.

Tip the pie filling into a large baking dish, cover with the potato and bake in the preheated oven for 30 minutes.

Smoked Salmon Tart

INGREDIENTS

butter, for greasing
flour, for dusting
250 g/9 oz ready-made shortcrust pastry
5 large eggs
300 ml/10 fl oz single cream
½ tsp chopped fresh dill
250 g/9 oz smoked salmon trimmings
200 g/7 oz baby spinach leaves, wilted
salt and freshly ground black pepper
fresh basil leaves, to garnish

Smoked salmon is usually eaten cold, but it is also delicious when cooked. This economical tart uses inexpensive smoked salmon trimmings.

METHOD

Preheat the oven to 200°C/400°F/Gas Mark 6. Grease a 23-cm/9-inch round flan tin.

Dust a work surface with flour and roll out the pastry to a round 5 cm/2 inches larger than the diameter of the tin. Use to line the tin, prick with a fork, then line with baking paper and baking beans and bake in the preheated oven for 10 minutes. Remove the paper and beans and bake for a further 2 minutes.

Meanwhile, beat the eggs with the cream, dill and a little salt and pepper, bearing in mind that smoked salmon is quite salty.

Remove the pastry case from the oven and reduce the oven temperature to 160°C/325°F/Gas Mark 3. Scatter the smoked salmon and the spinach evenly over the base of the pastry case, then pour in the egg mixture.

Return to the oven and bake for 30–35 minutes until the filling is set. Leave to cool for 5 minutes before serving, garnished with basil leaves.

SERVES 4–6

Luxury Fish Pie

INGREDIENTS

650 g/1 lb 7 oz white fish fillets, skinned

250 g/9 oz cooked, peeled prawns (optional)

200 g/7 oz spinach, cooked, drained and finely chopped

55 g/2 oz butter, plus extra for greasing

1 onion, finely chopped

150 ml/5 fl oz single cream

1 tbsp English mustard powder

juice of 1 lemon

1 kg/2 lb 4 oz creamy mashed potato

salt and freshly ground black pepper

Cod is the traditional ingredient in this pie, but you could use any other white fish. Prawns are not strictly necessary, but add extra colour, flavour and texture.

METHOD

Preheat the oven to 180°C/350°F/Gas Mark 4. Grease a 2-litre/3½-pint baking dish.

Cut the fish into bite-sized pieces and place in the base of the prepared dish. Scatter over the prawns and the spinach and season to taste with salt and pepper.

Melt the butter in a saucepan, add the onion and fry over a medium heat until softened. Add the cream and mustard powder and slowly stir in the lemon juice. Bring to the boil, stirring, then remove from the heat.

Pour the mixture into the dish, making sure that the fish and prawns are evenly covered.

Pipe the mashed potato onto the fish mixture, then bake in the preheated oven for 15–20 minutes until the topping is golden. Serve hot.

SERVES 6

Beef & Oyster Pie

In bygone days oysters were cheap and readily available and were often cooked with beef. This hearty pie includes another traditional ingredient – stout.

INGREDIENTS

- 450 g/1 lb stewing beef, trimmed and cubed
- 25 g/1 oz plain flour
- 1 tbsp vegetable oil
- 25 g/1 oz butter
- 1 onion, finely chopped
- 150 ml/5 fl oz stout
- 150 ml/5 fl oz beef stock
- 1 bouquet garni
- 12 oysters, shucked
- plain flour, for dusting
- 300 g/10½ oz ready-made shortcrust pastry
- 1 egg, beaten
- salt and freshly ground black pepper
- chopped fresh flatleaf parsley, to garnish

METHOD

Preheat the oven to 180°C/350°F/Gas Mark 4. Put the beef and flour into a polythene bag with some salt and pepper, secure the top of the bag and shake until the meat is completely coated in flour.

Heat the oil and butter together in a large casserole until the butter is melted. Add the meat and cook for 10 minutes until browned all over. Add the onion and cook for a further 2 minutes, or until just softened.

Add the stout, stock and bouquet garni. Cover and cook in the preheated oven for 1½ hours.

Transfer the contents of the casserole to a pie dish and stir in the oysters. Increase the oven temperature to 200°C/400°F/Gas Mark 6.

Roll out the pastry on a lightly floured work surface and use to cover the pie dish. Trim, crimping the edges, and decorate with cut-out pastry shapes. Brush with beaten egg and bake in the oven for 25 minutes. Serve piping hot, garnished with parsley.

SERVES 4–6

INGREDIENTS

butter, for greasing

plain flour, for dusting

250 g/9 oz ready-made shortcrust pastry

25 g/1 oz dried dulse, soaked in cold water for 10 minutes

300 ml/10 fl oz milk

4 large eggs

100 g/3½ oz mature Cheddar cheese, coarsely grated

salt and freshly ground black pepper

Seaweed Flan

A seaweed that can be found all along Ireland's western coastline, dulse is high in fibre and rich in vitamins and minerals. It's available dried, and can be reconstituted in cold water.

METHOD

Preheat the oven to 180°C/350°C/Gas Mark 4. Grease a 23-cm/9-inch flan tin. Roll out the pastry on a lightly floured work surface and use to line the prepared tin.

Drain the dulse, pat it dry and chop it very finely, then sprinkle it evenly in the base of the pastry case.

Put the milk into a bowl, add the eggs and beat well, then add the cheese and stir to combine. Add salt and pepper to taste, then pour the mixture into the pastry case.

Bake in the preheated oven for 20–25 minutes, or until set. Serve warm or cold.

SERVES 6–8

INGREDIENTS

flour, for dusting

500 g/1 lb 4 oz ready-made shortcrust pastry

450 g/1 lb boneless lamb, trimmed and diced, or cooked lamb, diced

1 large onion, finely chopped

2 carrots, diced

1 potato, diced

2 celery sticks, finely chopped

1 egg, beaten

salt and pepper

Individual Dingle Pies

These are great for a picnic or lunchbox and can be made with fresh lamb or with the leftovers of the Sunday roast.

METHOD

Preheat the oven to 180°C/350°F/Gas Mark 4.

Cut the pastry in half and roll out one piece on a work surface lightly dusted with flour. Cut out 6 rounds, using a small plate as a guide, re-rolling the trimmings as necessary.

Mix the meat and vegetables together and season to tase with salt and pepper.

Pile the mixture in the centre of each round, then roll out the remaining pastry and cut out 6 smaller rounds.

Lay the small rounds on top of the meat, then dampen the edges of the pastry bases and draw them up, pleating them to fit the pastry lids. Pinch the edges together, brush the pies with beaten egg and make a hole in the top of each to release the steam.

Place the pies on a baking sheet and bake in the preheated oven for 1 hour.

MAKES 6 PIES

INGREDIENTS

flour, for dusting
450 g/1 lb ready-made shortcrust pastry
25 g/1 oz butter, plus extra for greasing
1 garlic clove, crushed
450 g/1 lb spinach
225 g/8 oz Cheddar cheese, grated
2 small eggs, lightly beaten
5 tbsp double cream
grated nutmeg, to taste
salt and freshly ground black pepper

Cheese & Spinach Pie

This tasty pie makes a substantial lunch or a simple evening meal. It's great warm or cold.

METHOD

Preheat the oven to 180°C/350°F/Gas Mark 4. Grease a 23-cm/9-inch loose-based tart tin.

Roll out just over half the pastry on a work surface lightly dusted with flour and use to line the prepared tin.

Heat the butter in a large saucepan, add the garlic and fry until just giving off its aroma. Add the spinach and cook over a low heat until it begins to lose its volume. Add the cheese and stir to combine, then add most of the eggs, the cream, nutmeg and salt and pepper to taste.

Spoon the mixture into the pastry case, then roll out the remaining pastry, cut out a 23-cm/9-inch round and use to top the pie. Dampen the edges of the base and top and pinch the edges to seal. Glaze with the reserved beaten egg, sprinkle with salt and bake in the preheated oven for 40 minutes until golden.

SERVES 6–8

INGREDIENTS

butter, for greasing
250 g/9 oz ready-made shortcrust pastry
2 onions, cut into eighths lengthwise
200 g/7 oz small courgettes, halved lengthwise
2 tbsp olive oil
300 ml/10 fl oz double cream
4 eggs
180 g/6½ oz grated Cheddar cheese
250 g/9 oz spinach, cooked and chopped
salt and freshly ground black pepper

SERVES 6

Roasted Vegetable Quiche

This is an easy and very tasty lunch dish. You could use thawed frozen spinach if fresh is unavailable.

METHOD

Preheat the oven to 180°C/350°F/Gas Mark 4. Grease a 23-cm/9-inch tart tin.

Roll out the pastry and use to line the prepared tart tin. Prick the base with a fork and chill in the refrigerator for 15 minutes. Line the pastry case with baking paper and fill with baking beans, then bake blind in the preheated oven for 15 minutes. Remove the paper and beans and return to the oven for a further 5 minutes until golden. Set aside to cool. Increase the oven temperature to 200°C/400°F/Gas Mark 6.

Put the onions and courgettes into a large baking tray and drizzle with the oil, turning to coat. Roast in the oven for 30–40 minutes, turning halfway through the cooking time, until soft and golden. Remove from the oven and reduce the oven temperature to 180°C/350°F/Gas Mark 4.

Put the cream, eggs and half the cheese into a bowl and whisk, adding salt and pepper to taste. Sprinkle the remaining cheese in the base of the pastry case, top with onions, courgettes and spinach, spreading them out evenly, and pour over the cream mixture. Bake for 25–30 minutes until the filling is set and the top of the quiche is golden. Serve warm.

Salmon & Cream Cheese Tart

Salmon and cream cheese are a great combination. This rich tart is a good supper option.

INGREDIENTS

- butter, for greasing
- 300 g/10½ oz ready-made shortcrust pastry
- 4 eggs
- 400 ml/14 fl oz double cream
- 2 spring onions, finely sliced
- 450 g/1 lb cooked salmon
- 200 g/7 oz cream cheese
- freshly ground black pepper

METHOD

Preheat the oven to 200°C/400°F/Gas Mark 6. Grease a 22-cm/10-inch loose-based tart tin. Roll out the pastry and use to line the prepared tin. Fill the pastry case with baking paper and baking beans and bake blind in the preheated oven for 15 minutes. Remove the paper and beans and return to the oven for a further 5 minutes until golden. Set aside to cool and reduce the oven temperature to 180°C/350°F/Gas Mark 4.

Meanwhile, put the eggs and cream into a bowl and beat together, adding pepper to taste. Add the spring onions. Flake the salmon into large chunks and place in the base of the pastry case. Add tablespoons of the cheese, then pour in the egg mixture and bake for 25 minutes until lightly set. Leave to cool before serving.

SERVES 6–8

Biscuits & Buns

Harvest time in rural Ireland

INGREDIENTS

225 g/8 oz porridge oats, plus extra for dusting

60 g/2¼ oz wholemeal flour, plus extra for dusting

½ tsp bicarbonate of soda

1 tsp salt

½ tsp sugar

85 g/3 oz butter, plus extra for greasing

4–5 tbsp hot water

Crunchy Savoury Oatcakes

These are very quick and easy to prepare and are delicious with any kind of cheese or with smoked fish.

METHOD

Preheat the oven to 190°C/375°F/Gas Mark 5. Grease a baking sheet.

Put the oats, flour, bicarbonate of soda, salt and sugar into a bowl and mix to combine. Add the butter and rub it in until the mixture has the consistency of coarse breadcrumbs.

Gradually add the water and mix until the dough is thick but not sticky.

Roll out the dough to a thickness of 5 mm/¼ inch on a work surface lightly dusted with a mixture of oats and flour. Cut out 12 rounds with a biscuit cutter and place in the prepared baking sheet.

Bake in the preheated oven for 20–30 minutes until golden. Leave to cool on the sheet until firm, then transfer to a wire rack and leave to cool completely. Store in an airtight container.

MAKES 12

INGREDIENTS

350 g/12 oz self-raising flour
pinch of salt
200 g/7 oz demerara sugar
5-cm/2-inch piece fresh ginger, grated
1 tsp bicarbonate of soda
125 g/4½ oz butter, plus extra for greasing
75 g/2¾ oz golden syrup
1 egg, beaten
granulated sugar, for sprinkling

Ginger Nuts

These traditional biscuits have a lovely texture – fresh ginger adds extra spiciness.

METHOD

Preheat the oven to 160°C/325°F/Gas Mark 3. Lightly grease two large baking sheets.

Sift the flour and salt into a mixing bowl, then stir in the demerara sugar, ginger and bicarbonate of soda.

Put the butter and golden syrup into a small saucepan and heat over a very low heat until the butter has melted. Leave to cool slightly.

Pour the butter mixture onto the dry ingredients, add the egg and mix to a firm dough. With damp hands, roll the dough into 30 walnut-sized balls and place on the prepared baking sheets, well spaced to allow for spreading, then flatten slightly with your fingers. Sprinkle with a little granulated sugar.

Bake in the preheated oven for 15–20 minutes. Leave to cool on the sheets for 5 minutes, or until just beginning to firm up, then transfer to wire racks and leave to cool completely.

MAKES 30

INGREDIENTS

90 g/3¼ oz plain flour
2 tbsp cocoa powder
115 g/4 oz butter, plus extra for greasing
55 g/2 oz caster sugar
½ tsp vanilla extract

Chocolate Biscuits

Nothing says 'treat' better than a chocolate biscuit with a cup of tea or coffee. These are simplicity itself to prepare.

METHOD

Preheat the oven to 190°C/375°F/Gas Mark 5. Lightly grease two large baking sheets.

Sift the flour and cocoa powder together into a bowl. Put the butter, sugar and vanilla extract into a separate bowl and cream together until pale and fluffy.

Add the flour mixture to the butter mixture and stir until well combined. Drop teaspoons of the mixture onto the prepared baking sheets, well spaced to allow for spreading.

Bake in the preheated oven for 15–20 minutes until firm. Leave to cool on the sheets for 1 minute, then transfer to wire racks and leave to cool completely.

MAKES 12–15

INGREDIENTS

125 g/4½ oz butter
85 g/3 oz caster sugar
85 g/3 oz soft light brown sugar
1 egg, beaten
2 tbsp milk
250 g/9 oz plain flour
½ tsp bicarbonate of soda
pinch of salt
100 g/3½ oz plain chocolate, chopped into small pieces
100 g/3½ oz porridge oats
½ tsp vanilla extract
demerara sugar, for coating

Dark Chocolate Oaties

These moreish biscuits will keep for a few days in an airtight tin.

METHOD

Preheat the oven to 200°C/400°F/Gas Mark 6. Line a baking sheet with baking paper.

Put the butter, caster sugar and brown sugar into a mixing bowl and cream together until light and fluffy. Add the egg and mix well. Add the milk, with a little flour to prevent curdling.

Put the flour, bicarbonate of soda and salt into a bowl and mix to combine, then fold into the butter mixture with a metal spoon. Add the chocolate, oats and vanilla extract and mix well to combine.

Put some demerara sugar into a small bowl. Break off walnut-sized pieces of the dough and roll them into balls, then roll in the sugar to coat. Place them on the prepared baking sheet, evenly spaced, and bake in the preheated oven for 12–15 minutes. Leave to cool on the sheet for a few minutes, then transfer to a wire rack and leave to cool completely.

MAKES 18–20

INGREDIENTS

140 g/5 oz softened butter
140 g/5 oz sugar
1 tbsp milk
1 tsp golden syrup
140 g/5 oz self-raising flour
1 tsp bicarbonate of soda
115 g/4 oz rolled oats

MAKES 12

Crunchy Oat Biscuits

The homemade version of this popular traditional biscuit is so much better than the one sold in supermarkets.

METHOD

Preheat the oven to 150°C/300°F/Gas Mark 2. Line a large baking sheet with paper.

Put the butter and sugar into a bowl and cream together, then beat in the milk and golden syrup. Mix in the flour, bicarbonate of soda and the oats and mix to combine.

Roll walnut-sized pieces of the dough between your palms to make 12 balls, and place them on the prepared baking sheet, spaced well apart to allow for spreading. Flatten the balls slightly, then bake in the preheated oven for 10–15 minutes, until golden.

Leave to cool on the sheet for a few minutes, then transfer to a wire rack and leave to cool completely.

INGREDIENTS

85 g/3 oz plain flour
½ tsp salt
115 g/4 oz porridge oats
70 g/2½ oz raisins, sultanas, dried cranberries or choppied dried apricots
25 g/1 oz chopped walnuts, hazelnuts or cashew nuts
70 g/2½ oz soft light brown sugar
140 g/5 oz butter, plus extra for greasing
1 tsp golden syrup
½ tsp bicarbonate of soda
2 tbsp boiling water
2 tsp cider vinegar

MAKES 15–20

Oaty Fruit & Nut Biscuits

These oaty biscuits are very quick to rustle up. The type of dried fruit and nuts you use is up to you.

METHOD

Preheat the oven to 180°C/350°F/Gas Mark 4 and grease a large baking sheet.

Sift the flour and salt into a mixing bowl, add the oats, raisins, walnuts and sugar and stir to combine.

Put the butter and golden syrup into a small saucepan and heat until the butter is melted. Mix the bicarbonate of soda with the boiling water in a small cup.

Add the butter mixture to the dry ingredients, then add the bicarbonate of soda mixture and the vinegar. Mix thoroughly.

Drop teaspoons of the mixture onto the prepared baking sheet and bake in the middle of the preheated oven for 25–30 minutes. Leave to cool on the sheet for 5 minutes, then transfer to a wire rack and leave to cool completely.

INGREDIENTS

225 g/8 oz butter, plus extra for greasing
225 g/8 oz caster sugar
2 tsp clear honey
4 tbsp hot water
225 g/8 oz rolled oats
225 g/8 oz plain flour
1 tsp baking powder
1 tsp bicarbonate of soda

Oat & Honey Crunch Biscuits

These crunchy, slightly chewy biscuits are perfect for eating with your morning coffee. Add a handful of chocolate chips along with the oats for a touch of luxury.

METHOD

Preheat the oven to 190°C/375°F/Gas Mark 5 and grease two large baking sheets.

Put the butter and sugar into a mixing bowl and cream until pale and fluffy. Add the honey and water and stir to combine.

Add the oats and sift in the flour, baking powder and bicarbonate of soda.

Mix well, then roll the mixture into walnut-sized balls with your hands and arrange on the prepared baking sheets, well spaced to allow for spreading.

Bake in the preheated oven for 10–15 minutes. Leave to cool on the baking sheets for 10 minutes, then transfer to wire racks and leave to cool completely.

Store in an airtight tin for up to 1 week.

MAKES ABOUT 30

INGREDIENTS

175 g/6 oz self-raising flour, plus extra for dusting

½ tsp bicarbonate of soda

125 g/4 oz butter, plus extra for greasing

2 tsp golden syrup

85 g/3 oz granulated sugar

Portarlington Golden Biscuits

A nice, plain biscuit that you can rustle up from storecupboard ingredients.

METHOD

Preheat the oven to 200°C/400°F/Gas Mark 6 and grease a large baking sheet.

Sift the flour and bicarbonate of soda together into a bowl.

Put the butter, golden syrup and sugar into a small saucepan and heat until the sugar is dissolved. Bring to the boil, then pour into the flour mixture and stir well to combine.

Dust your hands with flour and roll the mixture into walnut-sized balls. Place them on the prepared baking sheet, well spaced to allow for spreading, and bake in the middle of the preheated oven for 10–15 minutes until golden. Leave to cool on the sheet for 5 minutes, then transfer to a wire rack and leave to cool completely.

MAKES 15–20

INGREDIENTS

350 g/12 oz plain flour
1 tsp cream of tartar
½ tsp bicarbonate of soda
225 g/8 oz butter, plus extra for greasing
225 g/8 oz caster sugar
1 egg, beaten

Porter Hope Biscuits

A great recipe for a biscuit tin standby.

METHOD

Preheat the oven to 180°C/350°F/Gas Mark 4 and grease two large baking sheets.

Put the flour, cream of tartar and bicarbonate of soda into a bowl and mix to combine. Rub in the butter, then stir in the sugar. Add the egg and mix to a firm dough. Break off walnut-sized pieces of the dough, roll into balls and flatten onto the prepared baking sheets using a fork. Space well to allow for spreading.

Bake in the middle of the preheated oven for 20 minutes (you will have to do this in batches), or until golden. Leave to cool on the sheets for 5 minutes, then transfer to a wire rack and leave to cool completely.

MAKES ABOUT 36

INGREDIENTS

225 g/8 oz softened butter, plus extra for greasing

100 g/3½ oz caster sugar

100 g/3½ oz self-raising flour, plus extra for dusting

55 g/2 oz desiccated coconut

225 g/8 oz oat flakes

Coconut Biscuits

These small crispy biscuits are the perfect accompaniment to a nice cup of tea.

METHOD

Preheat the oven to 180°C/350°F/Gas Mark 4. Grease two baking sheets.

Put the butter and sugar into a bowl and cream until light and fluffy. Add the flour, coconut and oat flakes and mix well.

Roll out the dough on a work surface lightly dusted with flour and cut out small rounds. Arrange them evenly on the prepared baking sheets (you may have to bake in batches) and bake in the preheated oven for 15–20 minutes until golden.

Leave to cool on the sheets for a few minutes, then transfer to a wire rack to cool completely.

MAKES ABOUT 36

INGREDIENTS

280 g/10 oz self-raising flour
115 g/4 oz caster sugar
225 g/8 oz softened butter
grated zest of 1 lemon

Lemon Biscuits

These little biscuits are perfect with a cup of tea or coffee, or as a sweet treat in a school lunchbox.

METHOD

Put all the ingredients into a bowl and mix well until a dough forms. Chill in the refrigerator for 30 minutes.

Meanwhile, preheat the oven to 180°C/350°F/Gas Mark 4 and line a baking sheet with baking paper.

Shape the dough into small balls and place them on the prepared tray (you will need to bake in batches).

Bake in the preheated oven for 10–15 minutes. Transfer to a wire rack and leave to cool, then store in airtight tins.

MAKES ABOUT 50

INGREDIENTS

200 g/7 oz plain flour, plus extra for dusting
25 g/1 oz oatmeal
55 g/2 oz mixed peel
pinch of ground ginger
pinch of mixed spice
pinch of bicarbonate of soda
175 g/6 oz treacle
85 g/3 oz butter, plus extra for greasing
55 g/2 oz caster sugar

Hunting Nuts

These solid biscuits fit handily into a pocket and were a traditional snack for hunters.

METHOD

Put the flour, oatmeal, mixed peel, spices and bicarbonate of soda into a bowl and mix to combine.

Put the treacle into a saucepan with the butter and sugar and heat over a low heat until melted. Pour into the dry ingredients and mix well together, then knead the dough into a hard ball. Set aside for 4 hours.

Preheat the oven to 200°C/400°F/Gas Mark 6 and grease a baking sheet. Roll out the dough on a work surface lightly dusted with flour to a thickness of 5 mm/¼ inch. Cut into 7 x 3-cm/2¾ x 1½-inch rectangles. Lay these on the prepared baking sheet and bake in the preheated oven for 8–10 minutes. Leave to cool on the sheet, then transfer to a wire rack and leave to cool completely.

MAKES 12

INGREDIENTS

115 g/4 oz softened butter, plus extra for greasing
55 g/2 oz caster sugar
55 g/2 oz plain flour
140 g/5 oz oatmeal
55 g/2 oz chopped almonds
½ tsp salt
pinch of bicarbonate of soda

Oaty Almond Biscuits

These crunchy biscuits make a lovely snack, and a tasty addition to a packed lunch.

METHOD

Preheat the oven to 190°C/375°F/Gas Mark 5. Grease a baking sheet.

Put the butter and sugar into a bowl and cream together until light and fluffy. Gradually add the remaining ingredients, mixing until well combined.

Turn out the dough onto a work surface lightly dusted with flour and roll out to a thickness of 5mm/¼ inch. Use a fluted cutter to cut out rounds. Arrange these on the prepared baking sheet and bake in the preheated oven for 10–15 minutes or until light golden in colour.

Leave to cool on the sheet for 5 minutes, then transfer to a wire rack and leave to cool completely.

MAKES 10

Ingredients

115 g/4 oz softened butter, plus extra for greasing
55 g/2 oz caster sugar
2 tsp golden syrup
140 g/5 oz porridge oats
55 g/2 oz plain flour, plus extra for dusting
15 g/½ oz desiccated coconut
pinch of bicarbonate of soda
pinch of salt
halved walnuts, to decorate

Filling
40 g/1½ oz softened butter
85 g/3 oz icing sugar
coffee essence, to taste

Icing
115 g/4 oz icing sugar
coffee essence, to taste
boiling water

Iced Coffee Oat Biscuits

These delicious iced sandwich biscuits make a lovely addition to an afternoon tea.

Method

Preheat the oven to 180°C/375°F/Gas Mark 4 and grease a baking sheet.

Put the butter and sugar into a bowl and cream together until light and fluffy. Beat in the golden syrup, then gradually add all the dry ingredients and mix well.

Turn out the dough onto a work surface lightly dusted with flour and roll out fairly thickly. Cut into 12 rounds, place on the prepared sheet and bake in the preheated oven for 10–15 minutes until golden. Leave to cool on the sheet, then transfer to a wire rack and leave to cool completely.

To make the filling, put the butter into a bowl and gradually beat in the icing sugar until the mixture is light and fluffy. Add coffee extract to taste, then use the mixture to sandwich the biscuits together.

To make the icing, sift the sugar into a bowl, then add some coffee essence and mix to a spreading consistency with a little boiling water. Spread a little on top of each biscuit and top each with a walnut half.

Makes 6

INGREDIENTS

115 g/4 oz softened butter, plus extra for greasing
115 g/4 oz caster sugar
1 tbsp golden syrup
grated rind of 1 orange
1 egg yolk, beaten
200 g/7 oz plain flour
½ tsp salt
½ tsp cream of tartar
½ tsp bicarbonate of soda

Filling

40 g/1½ oz softened butter
85 g/3 oz icing sugar, sifted
grated rind of 1 orange
½ tsp orange extract
a little orange food colouring

Orange Creams

This crunchy biscuit with a tangy buttercream filling is a citrus version of the ever-popular gipsy cream.

METHOD

Preheat the oven to 180°C/350°F/Gas Mark 4. Grease a large baking sheet

Put the butter and sugar into a mixing bowl and cream together until light and fluffy. Beat in the golden syrup and the orange rind, then beat in the egg yolk. Add the flour, salt, cream of tartar and bicarbonate of soda, mixing to incorporate.

Shape the mixture into 18 walnut-sized balls and place on the prepared sheet, spaced well apart to allow for spreading. Press lightly with a wet fork and bake in the preheated oven for 20–25 minutes until golden. Leave to cool on the sheet for 5 minutes, then transfer to a wire rack and leave to cool completely.

Meanwhile, make the filling. Put the butter into a bowl and cream until light and fluffy, then beat in the sugar, orange rind, orange extract and food colouring. Use the mixture to sandwich the biscuits together.

MAKES 9

Shah Biscuits

These very popular lightly spiced biscuits are great for dunking in a cup of tea or coffee.

INGREDIENTS

115 g/4 oz softened butter, plus extra for greasing
115 g/4 oz caster sugar
2 tsp golden syrup
1 egg yolk
200 g/7 oz plain flour, plus extra for dusting
½ tsp cream of tartar
½ tsp bicarbonate of soda
1 tsp ground ginger
pinch of mixed spice
pinch of ground cloves
pinch of salt

METHOD

Preheat the oven to 180°C/350°F/Gas Mark 4. Grease a baking sheet.

Put the butter and sugar into a bowl and cream together until light and fluffy, then beat in the golden syrup. Mix in the egg yolk, then work in the dry ingredients.

Using floured hands, roll the dough into walnut-sized balls and place them on the prepared sheet (you will have to bake in batches), spaced well apart to allow for spreading.

Bake in the preheated oven for about 20 minutes. Leave to cool on the sheet for a few minutes, then transfer to wire racks and leave to cool completely.

MAKES ABOUT 20

INGREDIENTS

1 sheet of rice paper, for baking
butter, for greasing
115 g/4 oz caster sugar
55 g/2 oz blanched almonds, finely chopped
15 g/½ oz ground almonds
1 tsp rice flour
1 large egg white
almond extract, to taste
whole blanched almonds, to decorate

Almond Macaroons

Not to be confused with macarons, these delightful old-fashioned biscuits get their distinctive chewy texture from the edible rice paper on which they are baked.

METHOD

Preheat the oven to 160°C/325°F/Gas Mark 3. Grease a baking sheet and line with rice paper.

Put the sugar, chopped almonds, ground almonds and rice flour into a bowl and mix to combine.

In a separate clean, grease-free bowl, whisk the egg white until soft peaks hold. Fold in the dry ingredients and add some almond extract. You should have a fairly stiff consistency.

Place teaspoons of the mixture on the prepared sheet, decorate each pile with a whole blanched almond, then bake in the preheated oven for about 40 minutes.

Remove the biscuits from the oven and tear away the excess rice paper. If it doesn't come away, trim it later with scissors. Place the biscuits on a wire tray and leave to cool completely.

MAKES 12

Ingredients

butter, for greasing
1 sheet of rice paper, for baking
1 large egg white
55 g/2 oz finely chopped walnuts
15 g/½ oz ground almonds
115 g/4 oz caster sugar
1 tsp rice flour
walnut halves, to decorate

Filling
40 g/1½ oz butter
140 g/5 oz icing sugar
coffee essence, to taste

Coffee Walnut Macaroons

These sandwich biscuits have a lovely chewy texture and a flavour that is reminiscent of a coffee and walnut sponge cake.

Method

Preheat the oven to 160°C/325°F/Gas Mark 3. Grease a baking tray and line with rice paper.

Whisk the egg white in a clean, grease-free bowl until soft peaks hold. Fold in the chopped walnuts, ground almonds, sugar and rice flour.

Place 12 teaspoons of the mixture on the prepared tray and decorate half with a walnut half. Bake in the preheated oven for about 40 minutes.

Remove the biscuits from the oven and tear away the excess rice paper. If it doesn't come away, trim it later with scissors. Place the biscuits on a wire tray and leave to cool completely.

Meanwhile, make the filling. Cream the butter with the icing sugar, adding a little coffee essence to taste. Use the mixture to sandwich the macaroons together.

MAKES 6

INGREDIENTS

70 g/2½ oz butter, plus extra for greasing
70 g/2½ oz caster sugar
115 g/4 oz plain flour
¼ tsp bicarbonate of soda
¼ tsp cream of tartar
12 walnut halves

Walnut Biscuits

These very simple biscuits are quick and easy to prepare and can be stored in a tin for up to a week.

METHOD

Preheat the oven to 180°C/350°F/Gas Mark 4. Grease a baking tray.

Put the butter and sugar into a bowl and cream until light and fluffy. Add the flour, bicarbonate of soda and cream of tartar and mix to a dough. Use your hands to roll the dough into balls a little smaller than walnuts.

Place the balls on the prepared tray, spaced evenly apart. Press a walnut half into the top of each and bake in the preheated oven for 15–20 minutes. Leave to cool on the tray for a few minutes, then transfer to a wire rack and leave to cool completely.

MAKES 12

Vanilla Biscuits

This crisp, golden biscuit is a great biscuit tin standby for an unexpected guest.

INGREDIENTS

- 115 g/4 oz softened butter, plus extra for greasing
- 85 g/3 oz sugar
- 55 g/2 oz porridge oats
- 115 g/4 oz self-raising flour
- ¼ tsp baking powder
- ¼ tsp vanilla extract
- 1 tsp golden syrup
- 3 tsp boiling water

METHOD

Preheat the oven to 180°C/350°F/Gas Mark 4. Grease a baking tray.

Put the butter and sugar into a bowl and cream until light and fluffy. Gradually add the remaining ingredients, working them in after each addition.

Shape the mixture into walnut-sized balls. Place on the prepared tray, spaced evenly apart, and flatten slightly with a wet fork.

Bake in the preheated oven for 15–20 minutes, or until golden and crisp.

MAKES 18–20

INGREDIENTS

125 g/4½ oz butter
55 g/2 oz caster sugar, plus extra for sprinkling
175 g/6 oz plain flour, plus extra for dusting

Shortbread Fingers

These crumbly, buttery fingers are incredibly easy to make, yet they never fail to impress.

METHOD

Preheat the oven to 190°C/375°F/Gas Mark 5. Line two large baking sheets with baking paper.

Put the butter and sugar into a mixing bowl and cream together until pale and smooth. Add the flour and stir to a smooth paste.

Turn out onto a work surface lightly dusted with flour and roll out to a thickness of 1 cm/½ inch. Cut into fingers and place on the prepared baking sheets. Sprinkle with sugar and chill for 15 minutes.

Bake in the preheated oven for 15–20 minutes until golden. Transfer to a wire rack and leave to cool.

MAKES 24

INGREDIENTS

25 g/1 oz rice flour
140 g/5 oz plain flour, plus extra for dusting
55 g/2 oz caster sugar, plus extra for sprinkling
¼ tsp baking powder
pinch of salt
55 g/2 oz blanched almonds, chopped
115 g/4 oz softened butter, plus extra for greasing

Almond Shortbread

Although it originates in Scotland, where it was known as 'bride's cake', shortbread has always been popular in Ireland. This nutty version has a lovely texture.

METHOD

Preheat the oven to 180°C/350°F/Gas Mark 4. Grease a 20-cm/8-inch sandwich tin.

Put the rice flour, plain flour, sugar, baking powder and salt into a mixing bowl and stir to combine. Add the almonds, stir in the butter and mix to a stiff dough.

Turn out the dough onto a work surface lightly dusted with flour and roll out to a 20-cm/8-inch round with a thickness of 1 cm/½ inch.

Place the round in the prepared tin, mark into 6 triangles with a sharp knife, pierce with a skewer several times and bake in the preheated oven for 30–40 minutes.

Leave to cool in the tin, then sprinkle with caster sugar, turn out of the tin and break into triangles to serve.

MAKES 6

INGREDIENTS

25 g/1 oz rice flour
140 g/5 oz plain flour, plus extra for dusting
55 g/2 oz caster sugar
¼ tsp baking powder
pinch of salt
55 g/2 oz blanched almonds, chopped
½ tsp vanilla extract
115 g/4 oz softened butter, plus extra for greasing

Coconut Shortbread

Desiccated coconut gives an unexpected taste sensation to this spin on traditional shortbread.

METHOD

Preheat the oven to 180°C/350°F/Gas Mark 4. Grease a 20-cm/8-inch sandwich tin.

Put the rice flour, plain flour, sugar, baking powder and salt into a mixing bowl and stir to combine. Add the almonds and vanilla extract, stir in the butter and mix to a stiff dough.

Turn out the dough onto a work surface lightly dusted with flour and roll out to a 20-cm/8-inch round with a thickness of 1 cm/½ inch.

Place the round in the prepared tin, mark into 6 triangles with a sharp knife and bake in the preheated oven for 30–40 minutes.

Leave to cool in the tin, then turn out and break into triangles to serve.

MAKES 6

INGREDIENTS

115 g/4 oz butter, plus extra for greasing
55 g/2 oz demerara sugar
115 g/4 oz porridge oats
70 g/2½ oz plain flour
¼ tsp bicarbonate of soda
pinch of salt

Oat Shortbread

This textured version of shortbread is very easy to prepare.

METHOD

Preheat the oven to 180°C/350°F/Gas Mark 4. Grease a 23 x 15-cm/9 x 6-inch baking tray.

Put the butter into a large saucepan and heat until melted. Remove from the heat, add the remaining ingredients and stir to combine.

Spread the mixture in the prepared tin, pressing down firmly. Bake in the preheated oven for about 45 minutes. Cut the shortbread into fingers while still hot, then leave to cool in the tin.

MAKES 12

INGREDIENTS

225 g/8 oz plain flour
pinch of salt
1 tsp baking powder
85 g/3 oz butter, plus extra for greasing
85 g/3 oz caster sugar
55 g/2 oz desiccated coconut
1 egg, beaten
150 ml/5 fl oz milk

Coconut Biscuits

Coconut gives a tropical flavour to this otherwise plain biscuit.

METHOD

Preheat the oven to 200°C/400°F/Gas Mark 6 and grease a large baking sheet.

Sift the flour, salt and baking powder into a mixing bowl, then rub in the butter until fine crumbs form. Add the sugar and coconut and mix well to combine.

Add the egg and milk and mix to a stiff batter. Drop 12 mounds of the batter onto the prepared sheet, well spaced to allow for spreading.

Bake in the preheated oven for 15–20 minutes until golden. Transfer to a wire rack and leave to cool.

MAKES 12

Sweet Oatcakes

This is the basic Irish sweet biscuit – the only grain used is oats.

INGREDIENTS

55 g/2 oz caster sugar
55 g/2 oz butter, softened, plus extra for greasing
1 egg, beaten
½ tsp bicarbonate of soda
½ tsp salt
175 g/6 oz porridge oats

METHOD

Preheat the oven to 200°C/400°F/Gas Mark 6. Grease a large baking sheet.

Put the sugar and butter into a bowl and cream until pale and fluffy. Add the egg and beat to combine. Add the bicarbonate of soda, salt and oats and mix to combine.

Shape into walnut-sized balls and place on the prepared sheet, well spaced to allow for spreading. Bake in the preheated oven for 20 minutes until browned on top.

Leave to cool on the sheet for 10 minutes, then transfer to a wire rack and leave to cool completely.

MAKES 12–15

Queen Cakes

Children love to help with baking and decorating these little cakes. They're very popular for afternoon tea and, of course, children's parties.

INGREDIENTS

175 g/6 oz self-raising flour
125 g/4½ oz caster sugar
125 g/4½ oz butter, softened
2 eggs, beaten
2 tbsp cold water
1 tsp vanilla extract
200 g/7 oz icing sugar
2 tbsp lukewarm water
liquid food colouring
hundreds and thousands, to decorate

METHOD

Preheat the oven to 200°C/400°F/Gas Mark 6. Line two 8-hole bun tins with paper cases.

Put the flour, caster sugar, butter, eggs, cold water and vanilla extract into a bowl and beat until smooth. Fill the paper cases two-thirds full with the batter.

Bake in the preheated oven for about 15 minutes until golden, then remove from the tins, transfer to a wire rack and leave to cool completely.

Sift the icing sugar into a bowl and mix in enough of the lukewarm water to make a thick, smooth paste. Add a few drops of food colouring, then spread the icing over the cakes and sprinkle with hundreds and thousands.

MAKES 16

Baking with Oats & Other Grains

In years gone by, wheat was a relatively expensive grain, and few Irish households could afford to use it regularly until the 20th century. However, good use was made of other grains.

Oats

Oaten bread will strengthen your arm.
(Traditional Irish saying)

Oats grow well in the damp Irish climate and in poor soil conditions, so they were a good substitute for wheat flour.

They add body and texture to every kind of bake, from bread to muffins to flapjacks, and are used to add crunch to the toppings for crumbles and fruit tarts.

Barley

Barley is also grown in Ireland, although it is not so hardy a grain as oats, and is used in baking to some extent. Barley flour is a bit sweeter than wheat flour, but produces a similar texture when baked. It has enough gluten to be used as the main ingredient in biscuits and muffins, but not enough to hold a loaf of bread together and should always be used in conjunction with a stronger flour.

Rice

This is a not a native grain and is not greatly used in Irish baking, although nothing beats the comfort of a traditional creamy baked rice pudding made with pearl rice.

Corn

Most people's idea of corn is sweetcorn, those golden kernels that can be added to soups and salads, or eaten directly off a grilled cob. While Italian polenta is now becoming popular, use of corn and its products in Ireland is generally limited to cornflour, which is a starch extracted from corn kernels and is useful mainly as a thickener in soups and stews. It can be utilised in baking to a limited extent – some shortbread recipes include it, and it can also be useful to add a little to soufflés, mousses and meringues.

Butterfly Cakes

These impressive-looking cakes are incredibly easy to make and are a very popular tea-time treat.

INGREDIENTS

175 g/6 oz self-raising flour
125 g/4½ oz caster sugar
125 g/4½ oz butter
2 eggs, beaten
2 tbsp cold water
1 tsp vanilla extract
5 tbsp strawberry or raspberry jam
5 tbsp whipped cream
icing sugar, for dusting

METHOD

Preheat the oven to 200°C/400°F/Gas Mark 6. Line two 8-hole bun tins with paper cases.

Put the flour, caster sugar, butter, eggs, water and vanilla extract into a bowl and beat until smooth. Fill the paper cases two-thirds full with the batter.

Bake in the preheated oven for about 15 minutes until golden, then remove from the tins, transfer to a wire rack and leave to cool completely.

Cut the tops off the cakes and set aside. Put a teaspoon of jam and a teaspoon of cream on top of each cake, then cut the reserved pieces in half and place two halves on each cake, set at an angle to imitate wings.

Dust with icing sugar just before serving.

MAKES 16

INGREDIENTS

175 g/6 oz self-raising flour
125 g/4½ oz caster sugar
3 tbsp cocoa powder
125 g/4½ oz butter
2 eggs, beaten
2 tbsp cold water
1 tsp vanilla extract
1 tbsp icing sugar, plus extra for dusting
5 tbsp whipped cream

MAKES 16

Chocolate Butterfly Cakes

This luxurious version of the butterfly cake combines chocolate with cream.

METHOD

Preheat the oven to 200°C/400°F/Gas Mark 6. Line two 8-hole bun tins with paper cases.

Put the flour, caster sugar, cocoa powder, butter, eggs, water and vanilla extract into a bowl and beat until smooth. Fill the paper cases two-thirds full with the batter.

Bake in the preheated oven for about 15 minutes until golden, then remove from the tins, transfer to a wire rack and leave to cool completely.

Cut the tops off the cakes and set aside. Mix the icing sugar with the cream and put a teaspoon of the mixture on each cake. Cut the reserved pieces in half and place two halves on each cake, set at an angle to represent wings.

Dust with icing sugar just before serving.

Jam Tarts

Every child's favourite, these delicious little tarts can be made with whatever type of jam you prefer. Resist the temptation to eat them straight out of the oven – the jam will be extremely hot.

INGREDIENTS

175 g/6 oz self-raising flour, plus extra for dusting
85 g/3 oz chilled butter, plus extra for greasing
100 g/3½ oz jam
milk, for brushing

METHOD

Preheat the oven to 200°C/400°F/Gas Mark 6. Grease 20 holes in two bun tins.

Put the flour into a mixing bowl, cut in the butter and rub it in until fine crumbs form. Add a few spoons of water and mix to a firm dough.

Roll out the dough on a work surface lightly dusted with flour and cut out 20 rounds with a 9-cm/3½-inch fluted cutter.

Ease the pastry rounds into the prepared tins and place a teaspoon of jam in each round.

Re-roll the pastry trimmings, cut out stars or other shapes and place these on the tarts. Brush the pastry with milk and bake the tarts in the preheated oven for 20–30 minutes until golden.

Leave to cool in the tins for 10 minutes, then turn out onto a wire rack and leave to cool until you're ready to serve them.

MAKES 20

INGREDIENTS

4 egg whites
pinch of salt
125 g/4½ oz granulated sugar
125 g/4½ oz caster sugar
300 ml/10 fl oz double cream, whipped
melted plain chocolate or strawberry sauce, for drizzling

Meringues

These are an afternoon tea favourite – they also make a great dessert, drizzled with melted chocolate or strawberry sauce.

METHOD

Preheat the oven to 120°C/250°F/Gas Mark ½ and line two large baking trays with baking paper.

Whisk the egg whites with the salt in a large grease-free bowl until they hold stiff peaks.

Gradually whisk in the granulated sugar – the meringue will begin to look glossy. Gradually add the caster sugar, whisking until the meringue is thick and holds stiff peaks.

Put the mixture into a piping bag fitted with a 2.5-cm/1-inch star nozzle and pipe 6 whirls onto each of the prepared trays.

Bake in the preheated oven until the meringues have a golden tinge and can be lifted off the paper easily. Switch off the oven and leave the meringues inside for 8 hours.

To serve, sandwich pairs of meringues together with a large spoonful of whipped cream, arrange on a serving plate and drizzle with melted chocolate.

MAKES 6

INGREDIENTS

butter, for greasing
350 g/12 oz self-raising flour
125 g/4½ oz white vegetable fat
1 tsp mixed spice
1 tsp ground ginger
85 g/3 oz demerara or soft light brown sugar
1 egg, beaten
1 tbsp milk

Spiced Buns

These tasty buns were traditionally made with beef dripping, but white vegetable fat makes a good substitute and gives them a great texture.

METHOD

Preheat the oven to 180°C/350°F/Gas Mark 4. Grease a large baking tray.

Put the flour into a mixing bowl and cut in the vegetable fat, rubbing it in with your fingertips until fine crumbs form. Add the mixed spice, ginger and sugar and stir to combine. Add the egg and enough milk to make a soft but not wet dough.

Divide the dough into about 20 equal pieces and shape each piece into a bun. Place the buns on the prepared tray and bake in the preheated oven for 15–20 minutes until golden. Serve warm or cold.

MAKES 20–24

INGREDIENTS

225 g/8 oz self-raising flour

125 g/4½ oz butter, plus extra for greasing

85 g/3 oz caster sugar

125 g/4½ oz mixed dried fruit

1 egg, beaten

2 tbsp milk

granulated sugar, for sprinkling

Rock Buns

The classic everyday bun – great with a cup of tea or coffee.

METHOD

Preheat the oven to 200°C/400°F/Gas Mark 6 and grease a large baking sheet.

Sift the flour into a mixing bowl, then rub in the butter until fine crumbs form. Add the caster sugar and dried fruit and mix well to combine.

Add the egg and milk and mix to a stiff batter. Drop 12 mounds of the batter onto the prepared sheet, well spaced to allow for spreading.

Sprinkle the buns with granulated sugar and bake in the preheated oven for 10–15 minutes until golden. Leave to cool on the sheet for 5 minutes, then transfer to a wire rack and leave to cool completely.

MAKES 12

INGREDIENTS

200 g/7 oz softened butter
200 g/7 oz caster sugar
3 eggs
200 g/7 oz self-raising flour
1 tsp vanilla extract
2 tbsp milk, if needed

Buttercream icing
250 g/9 oz icing sugar, sifted
125 g/4½ oz softened butter
2 tsp vanilla extract
1½ tbsp milk
gold or silver dragées, to decorate

MAKES 12

Vanilla Buns

These delectable little buns are perfect for a children's party. If you like, you could add a few drops of food colouring to the icing.

METHOD

Preheat the oven to 180°C/350°F/Gas Mark 4. Line a 12-hole bun tin with paper cases.

Put the butter and sugar into a mixing bowl and cream together until light and fluffy. Add the eggs, one at a time, and beat well to incorporate, beating in a little of the flour if the mixture starts to curdle. Add the vanilla extract, then fold in the flour using a metal spoon. Stir in some milk if the mixture is very stiff.

Spoon equal amounts of the batter into the prepared tin and bake in the preheated oven for 25 minutes, or until golden. Leave to cool in the tin for 5 minutes, then transfer to a wire rack and leave to cool completely.

Meanwhile, make the icing. Put half the sugar into a bowl with the butter and beat until light and fluffy. Beat in the remaining sugar, then add the vanilla extract and milk, beating to incorporate. Spread a tablespoon of the icing onto each cake, or pipe on swirls using a piping bag, then decorate with dragées.

INGREDIENTS

55 g/2 oz butter
85 g/3 oz caster sugar
1 egg
2 tbsp marmalade
175 g/6 oz plain flour
60 ml/2 fl oz milk
1 tsp baking powder

Marmalade Buns

These buns are best made with a bitter marmalade – Seville marmalade has always been a popular choice in Ireland.

METHOD

Preheat the oven to 180°C/350°F/Gas Mark 4. Line a 12-hole bun tin with paper cases.

Put the butter and sugar into a mixing bowl and cream together until light and fluffy. Add the egg and mix to incorporate, then stir in the marmalade. Sift the flour and the baking powder into the wet mixture, beating to incorporate.

Place equal amounts of the batter in the holes of the prepared tin, then bake in the preheated oven for 20 minutes.

Leave to cool in the tin for a few minutes, then turn out onto a wire rack and leave to cool completely.

MAKES 12

INGREDIENTS

115 g/4 oz softened butter
115 g/4 oz caster sugar
2 eggs, beaten
140 g/5 oz plain flour
¾ tsp baking powder
1 tbsp milk
55 g/2 oz chopped glacé cherries

Cherry Buns

These little cakes were often served on 6 January, celebrated in Ireland as Women's Christmas *(Nollaig na mBan)*, when women traditionally did no housework or cooking.

METHOD

Preheat the oven to 200°C/400°F/Gas Mark 6. Line a 12-hole bun tin with paper cases.

Put the butter and sugar into a mixing bowl and cream until light and fluffy. Gradually add the eggs, alternating with some of the flour to prevent curdling.

Stir in the remaining flour and the baking powder, with enough milk to achieve a dropping consistency. Add the cherries and mix well.

Spoon the mixture into the prepared tin and bake in the preheated oven for 20 minutes. Leave to cool in the tin for about 10 minutes, then turn out onto a wire rack and leave to cool completely.

MAKES 12

INGREDIENTS

zest and juice of 2 large oranges
100 ml/3½ fl oz milk
225 g/8 oz self-raising flour
pinch of salt
115 g/4 oz caster sugar
55 g/2 oz ground almonds
2 eggs
6 tbsp sunflower oil
½ tsp almond extract
40 g/1½ oz demerara sugar

Orange & Almond Muffins

Muffins are very easy to make – the secret is not to overmix the batter.

METHOD

Preheat the oven to 200°C/400°F/Gas Mark 6. Line a 12-hole muffin tin with paper cases.

Put the orange juice and zest into a jug and make up to 250 ml/9 fl oz with the milk.

Put the flour and salt into a large bowl and stir in the caster sugar and ground almonds. Beat the eggs in a large jug, then beat in the orange and milk mixture, the oil and the almond extract. Make a well in the centre of the dry ingredients and pour in the liquid ingredients. Stir until just combined – a little flour should still be showing.

Spoon the batter into the prepared tin and sprinkle with the demerara sugar. Bake in the preheated oven for 20 minutes until risen and golden brown. Leave to cool in the tin for 5 minutes, then transfer to a wire rack and leave to cool completely.

MAKES 12

INGREDIENTS

280 g/10 oz self-raising flour
pinch of salt
115/g 4 oz caster sugar
2 eggs
250 ml/9 fl oz buttermilk
6 tbsp sunflower oil
1 tsp vanilla extract
150 g/5½ oz frozen mixed berries
icing sugar, for dusting

Buttermilk Berry Muffins

In the past, fresh berries would have been used, but incorporating frozen fruit means these muffins can be enjoyed all year round.

METHOD

Preheat the oven to 200°C/400°F/Gas Mark 6. Line a 12-hole muffin tin with paper cases.

Put the flour and salt into a mixing bowl, then stir in the caster sugar. Beat the eggs in a large jug, then beat in the buttermilk, oil and vanilla extract.

Make a well in the centre of the dry ingredients and pour in the liquid ingredients. Add the berries and stir until just combined – a little flour should still be showing.

Spoon the batter into the prepared tin and bake in the preheated oven for 20 minutes until risen and golden brown. Leave to cool in the tin for 5 minutes, then transfer to a wire rack and leave to cool completely. Dust with icing sugar just before serving.

MAKES 12

INGREDIENTS

280 g/10 oz self-raising flour
pinch of salt
115 g/4 oz caster sugar
2 tbsp poppy seeds
2 eggs
250 ml/9 fl oz milk
6 tbsp sunflower oil
grated rind of 2 lemons

Lemon & Poppy Seed Muffins

When ingredients were limited, poppy seeds were a popular storecupboard addition to a variety of cakes and breads.

METHOD

Preheat the oven to 200°C/400°F/Gas Mark 6. Line a 12-hole muffin tin with paper cases.

Put the flour and salt into a mixing bowl, then stir in the sugar and the poppy seeds. Beat the eggs in a large jug, then beat in the milk, oil and lemon rind. Make a well in the centre of the dry ingredients and pour in the liquid ingredients. Stir until just combined – a little flour should still be showing.

Spoon the batter into the prepared tin and bake in the preheated oven for 20 minutes until risen and golden brown. Leave to cool in the tin for 5 minutes, then transfer to a wire rack and leave to cool completely.

MAKES 12

INGREDIENTS

280 g/10 oz self-raising flour
pinch of salt
115 g/4 oz soft light brown sugar
1 large eating apple, peeled, cored and finely chopped
2 eggs
250 ml/9 fl oz buttermilk
6 tbsp sunflower oil
1 tsp vanilla extract
150 g/5½ oz blackberries
40 g/1½ oz demerara sugar

Blackberry & Apple Muffins

These muffins showcase two popular autumn ingredients – blackberries and apples. You could use frozen blackberries out of season.

METHOD

Preheat the oven to 200°C/400°F/Gas Mark 6. Line a 12-hole muffin tin with paper cases.

Put the flour and salt into a mixing bowl, then stir in the brown sugar and the apple. Beat the eggs in a large jug, then beat in the buttermilk, oil and vanilla extract.

Gently stir in the blackberries, then make a well in the centre of the dry ingredients and pour in the liquid ingredients. Stir until just combined – a little flour should still be showing.

Spoon the batter into the prepared tin, sprinkle with the demerara sugar and bake in the preheated oven for 20 minutes until risen and golden brown. Leave to cool in the tin for 5 minutes, then transfer to a wire rack and leave to cool completely.

MAKES 12

INGREDIENTS

55 g/2 oz raisins
3 tbsp fresh orange juice
140 g/5 oz plain white flour
140 g/5 oz plain wholemeal flour
1 tbsp baking powder
115 g/4 oz caster sugar
2 ripe bananas
100 ml/3½ fl oz milk
2 eggs
6 tbsp sunflower oil
grated rind of 1 orange

Wholemeal Banana Muffins

These wholemeal muffins are a great way of using up overripe bananas – the riper the better.

METHOD

Put the raisins into a bowl, add the orange juice and set aside for 1 hour.

Preheat the oven to 200°C/400°F/Gas Mark 6. Line a 12-hole muffin tin with paper cases.

Put the white flour, wholemeal flour and baking powder into a large bowl and stir in the sugar.

Mash the bananas in a jug and add enough milk to make up to 200 ml/7 fl oz.

Beat the eggs in a jug, then beat in the banana mixture, raisins and orange rind.

Make a well in the centre of the dry ingredients and pour in the liquid ingredients. Stir until just combined – a little flour should still be showing.

Spoon the batter into the prepared tin and bake in the preheated oven for 20 minutes until risen and golden brown. Leave to cool in the tin for 5 minutes, then transfer to a wire rack and leave to cool completely.

MAKES 12

INGREDIENTS

140 g/5 oz self-raising flour
1 tsp mixed spice
115 g/4 oz soft light brown sugar
175 g/6 oz porridge oats
1 large eating apple, cored and finely chopped
2 eggs
125 ml/4 fl oz milk
125 ml/4 fl oz apple juice
6 tbsp sunflower oil

Spiced Apple & Oat Muffins

This is a great breakfast muffin with a lovely texture and a hint of spice.

METHOD

Preheat the oven to 200°C/400°F/Gas Mark 6. Line a 12-hole muffin tin with paper cases.

Sift the flour and mixed spice into a bowl, then stir in the sugar and 140 g/5 oz of the oats. Add the apple and stir.

Beat the eggs in a jug, then beat in the milk, apple juice and oil. Make a well in the centre of the dry ingredients and pour in the liquid ingredients. Stir until just combined – a little flour should still be showing.

Spoon the batter into the prepared tin, sprinkle with the remaining oats and bake in the preheated oven for 20 minutes until risen and golden brown. Leave to cool in the tin for 5 minutes, then transfer to a wire rack and leave to cool completely.

MAKES 12

TRAYBAKES

Clonakilty, County Cork

Almond Fingers

These are like tiny Bakewell tarts, with a satisfying contrast between crisp pastry and soft, almondy filling.

INGREDIENTS

butter, for greasing
250 g/9 oz ready-made shortcrust pastry
100 g/3½ oz raspberry jam
2 egg whites
175 g/6 oz caster sugar
85 g/3 oz ground almonds
1 tsp almond extract
25 g/1 oz flaked almonds

METHOD

Preheat the oven to 180°C/350°F/Gas Mark 4. Grease a 23 x 15-cm/9 x 6-inch baking tray.

Roll out the pastry and use to line the prepared baking tray. Spread the jam evenly over the base.

Whisk the egg whites until soft peaks hold, then fold in the sugar, ground almonds and almond extract. Spread the mixture over the jam. Sprinkle with the flaked almonds and bake in the preheated oven for about 40 minutes. Leave to cool in the tin, then cut into fingers to serve.

MAKES 12

INGREDIENTS

butter, for greasing
250 g/9 oz ready-made shortcrust pastry
3 tbsp apricot jam
2 egg whites
175 g/6 oz caster sugar
70 g/2½ oz desiccated coconut
1 tsp ground rice
½ tsp vanilla extract
25 g/1 oz flaked almonds

Coconut Fingers

Coconut is a very useful storecupboard ingredient, which adds sweetness, texture and a distinctive flavour to a variety of sweet bakes.

METHOD

Preheat the oven to 180°C/350°F/Gas Mark 4. Grease a 23 x 15-cm/9 x 6-inch baking tray.

Roll out the pastry and use to line the prepared baking tray. Spread the jam over the base.

Put the egg whites into a clean, grease-free bowl and whisk until soft peaks hold. Fold in the sugar, coconut, ground rice and vanilla extract. Spread the mixture evenly over the jam, sprinkle with the flaked almonds and bake in the preheated oven for about 40 minutes. Leave to cool in the tin, then cut into fingers to serve.

MAKES 12

INGREDIENTS

275 g/9¾ oz white self-raising flour

150 g/5½ oz butter, softened, plus extra for greasing

150 g/5½ oz soft light brown sugar

1 tsp ground cinnamon

1 cooking apple, grated

1 egg, beaten

1 tbsp milk

caster sugar, for sprinkling

Apple Fingers

These spongy cakes make a great lunchbox treat, or can be heated up and served with custard or cream for dessert.

METHOD

Preheat the oven to 200°C/400°F/Gas Mark 6 and grease a Swiss roll tin.

Put the flour into a mixing bowl, add the butter, brown sugar, cinnamon and apple and mix well to combine.

Add the egg and milk and mix to a soft dough. Spread the dough in the prepared tin and bake in the preheated oven for 30 minutes, turning the tin halfway through the baking time.

Transfer the tin to a wire rack, sprinkle with caster sugar and mark the cake into 12 fingers with a knife. Leave to cool in the tin, then cut the fingers along the marks. Replace the tin on the rack and leave to cool for a further 30 minutes before removing the fingers.

MAKES 12

INGREDIENTS

350 g/12 oz rolled oats
175 g/6 oz demerara sugar
pinch of salt
225 g/8 oz butter, plus extra for greasing
2 tbsp golden syrup

Flapjacks

These are a classic family favourite and are very easy to make. They can be stored in an airtight tin for up to two weeks.

METHOD

Preheat the oven to 180°C/325°F/Gas Mark 4. Grease a baking tray.

Put the oats, sugar and salt into a mixing bowl and mix to combine.

Put the butter and golden syrup into a saucepan and heat over a medium heat until the butter is melted.

Pour the butter mixture over the dry ingredients and mix well. Press the mixture into the prepared tray, then bake in the preheated oven for 30 minutes.

Leave to cool in the tray for about 10 minutes, then cut into squares, transfer to a wire rack and leave to cool completely.

MAKES ABOUT 24

INGREDIENTS

100 g/3½ oz porridge oats
25 g/1 oz plain flour
55 g/2 oz ground almonds
pinch of salt
85 g/3 oz butter, melted, plus extra for greasing
1 tsp almond extract
1 tbsp golden syrup, plus extra if needed
3 tbsp raspberry jam
flaked almonds, to decorate

Bakewell Flapjacks

A combination of two traditional family favourites, flapjacks and Bakewell tart, these are sure to become a regular weekend bake.

METHOD

Preheat the oven to 160°C/325°F/Gas Mark 3 and grease a 14-cm/5½-inch square baking tin.

Put the oats, flour, ground almonds and salt into a mixing bowl and stir to combine. Add the butter, almond extract and golden syrup and mix well, adding a little more syrup if the mixture is too dry to come together.

Spread half the mixture in the base of the prepared tin and level using the back of a wet spoon. Spread the jam evenly over this layer, leaving a 5-mm/¼-inch border. Spread the remaining oat mixture on top and sprinkle with flaked almonds.

Bake in the preheated oven for 15–20 minutes. It will start to brown very quickly towards the end of the cooking time, so keep an eye on it to prevent burning.

Leave to cool in the tin for 10 minutes, then use a sharp knife to mark into 8 bars. Leave to cool for a further 20 minutes, then carefully remove from the tin, transfer to a wire rack and leave to cool completely.

MAKES 8

INGREDIENTS

225 g/8 oz ready-to-eat dried apricots, finely chopped
1 tbsp clear honey
5 tbsp water
1 tbsp lemon juice
175 g/6 oz butter, softened, plus extra for greasing
85 g/3 oz caster sugar
175 g/6 oz semolina
175 g/6 oz wholemeal self-raising flour
1 tsp ground cinnamon

Fruit Slices

You can use any dried fruit for these, but apricots are particularly tangy and delicious.

METHOD

Preheat the oven to 160°C/325°F/Gas Mark 3 and grease a 28 x 20-cm/11 x 8-inch deep baking tin.

Put the apricots, honey, water and lemon juice into a saucepan and heat over a low heat, stirring until the honey has dissolved and the mixture is creamy. Remove from the heat and set aside until needed.

Put the butter and sugar into a mixing bowl and cream together until pale and fluffy. Add the semolina, flour and cinnamon and stir until the mixture comes together and is crumbly in texture.

Spread half the flour mixture in the prepared tin, pushing it into the corners, then spread the apricot mixture on top. Finish with the remaining flour mixture, levelling the top, then bake in the preheated oven for 40–45 minutes until golden.

Leave to cool in the tin for 10 minutes, then use a sharp knife to mark into 16 bars. Leave in the tin for a further 20 minutes, then carefully remove the bars, transfer to a wire rack and leave to cool completely.

MAKES 16

INGREDIENTS

125 g/4½ plain flour, plus extra for dusting
pinch of salt
180 g/6¼ oz butter, plus extra for greasing
cold water, for mixing
125 g/4½ oz caster sugar
1 egg, beaten
175 g/6 oz porridge oats
2 tbsp apricot jam

Apricot Oat Fingers

These crumbly slices have a tangy layer of apricot jam.

METHOD

Preheat the oven to 220°C/425°F/Gas Mark 7 and grease a Swiss roll tin.

Sift the flour and salt into a mixing bowl, then rub in 55 g/2 oz of the butter until fine crumbs form. Add enough water to make a firm dough and mix it in with a knife. Set aside until needed.

Put the remaining butter into a saucepan and heat until melted. Remove from the heat and stir in the sugar and egg, then add the oats and mix well.

Turn out the dough onto a work surface lightly dusted with flour and roll out thinly. Use to line the prepared tin. Spread the jam on top, then cover with the oat mixture, levelling the surface. Bake in the preheated oven for 20–30 minutes until light brown on top.

Leave to cool in the tin for 10 minutes, then use a sharp knife to mark into 12 slices. Leave in the tin for a further 20 minutes, then remove the fingers, transfer to a wire rack and leave to cool completely.

MAKES 12

INGREDIENTS

400 g/14 oz ready-made mincemeat
icing sugar, for dusting

Base
140 g/5 oz softened butter, plus extra for greasing
85 g/3 oz golden caster sugar
140 g/5 oz plain flour
85 g/3 oz cornflour

Topping
85 g/3 oz chilled butter, cubed
115 g/4 oz white self-raising flour
85 g/3 oz golden caster sugar
25 g/1 oz flaked almonds

Mincemeat Crumble Bars

This is a great way of using up any mincemeat that's left over from Christmas.

METHOD

Grease a rectangular 28 x 20-cm/11 x 8-inch shallow cake tin.

To make the base, put the butter and sugar into a bowl and cream until light and fluffy. Add the flour and cornflour and bring together with your hands to form a ball of dough. Press the dough into the prepared tin, working it into the corners. Chill in the refrigerator for 20 minutes.

Meanwhile, preheat the oven to 200°C/400°F/Gas Mark 6. Bake the base in the preheated oven for 15 minutes, or until golden and puffed (do not switch off the oven). Leave to cool for 10 minutes, then spread the mincemeat over the base.

To make the topping, put the butter, flour and sugar into a mixing bowl and rub together until coarse crumbs form. Add the almonds and stir to combine.

Scatter the topping over the mincemeat, covering it completely. Return to the oven for a further 20 minutes, or until the top is golden brown. Leave to cool in the tin for 5 minutes, then cut into slices and leave to cool completely. Dust with icing sugar just before serving.

MAKES 12

INGREDIENTS

175 g/6 oz butter, plus extra for greasing

200 g/7 oz soft light brown sugar

150 g/5½ oz caster sugar

3 eggs, beaten

5 tbsp crunchy peanut butter

2 tsp vanilla extract

250 g/9 oz self-raising flour

pinch of salt

200 g/7 oz salted peanuts

Peanut Butter Bars

The salted peanuts in these bars provide a lovely contrast with the sweet cake.

METHOD

Preheat the oven to 180°C/350°F/Gas Mark 4. Grease a 23 x 30-cm/9 x 12-inch cake tin and line the base with baking paper.

Put the butter into a small saucepan over a low heat and heat until melted. Remove from the heat and leave to cool slightly.

Put the brown sugar and caster sugar into a bowl and stir to combine, then add the butter and mix well. Add the eggs and the peanut butter and mix well, then stir in the vanilla extract.

Sift in the flour and salt and mix well, then mix in about half the peanuts and stir to combine. Spread the batter in the prepared tin and sprinkle over the remaining peanuts. Bake in the preheated oven for 30–35 minutes, or until firm. Leave to cool in the tin for 10 minutes, then turn out onto a wire rack and leave to cool completely. Cut into bars to serve.

MAKES 16

INGREDIENTS

115 g/4 oz softened butter, plus extra for greasing

140 g/5 oz rolled oats

115 g/4 oz demerara sugar

85 g/3 oz raisins

Fruity Flapjacks

You could use any dried fruit in these chewy flapjacks.

METHOD

Preheat the oven to 190°C/375°F/Gas Mark 5. Grease a 28 x 18-cm/11 x 7-inch shallow cake tin and line with baking paper.

Put all of the ingredients into a bowl and mix to combine. Spoon the mixture into the prepared tin and work it into the corners, pressing down with the back of a spoon.

Bake in the preheated oven for 15–20 minutes or until golden in colour. Remove from the oven and mark out 14 bars with a sharp knife. Leave to cool in the tin for 10 minutes, then transfer the bars to a wire rack and leave to cool completely.

MAKES 14

INGREDIENTS

115 g/4 oz butter, plus extra for greasing
60 g/2¼ oz caster sugar
1 tbsp golden syrup
350 g/12 oz rolled oats
85 g/3 oz chocolate chips
85 g/3 oz raisins

Chocolate Chip Flapjacks

Chocolate chips are a lovely addition to the traditional plain flapjack.

METHOD

Preheat the oven to 180°C/350°F/Gas Mark 4. Grease a 20-cm/8-inch shallow square cake tin.

Put the butter, sugar and golden syrup into a saucepan over a low heat and stir until melted and combined.

Remove from the heat, add the oats and stir to coat. Add the chocolate chips and raisins and mix well to combine.

Spoon the mixture into the prepared tin and work into the corners, pressing down with the back of a spoon.

Bake in the preheated oven for 30 minutes. Leave to cool in the tin for 10 minutes, then mark into fingers. Set aside, still in the tin, until almost cold, then cut into bars and transfer to a wire rack to cool completely.

MAKES 12

INGREDIENTS

150 g/5½ oz self-raising flour

pinch of salt

100 g/3½ oz chilled butter, cubed, plus extra for greasing

150 g/5½ oz soft light brown sugar

1 egg, beaten

4 tbsp milk

100g/3½ oz halved hazelnuts

demerara sugar, for sprinkling

Hazelnut Squares

These delicious squares have a lovely texture from the hazelnuts and the crunchy sugar topping.

METHOD

Preheat the oven to 180°C/350°F/Gas Mark 4. Grease a 23-cm/9-inch square cake tin and line with baking paper. Put the flour and salt into a mixing bowl, add the butter and rub it in with your fingertips until the mixture resembles breadcrumbs. Add the brown sugar and stir to combine.

Add the egg, milk and nuts to the bowl and stir until you achieve a soft consistency. Spoon the batter into the prepared tin, levelling the surface. Sprinkle generously with demerara sugar and bake in the preheated oven for 25 minutes, or until firm.

Leave to cool in the tin for 10 minutes, then turn out onto a wire rack and leave to cool completely. Cut into squares to serve.

MAKES 16

INGREDIENTS

300 g/10½ oz ready-made shortcrust pastry

300 g/10½ oz stale cake or bread

75 g/2¾ oz plain flour, plus extra for dusting

pinch of salt

½ tsp baking powder

2 tsp mixed spice

100 g/3½ oz granulated sugar

175 g/6 oz raisins

55 g/2 oz butter, melted, plus extra for greasing

1 egg, beaten

2 tsbp milk, plus extra if needed

caster sugar, for sprinkling

MAKES 9 SQUARES

Gur Cake

This filling Dublin specialty is a good way to use up stale Madeira cake or sponge cake. It's traditionally eaten as a snack, but can also be served warm with cream or ice cream as a dessert.

METHOD

Preheat the oven to 190°C/375°F/Gas Mark 5. Grease a 30 x 18-cm/12 x 7-inch baking tin. Divide the pastry into two pieces, then roll out one piece on a work surface lightly dusted with flour and use to line the prepared tin.

Put the cake into a food processor and pulse until coarse crumbs form. Put the crumbs into a mixing bowl and add the flour, salt, baking powder, mixed spice, granulated sugar and raisins, mixing well to combine. Add the butter, egg and milk and mix until stiff.

Spread the mixture over the pastry in the tin, then roll out the remaining pastry and use to cover the cake. Slash the pastry lid with a sharp knife several times, then bake in the preheated oven for 50 minutes–1 hour until the pastry is crisp and golden.

Sprinkle with caster sugar and leave to cool in the tin, then cut into squares and serve.

INGREDIENTS

Base
140 g/5 oz plain flour
115 g/4 oz chilled butter, plus extra for greasing
115 g/4 oz caster sugar

Topping
2 eggs
1 tsp vanilla extract
225 g/8 oz soft light brown sugar
1 tbsp plain flour
pinch of salt
¼ tsp baking powder
115 g/4 oz desiccated coconut
115 g/4 oz chopped walnuts

Coconut & Walnut Bars

These bars have a lovely shortbread-style base, which requires pre-baking. The bars are best eaten the day after baking.

METHOD

Preheat the oven to 180°C/350°F/Gas Mark 4. Grease a Swiss roll tin.

To make the base, put the flour into a bowl, add the butter and mix with your fingertips until crumbs form. Add the caster sugar and mix, then turn the mixture into the prepared tin, pressing it flat with the back of a spoon. Bake in the preheated oven for 10 minutes.

Meanwhile, to make the topping, put the eggs into a mixing bowl and whisk until light in colour. Add the vanilla extract, brown sugar, flour, salt and baking powder and beat until smooth. Stir in the coconut and nuts and spread the mixture over the base. Return to the oven and bake for a further 20–30 minutes until the topping is golden and firm.

Leave to cool in the tin for 5 minutes, then cut into bars and transfer to a wire rack to cool completely.

MAKES 16

INGREDIENTS

butter, for greasing
flour, for dusting
280 g/10 oz ready-made shortcrust pastry
2 Bramley apples, peeled, cored and finely chopped
250 g/8 oz currants
55 g/2 oz mixed peel
115 g/4 oz caster sugar
grated rind of 1 lemon
juice of ½ lemon
2 tsp golden syrup
beaten egg, for brushing
icing sugar, for dusting

MAKES 16

Currant Squares

These pastry squares have a delicious sweet and sticky filling.

METHOD

Preheat the oven to 190°C/375°F/Gas Mark 5. Grease a Swiss roll tin.

Roll out the pastry on a work surface lightly dusted with flour, then divide in two and use one piece to line the prepared tin.

Put the apples into a bowl with the currants, mixed peel, caster sugar, lemon rind, lemon juice and golden syrup and mix to combine. Spread the mixture over the pastry in the tin and cover with the remaining piece of pastry, trimming any excess. Brush with beaten egg and bake in the preheated oven for about 40 minutes until golden.

Leave to cool in the tin for 10 minutes, then dust with icing sugar, cut into squares and transfer to a wire rack to cool completely.

INGREDIENTS

225 g/8 oz chopped dried dates
55 g/2 oz granulated sugar
1 tbsp water
115 g/4 oz chilled butter, cubed, plus extra for greasing
115 g/4 oz porridge oats
115 g/4 oz plain flour
½ tsp bicarbonate of soda
55 g/2 oz soft light brown sugar

Date Fingers

Dried dates were introduced to Ireland during the Middle Ages, providing cooks with a welcome sweet ingredient.

METHOD

Preheat the oven to 190°C/375°F/Gas Mark 5. Grease a 20-cm/8-inch shallow square cake tin.

Put the dates into a saucepan with the granulated sugar and water and heat gently over a low heat until reduced to a soft paste.

Meanwhile, put the butter into a bowl with the oats, flour, bicarbonate of soda and brown sugar and rub together until crumbs form. Press half the mixture into the prepared tin, spread with the date mixture and cover with the remaining crumb mixture. Press level with the back of a spoon and bake in the preheated oven for 30–40 minutes.

Leave to cool in the tin for about 5 minutes, then cut into fingers and transfer to a wire rack to cool completely.

MAKES 12

INGREDIENTS

175 g/6 oz butter, plus extra for greasing

125 g/4½ oz caster sugar, plus extra for sprinkling

1½ tbsp golden syrup

150 g/5½ oz white self-raising flour

150 g/5½ oz wholemeal self-raising flour

125 g/4½ oz sultanas

55 g/2 oz chopped walnuts

55 g/2 oz chopped glacé cherries

MAKES 16

Nutty Fruit Slices

These fruit slices are a traybake version of a satisfying fruit bread. You can use any fruit or nuts you like.

METHOD

Preheat the oven to 180°C/350°F/Gas Mark 4. Grease a Swiss roll tin.

Put the butter, sugar and golden syrup into a large saucepan over a low heat and heat until melted. Do not let it boil. Remove from the heat, add the remaining ingredients and mix well.

Spread the mixture in the prepared tin and bake in the preheated oven for 20 minutes or until golden and firm.

Leave to cool in the tin for 10 minutes, then cut into slices and leave to cool completely before removing from the tin.

INGREDIENTS

55 g/2 oz butter, plus extra for greasing
115 g/4 oz rolled oats
175 g/6 oz caster sugar
85 g/3 oz desiccated coconut
1 tsp baking powder
pinch of salt
1 egg, beaten

Coconut Flapjacks

These are the simplest of simple flapjacks, prepared without golden syrup. The coconut adds great flavour.

METHOD

Preheat the oven to 180°C/350°F/Gas Mark 4. Grease a Swiss roll tin.

Put the butter into a small saucepan over a low heat and heat until melted.

Meanwhile, put the dry ingredients into a bowl and stir to combine. Add the butter and egg and mix well.

Spread the mixture in the prepared tin, levelling with the back of a spoon, and bake in the preheated oven for 20 minutes, or until light brown in colour. Leave to cool in the tin for 10 minutes, then cut into squares and leave to cool completely before turning out of the tin.

MAKES 18

INGREDIENTS

1 Bramley apple, peeled, cored and diced
2 tbsp water
100 g/3½ oz softened butter
175 g/6 oz caster sugar
1 egg, beaten
280 g/10 oz self-raising flour
125 ml/4 fl oz milk
200 g/7 oz fresh blackberries

Topping
85 g/3 oz white self-raising flour
100 g/3½ oz demerara sugar
zest of 1 lemon
55 g/2 oz chilled butter, cubed

MAKES 16

Apple & Blackberry Crumble Squares

These squares combine sponge cake and autumn fruit crumble for a lovely sweet treat.

METHOD

Preheat the oven to 180°C/350°F/Gas Mark 4. Line a 20 x 30-cm/9 x 12-inch shallow cake tin with baking paper.

To make the topping, put the flour, sugar and lemon zest into a bowl, add the butter and rub it in with your fingertips until crumbs form.

Put the apple into a small saucepan with the water and cook over a low heat until the apple is softening.

Put the butter and sugar into a bowl and cream together until light and fluffy. Gradually beat in the egg, adding in a little of the flour to prevent curdling. Add the flour and the milk and beat until everything is combined.

Add the apple and mix well, then spoon the mixture into the prepared tin and level the surface. Dot with the blackberries, sprinkle over the topping and bake in the preheated oven for 45 minutes until golden. Leave to cool in the tin for 10 minutes, then cut into squares and leave to cool completely before turning out.

INGREDIENTS

250 g/9 oz self-raising flour
25 g/1 oz porridge oats
280 g/10 oz soft light brown sugar
200 g/7 oz chilled butter, cubed
85 g/3 oz desiccated coconut
2 eggs, beaten
350 g/12 oz fresh or frozen raspberries

Raspberry & Coconut Squares

A delectable combination of raspberry and coconut in a deliciously crumbly square.

METHOD

Preheat the oven to 180°C/350°F/Gas Mark 4. Line a 20-cm/8-inch shallow square cake tin with baking paper.

Put the flour, oats and sugar into a large bowl. Rub in the butter with your fingertips until large crumbs form. Stir in the coconut, then fill a tumbler with some of the mixture and reserve.

Stir the eggs into the remaining mixture, then spread it over the base of the prepared tin. Smooth the surface with the back of a spoon, then scatter over the raspberries. Sprinkle with the reserved mixture and bake in the preheated oven for 1 hour–1 hour 15 minutes until golden and a skewer inserted into the centre comes out clean.

Leave to cool in the tin, then turn out and cut into squares.

MAKES 9

Ingredients

175 g/6 oz chilled butter, cubed, plus extra for greasing
300 g/10½ oz soft light brown sugar
300 g/10½ oz self-raising flour
1 Bramley apple, peeled and cored
250 ml/8½ fl oz milk
1 tsp bicarbonate of soda
2 eggs, lightly beaten
pinch of salt
1 tsp grated nutmeg, plus extra for dusting
1 tsp ground cinnamon
60 g/2¼ oz walnuts, roughly chopped

Apple & Walnut Squares

This lightly spiced traybake has all the lovely flavour of a good apple pie and is delicious served with cream or ice cream.

Method

Preheat the oven to 180°C/350°F/Gas Mark 4. Grease a 23-cm/9-inch shallow square cake tin and line with baking paper. Put the butter, sugar and flour into a food processor and process until fine crumbs form. Spoon half the mixture into the prepared tin, pressing down with the back of a spoon.

Chop three-quarters of the apple into small pieces and finely slice the remainder.

Put the milk, bicarbonate of soda, eggs, salt and spices into a bowl and beat together until combined. Add the remaining crumble mixture, the walnuts and the chopped apple and mix to combine. Spread the batter over the base and arrange the apple slices on top. Dust with a little nutmeg and bake in the preheated oven for 1 hour–1 hour 10 minutes until a skewer inserted into the centre of the cake comes out clean. Cover with baking paper after about 45 minutes.

Leave to cool in the tin, then turn out and cut into squares.

MAKES 12

Cherry Bakewell Squares

Bakewell tart is traditionally made with raspberry jam, but these iced squares are a delicious alternative.

INGREDIENTS

- 300 g/10½ oz ready-made shortcrust pastry
- 200 g/7 oz softened butter
- 200 g/7 oz caster sugar
- 5 eggs
- 100 g/3½ oz self-raising flour, plus extra for dusting
- 125 g/4½ oz ground almonds
- 1 tsp baking powder
- 1 tsp almond extract
- 175 g/6 oz morello or black cherry jam

Icing
- 300 g/10½ oz icing sugar
- 1 tbsp lemon juice
- cold water, as needed

METHOD

Roll out the pastry on a work surface lightly dusted with flour into a rectangle large enough to line the base and sides of a 23 x 33-cm/9 x 13-inch cake tin. Press the pastry into the tin and chill for 20 minutes.

Meanwhile, preheat the oven to 200°C/400°F/Gas Mark 6. Line the pastry case with baking paper, fill with baking beans and bake blind in the preheated oven for 15 minutes. Remove the paper and beans and bake for a further 5 minutes. Reduce the oven temperature to 180°C/350°F/Gas Mark 4.

Put the butter and sugar into a mixing bowl and beat until light and fluffy. Beat in the eggs one at a time, adding a little flour if the mixture starts to curdle. Add the remaining dry ingredients and the almond extract and mix until smooth.

Spread the jam over the base of the pastry case, then top with the cake batter and level out with the back of a spoon. Bake for 25–30 minutes until golden, and a skewer inserted in the centre comes out clean. Leave to cool in the tin.

Meanwhile, to make the icing, mix the icing sugar with the lemon juice and enough cold water to make a thick icing. Turn out the cake onto a plate, then spread the icing over the top. Leave to set for 1 hour, then cut into squares and serve.

MAKES 15

CHOCOLATE

the Claddagh, Galway, County Galway

INGREDIENTS

butter, for greasing
150 g/5½ oz plain flour
300 g/10½ oz sugar
70 g/2½ oz cocoa powder
2 tsp bicarbonate of soda
1 tsp baking powder
1 tsp salt
125 ml/4 fl oz sunflower oil
2 eggs
3 tsp orange extract
225 ml/8 fl oz buttermilk
125 ml/4 fl oz freshly squeezed orange juice
125 ml/4 fl oz water
chocolate curls and icing sugar, to decorate

Buttercream
85 g/3 oz icing sugar
90 ml/3 fl oz water
3 egg yolks
grated rind of 1 orange
175 g/6 oz softened butter, creamed until smooth

SERVES 8

Orange Chocolate Layer Cake

This luscious and impressive cake is great for a special occasion.

METHOD

Preheat the oven to 180°C/350°F/Gas Mark 4. Grease two 23-cm/9-inch round cake tins and line with baking paper.

Put the flour, sugar, cocoa powder, bicarbonate of soda, baking powder and salt into a mixing bowl and stir. Put the oil, eggs, orange extract, buttermilk, orange juice and water into a separate bowl and whisk to combine. Add the dry ingredients to the wet ingredients and beat well to combine.

Pour half the batter into each tin and bake in the preheated oven for 20–25 minutes until a skewer inserted into the centre of each cake comes out clean. Leave to cool in the tins, then turn out and level the top of each cake using a sharp knife.

To make the buttercream, put the sugar and water into a saucepan and cook over a medium heat until it reaches a temperature of 102°C/215°F. Whisk the egg yolks and orange rind together until thick and creamy, then slowly pour in the syrup, beating until cool and fluffy. Gradually add the egg yolk mixture to the butter, beating until shiny and firm.

To assemble the cake, spread one cake with buttercream, then place the second cake on top and spread the remaining buttercream over the top and sides. Decorate with chocolate curls and dust with icing sugar.

INGREDIENTS

Meringue
1 tbsp cocoa powder
120 g/4¼ oz icing sugar
3 egg whites

Cake
50 g/1¾ oz plain flour
40 g/1½ oz cocoa powder
4 eggs, separated, whites whisked to stiff peaks
120 g/4¼ oz caster sugar
chocolate curls, to decorate

Filling
600 ml/1 pint double cream
2 tbsp cocoa powder
70 g/2½ oz vanilla sugar

SERVES 6

Chocolate Meringue Layer Cake

The whisked egg whites give a very light texture to the sponge.

METHOD

Preheat the oven to 160°C/325°F/Gas Mark 3. Line two baking sheets with baking paper and draw an 18-cm/7-inch circle on each. Put the cocoa powder and 50 g/1¾ oz of the sugar into a bowl and mix to combine. Gradually whisk the remaining sugar into the egg whites until stiff peaks hold. Fold in the cocoa mixture. Spoon into a piping bag fitted with a 1-cm/½-inch plain nozzle and pipe a spiral onto each baking sheet. Bake for 1 hour 30 minutes until crisp. Peel away the paper. Increase the oven temperature to 180°C/350°F/Gas Mark 4.

To make the cake, grease and line an 18-cm/7-inch round springform cake tin. Sift the flour and cocoa powder into a bowl, then whisk the egg yolks and sugar in a separate bowl until thick. Fold in a third of the flour mixture, a third of the egg yolks and a third of the egg whites, repeating twice. Pour into the prepared tin and bake for 40–45 minutes. Leave to cool in the tin for 5 minutes, then turn out to cool completely.

Whip the filling ingredients together until soft peaks hold. Slice the cake in two horizontally. Place a meringue circle on a plate, spread with filling, then place a cake layer on top. Repeat, then spread the remaining filling over the top and sides of the cake. Decorate with chocolate curls.

INGREDIENTS

Pastry
70 g/2½ oz plain flour
25 g/1 oz ground walnuts
25 g/1 oz vanilla sugar
25 g/1 oz chilled butter, cubed
2 tsp cold water

Filling
450 g/1 lb full-fat soft cheese
150 g/5½ oz caster sugar
2 tsp plain flour
3 eggs, separated, whites whisked to stiff peaks
85 g/3 oz plain chocolate, melted
90 ml/3 fl oz double cream

SERVES 6–8

Chocolate Cheesecake

This baked cheesecake has to be prepared the day before it is eaten, so it is a perfect dinner-party dessert.

METHOD

To make the pastry, put the dry ingredients into a large bowl, add the butter and rub in with your fingertips until coarse crumbs form. Add enough water to mix to a dough, then wrap the dough in clingfilm and chill in the refrigerator for 1 hour.

Meanwhile, preheat the oven to 200°C/400°F/Gas Mark 6 and grease the base of a 20-cm/8-inch round springform cake tin. Roll out the dough to a round big enough to line the base of the tin, place on the base without clipping on the springform and trim the edges. Bake in the preheated oven for 15 minutes or until golden. Leave to cool on the base of the tin, then grease the springform and clip it onto the base. Reduce the oven temperature to 160°C/325°F/Gas Mark 3.

To make the filling, put the cheese into a large bowl and beat until soft and fluffy. Add the sugar and flour and mix to combine, then beat in the egg yolks, one at a time, beating well after each addition. Stir in the chocolate and cream, gently fold in a third of the egg whites, then fold in the remainder. Pour the mixture onto the pastry in the prepared tin and bake for 1 hour or until the filling is firm.

Leave to cool in the tin for at least 2 hours before removing the springform. Chill in the refrigerator overnight.

INGREDIENTS

butter, for greasing
5 eggs, separated, whites whisked to stiff peaks
175 g/6 oz caster sugar
85 g/3 oz plain chocolate, melted
85 g/3 oz plain flour
½ tsp ground cinnamon, plus extra for dusting
½ tsp ground cloves
½ tsp ground nutmeg
icing sugar, for dusting

Chocolate Spice Cake

This unusual spiced cake is a great afternoon tea centrepiece.

METHOD

Preheat the oven to 180°C/350°F/Gas Mark 4. Grease a 20-cm/8-inch round springform cake tin and line with baking paper.

Put the egg yolks into a bowl with the sugar and beat until thick. Fold in the chocolate, flour and spices with a metal spoon. Gently fold in a third of the egg whites, then fold in the remainder.

Pour the batter into the prepared tin and bake in the preheated oven for 40–50 minutes, until a skewer inserted into the centre of the cake comes out clean. Leave to cool in the tin for 15 minutes, then unclip and remove the springform and leave to cool completely. Dust with icing sugar and a sprinkling of cinnamon just before serving.

SERVES 6–8

INGREDIENTS

butter, for greasing
flour, for dusting
250 g/9 oz ready-made sweet shortcrust pastry
400 ml/14 fl oz double cream
140 g/5 oz plain chocolate, roughly chopped
2 tbsp whiskey
2 tbsp icing sugar
white chocolate curls, to decorate

Chocolate Whiskey Mousse Tart

A rich tart that should be served after a light meal – the whiskey is just a suggestion but it adds a great aroma.

METHOD

Preheat the oven to 200°C/400°F/Gas Mark 6. Grease a 23-cm/9-inch round tart tin.

Roll out the pastry on a work surface lightly dusted with flour and use to line the prepared tin. Prick the pastry case with a fork, then line with baking paper, fill with baking beans and bake in the preheated oven for 10 minutes. Remove the paper and beans and return to the oven for a further 2 minutes, then leave to cool in the tin.

Meanwhile, put 175 ml/6 fl oz of the cream into a saucepan and bring to a simmer over a low heat. Remove from the heat and add the chocolate, stirring until melted and combined. Leave to cool to room temperature, then stir in the whiskey.

Whip the remaining cream with the icing sugar until stiff peaks form. Gently fold in the chocolate mixture until combined.

Pour the chocolate filling into the pastry case and chill for 1½ hours, or until set. Serve chilled, decorated with white chocolate curls. The tart will keep in the refrigerator for up to 2 days.

SERVES 6–8

INGREDIENTS

butter, for greasing
250 g/9 oz ready-made shortcrust pastry
250 ml/8½ fl oz milk
115 g/4 oz caster sugar
200 g/7 oz plain chocolate, broken into pieces
2 eggs, separated, whites whisked to stiff peaks
1 tbsp powdered gelatine
3 tbsp cold espresso coffee
350 ml/12 fl oz double cream, whipped

Topping
250 ml/8½ fl oz double cream, whipped
grated chocolate

SERVES 8

Chocolate Chiffon Pie

This was a popular dinner party dessert in the 1960s – it originated in the United States and the recipe was brought to Ireland by visiting emigrants.

METHOD

Preheat the oven to 190°C/375°F/Gas Mark 5. Grease a 23-cm/9-inch fluted deep pie tin. Roll out the pastry on a work surface lightly dusted with flour and use to line the prepared tin. Line the pastry with baking paper, fill with baking beans and bake in the preheated oven for 15 minutes. Remove the beans and paper and bake for a further 15 minutes until light golden in colour. Leave to cool in the tin.

Put the milk, 80 g/3 oz of the sugar and the chocolate into a large saucepan over a medium heat and stir until the chocolate has melted and the mixture is thick and smooth. Remove from the heat and leave to cool for about 5 minutes, then whisk in the egg yolks.

Put the gelatine into a small saucepan with the coffee and heat over a low heat until the gelatine has dissolved, then stir into the chocolate mixture. Chill until beginning to set. Whisk the remaining sugar into the egg whites until firm. Gently fold the cream and then the egg whites into the chocolate mixture. Pour into the pastry case and top with whipped cream and grated chocolate. Chill until ready to serve.

INGREDIENTS

Pastry
225 g/8 oz plain flour, plus extra for dusting
2 tbsp caster sugar
1 tsp salt
55 g/2 oz ground almonds
150 g/5½ oz butter, cubed, plus extra for greasing
1 egg yolk

Filling
200 ml/7 fl oz double cream
1½ tbsp brandy
200 g/7 oz plain chocolate, broken into pieces
2 egg whites, whisked to stiff peaks
55 g/2 oz caster sugar

Topping
300 ml/10 fl oz whipped double cream
chocolate curls

SERVES 10

Chocolate Tart

It's worth taking the time to make the rich pastry for this teatime treat from scratch.

METHOD

To make the pastry, sift the flour, sugar, salt and ground almonds into a mixing bowl. Make a well in the centre, add the butter and egg yolk and work into the dry ingredients to make a dough. Wrap in clingfilm and chill in the refrigerator for 1 hour.

Preheat the oven to 190°C/375°F/Gas Mark 5. Grease a 25-cm/10-inch tart tin. Roll out the dough on a work surface lightly dusted with flour and use to line the prepared tin. Line the pastry with baking paper, fill with baking beans and bake blind in the preheated oven for 15 minutes. Remove the paper and beans and bake for a further 15 minutes until light golden in colour. Leave to cool in the tin.

Meanwhile, to make the filling, pour the cream and brandy into a large saucepan and bring just to the boil. Add the chocolate and stir until the mixture is thick and smooth. Chill in the refrigerator for 1 hour, then whisk the mixture until light and fluffy. Whisk the sugar into the egg whites, gently fold a third into the chocolate mixture, then fold in the remainder. Remove the pastry case from the tin and fill with the chocolate mixture.

Top the tart with whipped cream and sprinkle with chocolate curls. Chill until ready to serve.

INGREDIENTS

175 g/6 oz plain chocolate
6 eggs, separated
175 g/6 oz caster sugar, plus extra for sprinkling
1 tbsp cocoa powder, sifted

Filling
300 ml/10 fl oz double cream
2 tbsp icing sugar
a mixture of icing sugar and cocoa powder, to decorate

SERVES 8

Chocolate Swiss Roll

This light and airy flourless version of a classic Swiss roll is simply delicious.

METHOD

Preheat the oven to 180°C/350°F/Gas Mark 4. Grease a 23 x 33-cm/9 x 13-inch Swiss roll tin and line with baking paper. Put the chocolate in a heatproof bowl set over a saucepan of gently simmering water and heat until melted.

Put the egg whites into a large grease-free bowl and whisk until soft peaks hold. Set aside until needed. Put the egg yolks and caster sugar into a large heatproof bowl set over a saucepan of gently simmering water. Whisk until the mixture is thick enough to leave a trail when the whisk is lifted. Stir in the chocolate, then gently fold in the egg whites. Fold in the cocoa powder. Pour the batter into the prepared tin and bake in the preheated oven for 20–25 minutes until the centre of the cake springs back when lightly touched with your finger.

Lay a sheet of baking paper on the work surface and sprinkle with a little caster sugar. Turn out the sponge onto the paper, then carefully peel away the lining paper. Trim the edges and cover the sponge with a damp tea towel. Leave to cool.

To make the filling, whip the cream with the icing sugar until it holds soft peaks, then spread it over the sponge. Starting from one of the narrow ends, carefully roll up the sponge using the paper to help – don't worry if it cracks a little. Transfer to a serving plate, dust with a mixture of icing sugar and cocoa powder and serve.

INGREDIENTS

Meringues
2 egg whites
100 g/3½ oz caster sugar
2 tsp cocoa powder
vegetable oil, for greasing

Filling
125 ml/4 fl oz double cream
1½ tbsp caster sugar
2 tsp cocoa powder

MAKES 6

Chocolate Meringues

Meringues are very easy to make although they take a long time to cook. They can be stored (unfilled) at room temperature for up to two weeks or frozen for up to a month.

METHOD

Preheat the oven to 110°C/225°F/Gas Mark ¼. Grease a large baking sheet and line with baking paper.

Put the egg whites into a clean grease-free bowl and whisk until stiff peaks hold. Gradually add the sugar, beating well after each addition, until stiff and glossy. Gently fold in the cocoa powder. Spoon the mixture into a piping bag fitted with a 1-cm/½-inch star nozzle and pipe 4-cm/1½-inch spirals onto the prepared baking sheet.

Bake in the preheated oven for 3 hours until the meringues are dry and can be easily detached from the baking paper. Transfer to a wire tray and leave to cool completely.

To make the filling, whip the cream with the sugar and fold in the cocoa powder. Use to sandwich the meringues.

Chocolate Walnut Loaf

This nutty cut-and-come-again loaf has a cake-like texture, but the exterior is crusty, like a loaf of bread.

INGREDIENTS

- 210 g/7½ oz plain flour
- 150 g/5½ oz cocoa powder
- 2 tsp baking powder
- ½ tsp salt
- 225 g/8 oz softened butter, plus extra for greasing
- 200 g/7 oz granulated sugar
- 4 large eggs
- 1 tsp vanilla extract
- 250 g/9 oz ground walnuts
- 115 g/4 oz chopped walnuts
- 55 g/2 oz plain chocolate chips

METHOD

Preheat the oven to 180°C/350°F/Gas Mark 4. Grease a 450-g/1-lb loaf tin.

Put the flour, cocoa powder, baking powder and salt into a mixing bowl and stir to combine.

Put the butter and sugar into a separate bowl and cream together until light and fluffy. Add the eggs, one at a time, beating well after each addition. Stir in the vanilla extract, then gradually mix in the ground walnuts. Fold in the flour mixture with a metal spoon and mix until just combined, then fold in the chopped walnuts and the chocolate chips.

Scrape the batter into the prepared tin and bake in the preheated oven for 1 hour–1 hour 20 minutes, or until a skewer inserted into the centre of the cake comes out clean. Leave to cool in the tin for 10 minutes, then turn out onto a wire rack and leave to cool completely.

MAKES 1 LOAF

INGREDIENTS

280 g/10 oz plain flour
1 tsp salt
1 tsp baking powder
½ tsp bicarbonate of soda
115 g/4 oz softened butter, plus extra for greasing
200 g/7 oz granulated sugar
2 large eggs
60 ml/2 fl oz natural yogurt
¼ tsp vanilla extract
200 g/7 oz stoned cherries, roughly chopped
100 g/3½ oz plain chocolate chunks

Chocolate Cherry Loaf

This is a delicious cake at any time of the day – the chocolate is complemented by the luscious cherries.

METHOD

Preheat the oven to 180°C/350°F/Gas Mark 4. Grease a 450-g/1-lb loaf tin.

Put the flour, salt, baking powder and bicarbonate of soda into a mixing bowl and stir to combine.

Put the butter into a separate bowl with the sugar and cream together until light and fluffy. Beat in the eggs, one at a time, making sure that the first is incorporated before adding the second. Stir in the yogurt and the vanilla extract. Add the cherries and the chocolate chunks and mix to combine.

Gradually fold in the flour mixture with a metal spoon and mix until just combined. Pour the batter into the prepared tin and level the top with a spatula. Bake in the preheated oven for 1 hour, or until a skewer inserted into the centre of the loaf comes out clean. Leave to cool in the tin for 15 minutes, then turn out onto a wire rack and leave to cool completely.

MAKES 1 LOAF

Chocolate & Raspberry Sandwich Cake

This moist cake uses frozen raspberries, so it can be enjoyed at any time of the year. The cakes can be frozen and sandwiched together with the filling later.

INGREDIENTS

225 ml/8 fl oz sunflower oil, plus extra for greasing
250 g/9 oz caster sugar
3 large eggs
225 ml/8 fl oz milk
250 g/9 oz self-raising flour
4 tbsp cocoa powder
1½ tsp bicarbonate of soda

Filling
150 g/5½ oz raspberry jam
100 g/3½ oz frozen raspberries, thawed
300 ml/10 fl oz double cream
2 tbsp icing sugar

SERVES 8

METHOD

Preheat the oven to 180°C/350°F/Gas Mark 4. Grease two 20-cm/8-inch round springform cake tins and line with baking paper.

Put the oil, sugar, eggs and milk into a bowl and whisk until smooth. Sift the flour, cocoa powder and bicarbonate of soda into a separate large bowl, then gradually add the liquid ingredients, beating constantly. Divide the mixture between the prepared tins, then bake in the preheated oven for 35–40 minutes until risen and springy in the centre. Leave to cool in the tins for 10 minutes, then turn out onto a wire rack and leave to cool completely. Level the tops of the cakes with a sharp knife.

To make the filling, put the jam and raspberries into a bowl and stir to combine. Pour the cream and sugar into a separate bowl and whip until soft peaks form. Fold half the raspberry mixture through the cream to create a ripple effect.

Spread most of the reserved raspberry mixture over one of the cakes, then spread over half the cream, smoothing with a palette knife. Place the second cake on top and swirl the remaining cream and remaining raspberry mixture over it. The cake will keep in the refrigerator for 2 days.

Chocolate Potato Cake

This delicious cake relies on potatoes for its light texture.

INGREDIENTS

175 g/6 oz butter, softened, plus extra for greasing
175 g/6 oz caster sugar
2 eggs, beaten
150 g/5 oz self-raising flour
25 g/1 oz cocoa power
1 heaped tsp baking powder
55 g/2 oz mashed potatoes
3 tbsp milk
icing sugar, for dusting

METHOD

Preheat the oven to 190°C/350°F/Gas Mark 5. Grease a 25-cm/10-inch round cake tin and line with baking paper.

Put the butter and caster sugar into a mixing bowl and cream together until pale and fluffy. Gradually add the beaten eggs, beating well after each addition.

Sift in the flour, cocoa powder and baking powder and lightly fold in with a metal spoon. Add the mashed potatoes and milk and stir to combine.

Pour the batter into the prepared tin and bake in the preheated oven for 35–40 minutes, or until a skewer inserted into the centre comes out clean.

Leave to cool in the tin for 10 minutes, then turn out onto a wire rack and leave to cool completely. Dust with icing sugar just before serving.

SERVES 8–10

INGREDIENTS

butter, for greasing
plain flour, for dusting
250 g/9 oz ready-made shortcrust pastry
150 g/5½ oz plain chocolate
2 eggs, beaten
1 tbsp single cream
2 large ripe pears
whipped cream, to serve

Chocolate & Pear Tart

Use a good quality chocolate with a high percentage of cocoa solids to complement the sweetness of the pears.

METHOD

Preheat the oven to 180°C/350°F/Gas Mark 4. Grease a 20-cm/8-inch round loose-based tart tin.

Roll out the pastry on a work surface lightly dusted with flour and use to line the tart tin. Line with baking paper and fill with baking beans, then bake in the preheated oven for 15 minutes. Remove from the oven and increase the oven temperature to 190°C/375°F/Gas Mark 5.

Put the chocolate into a bowl set over a saucepan of gently simmering water and heat until melted. Remove from the heat and leave to cool slightly, then beat in the eggs. Fold in the cream. Spread the mixture over the base of the pastry case.

Peel and core the pears and cut them lengthways into thin slices. Arrange the pear slices on the chocolate in an overlapping pattern and sprinkle over the caster sugar.

Bake for about 25 minutes until the pears are golden brown. Leave to cool completely, then serve with whipped cream.

SERVES 6

INGREDIENTS

butter, for greasing
250 g/9 oz stale brioche, thickly sliced
100 g/3½ oz Seville marmalade
55 g/2 oz plain chocolate chips
2 eggs
2 tbsp caster sugar
zest of 1 orange
150 ml/5 fl oz double cream
225 ml/8 fl oz milk
1 tsp vanilla extract
1 tbsp demerara sugar
whipped cream or custard, to serve

Chocolate & Marmalade Bread Pudding

This well-flavoured bread pudding could be made with sliced white bread, but brioche gives it a touch of luxury.

METHOD

Preheat the oven to 160°C/325°F/Gas Mark 3 and grease a baking dish.

Spread half the brioche slices with marmalade, then sandwich them and cut them into triangles. Arrange them evenly in the prepared dish and scatter over the chocolate chips.

Put the eggs, caster sugar, orange zest, cream, milk and vanilla extract into a jug and whisk to combine. Pour over the bread and leave to soak for about 10 minutes. Sprinkle over the demerara sugar.

Bake in the centre of the preheated oven for about 45 minutes, or until the pudding has just set. Leave it to cool slightly, then cut into slices and serve with cream or custard.

SERVES 6

INGREDIENTS

100 g/3½ oz softened butter, plus extra for greasing

100 g/3½ oz plain chocolate, roughly chopped

4 large eggs

125 g/4½ oz caster sugar

75 g/2¾ oz ground almonds

2 tbsp cocoa powder, plus extra for dusting

whipped cream, to serve

Sunken Chocolate Cake

This luscious classic dessert cake is baked without any flour.

METHOD

Preheat the oven to 180°C/350°F/Gas Mark 4. Grease a 20-cm/8-inch round springform cake tin and line the base with baking paper.

Put the butter and chocolate into a heatproof bowl set over a saucepan of gently simmering water and heat until melted and combined (make sure the bowl doesn't touch the water). Set aside to cool slightly.

Put the eggs into a bowl with the sugar and whisk with a hand-held electric mixer until at least doubled in volume. Put the almonds and cocoa powder into a separate bowl and stir to combine. Gradually add this mixture to the egg and sugar mixture, whisking constantly.

Pour the butter and chocolate mixture into the batter, whisking constantly until incorporated, then pour the batter into the prepared tin. Bake in the preheated oven for about 25 minutes until the top is cracking and a skewer inserted into the centre of the cake comes out almost clean (the cake has quite a fudgy texture).

Leave to cool in the tin – the top of the cake will develop more cracks and the cake will sink a little. Unclip and remove the springform and place the cake on a serving plate. Dust with cocoa powder and serve with whipped cream.

SERVES 6–8

Baileys Chocolate Cheesecake

This indulgent baked cheesecake is a perfect dessert for a celebration meal.

INGREDIENTS

660 g/1 lb 8 oz full-fat cream cheese
250 g/9 oz caster sugar
25 g/1 oz cocoa powder, plus extra for dusting
3 tbsp plain flour
3 eggs
125 ml/4 fl oz soured cream
4 tbsp Baileys Irish Cream liqueur

Base
200 g/7 oz digestive biscuits, crushed
40 g/1½ oz icing sugar
35 g/1¼ oz cocoa powder
100 g/3½ oz butter, melted

METHOD

Preheat the oven to 180°C/350°F/Gas Mark 4. To make the base, put the crushed biscuits, icing sugar and cocoa powder into a mixing bowl, add the butter and stir to combine.

Press the mixture into the base of a 23-cm/9-inch round springform cake tin and bake in the preheated oven for 10 minutes. Set aside and increase the oven temperature to 230°C/450°F/Gas Mark 8.

Put the cream cheese, caster sugar, cocoa powder and flour into a mixing bowl and beat with a hand-held electric mixer until smooth. Add the eggs one at a time, beating well after each addition. Add the soured cream and liqueur and beat until well combined.

Pour the mixture into the tin and bake for 10 minutes, then reduce the oven temperature to 120°C/250°F/Gas Mark ½ and bake for a further 1 hour.

Use a knife to loosen the cake from the side of the tin, then leave to cool completely. Unclip and remove the springform (don't worry if the surface of the cake cracks a little) and chill in the fridge for a few hours. Dust with cocoa powder just before serving.

SERVES 10

INGREDIENTS

butter, for greasing
flour, for dusting
225 g/8 oz ready-made shortcrust pastry
250 ml/8½ fl oz milk
2 tbsp cold water
1 tbsp powdered gelatine
3 egg yolks
55 g/2 oz caster sugar
85 g/3 oz plain chocolate, roughly chopped
1 tbsp rum
125 ml/4 fl oz double cream, plus extra to serve

Chocolate Rum Pie

Rum adds great depth of flavour to this easy chocolate tart with its light mousse filling.

METHOD

Preheat the oven to 200°C/400°F/Gas Mark 6. Grease a 20-cm/8-inch fluted tart tin. Roll out the pastry on a work surface lightly dusted with flour and use to line the prepared tin. Line the pastry case with baking paper, fill with baking beans and chill in the refrigerator for 30 minutes. Bake blind in the preheated oven for 15 minutes, then remove the paper and beans and bake for a further 15 minutes, or until crisp and brown. Leave to cool in the tin.

Meanwhile, heat the milk in a medium saucepan until hot but not boiling. Put the cold water into a cup and sprinkle over the gelatine. Put the egg yolks and sugar into a bowl and beat until light and creamy. Gradually stir in the hot milk, then return to the pan, add the chocolate and gelatine mixture and stir over a low heat until all the ingredients have melted and combined. Pour into a bowl and set aside to cool.

When the mixture is beginning to set, stir in the rum. Whip the cream until soft peaks hold, then fold into the chocolate mixture. Pour into the pastry case and leave in a cool place until set. Serve with cream.

SERVES 6-8

INGREDIENTS

flour, for dusting

250 g/9 oz ready-made shortcrust pastry

300 g/10½ oz plain chocolate, roughly chopped

200 g/7 oz butter, plus extra for greasing

2 eggs

2 egg yolks

55 g/2 oz soft light brown sugar

Pinch of salt

150 g/5½ oz thick-cut Seville marmalade

whipped cream, to serve

SERVES 8

Chocolate Marmalade Tart

Chocolate and orange complement each other perfectly here. Use a good thick-cut Seville marmalade, for texture as well as flavour.

METHOD

Preheat the oven to 180°C/350°F/Gas Mark 4. Grease a 23-cm/9-inch tart tin. Roll out the pastry on a work surface lightly dusted with flour and use to line the tin. Line the pastry case with baking paper, fill with baking beans and chill in the refrigerator for 15 minutes. Bake in the preheated oven for 15–20 minutes, then remove the paper and beans and bake for a further 10 minutes until golden and cooked through. Leave to cool in the tin. Do not switch off the oven.

Put the chocolate and butter into a heatproof bowl set over a saucepan of gently simmering water (the bowl should not come into contact with the water) and stir until melted and combined. Set aside to cool.

Put the eggs, egg yolks, sugar and salt into a mixing bowl and beat with a hand-held electric mixer until tripled in volume. Using a metal spoon, fold a third of the chocolate mixture into the egg mixture, then gently fold in the remaining chocolate mixture.

Spread the marmalade over the base of the pastry case, then slowly pour over the filling. Bake for 15 minutes until the filling is just set and the edges have cracked slightly. The centre will be slightly wobbly. Leave to cool completely before serving with whipped cream.

INGREDIENTS

225 g/8 oz granulated sugar
5 tbsp water
70 g/2½ oz cocoa powder
225 g/8 oz softened butter, plus extra for greasing
225 g/8 oz caster sugar
5 eggs, separated, whites whisked to stiff peaks
225 g/8 oz plain flour
¼ tsp bicarbonate of soda
pinch of salt
icing sugar, for dusting

Chocolate Pound Cake

Pound cakes traditionally called for a pound (450 g) of each of the main ingredients. This version uses half that quantity. You will need a sugar thermometer.

METHOD

Put the granulated sugar into a saucepan with the water and bring to the boil, stirring constantly. Cook until the temperature of the syrup reaches 102°C/215°F. Remove from the heat and set the base of the pan in cold water. Add the cocoa powder, stir until smooth and set aside to cool.

Preheat the oven to 160°C/325°F/Gas Mark 3. Grease a 900-g/2-lb loaf tin and line with baking paper. Put the butter into a mixing bowl and cream until smooth. Add the caster sugar and beat until pale and fluffy. Add the egg yolks, one at a time, beating well after each addition. Stir in the chocolate syrup, then fold in the flour, bicarbonate of soda and salt with a metal spoon. Gently fold in a third of the egg whites, then fold in the remainder.

Pour the batter into the prepared tin and bake in the preheated oven for 1 hour 30 minutes, or until a skewer inserted into the centre of the cake comes out clean. Leave to cool in the tin for 15 minutes, then turn out onto a wire tray and leave to cool completely before removing the lining paper. Transfer to a serving plate and dust with icing sugar.

MAKES 1 LOAF

INGREDIENTS

175 g/6 oz butter, plus extra for greasing
225 g/8 oz soft light brown sugar
275 g/9¼ oz self-raising flour
2 tsp cocoa powder
1½ tsp bicarbonate of soda
3 eggs, beaten
2 ripe bananas, mashed
¼ tsp vanilla extract
100 g/3½ oz plain chocolate chips

SERVES 8

Chocolate Banana Cake

This is incredibly easy to make and is a step above the usual banana loaf.

METHOD

Preheat the oven to 150°C/300°F/Gas Mark 2. Grease a 20-cm/8-inch round cake tin.

Put the butter into a saucepan with the sugar and heat, stirring, until melted. Stir in the flour, cocoa powder and bicarbonate of soda. Remove from the heat and stir in the eggs, bananas and vanilla extract. Leave to cool slightly.

Stir in the chocolate chips, then spoon the batter into the prepared tin and bake in the preheated oven for 1 hour, or until a skewer inserted into the centre of the cake comes out clean. Leave to cool in the tin for 15 minutes, then turn out onto a wire rack and leave to cool completely.

Guinness Chocolate Cake

Guinness gives this delicious cake a depth of unusual flavour. Great for a celebration.

INGREDIENTS

300 g/10½ oz butter, plus extra for greasing
100 g/3½ oz cocoa powder
150 ml/5 fl oz Guinness
250 g/9 oz plain flour
2 tsp bicarbonate of soda
375 g/13 oz golden caster sugar
3 large eggs, beaten
150 ml/5 fl oz soured cream
2 tsp vanilla extract

Frosting
125 g/4½ oz butter, softened
225 g/8 oz full-fat cream cheese
225 g/8 oz icing sugar

METHOD

Preheat the oven to 180°C/350°F/Gas Mark 4. Grease a 23-cm/9-inch round loose-based cake tin and line the base with baking paper. Put the butter into a saucepan over a medium heat and heat until melted. Whisk in the cocoa powder and then the Guinness. Remove from the heat.

Put the flour, bicarbonate of soda and caster sugar into a large mixing bowl. Make a well in the centre and add the butter mixture, then add the eggs, soured cream and vanilla extract. Stir well to combine, then pour the batter into the prepared tin and bake in the preheated oven for 1 hour, or until a skewer inserted into the centre comes out clean (do keep an eye on the cake – because of its dark colour it will be difficult to tell if it's burning). Leave to cool in the tin for 10 minutes, then turn out onto a wire rack and leave to cool completely.

Meanwhile, make the frosting. Put the butter into a bowl with the cream cheese and beat well until light and creamy. Sift in the icing sugar and beat until smooth. Spread the frosting over the top of the cake and serve.

SERVES 10

Celebration Bakes

New Year's Eve fireworks over the Ha'penny Bridge, Dublin

INGREDIENTS

1 kg/2 lb 4 oz mixed dried fruit, including cherries or cranberries

juice and grated zest of 1 orange

juice and grated zest of 1 lemon

150 ml/5 fl oz Irish whiskey, plus extra for 'feeding' the cake

250 g/9 oz butter, softened

200 g/7 oz soft light brown sugar

175 g/6 oz plain flour

½ tsp baking powder

100 g/3½ oz ground almonds

100 g/3½ oz flaked almonds

2 tsp mixed spice

1 tsp ground cinnamon

½ tsp ground cloves

4 large eggs, beaten

1 tsp almond extract

SERVES 12–15

Christmas Cake

This traditional Christmas cake is 'fed' with whiskey over a period of weeks. Make it at least 6 weeks in advance.

METHOD

Put the dried fruit, orange juice and zest, lemon juice and zest, whiskey, butter and sugar into a large saucepan and bring to the boil over a medium heat. Reduce the heat and simmer for 5 minutes. Transfer the contents of the pan to a large mixing bowl and leave to stand for 30 minutes.

Preheat the oven to 150°C/300°F/Gas Mark 2. Line a large cake tin with a double layer of baking paper and wrap a double layer of brown paper around the tin, securing it with kitchen string.

Add the flour, baking powder, ground almonds, flaked almonds, mixed spice, cinnamon, cloves, eggs and almond extract to the fruit mixture and stir until well combined. Tip into the prepared tin, level the top and bake in the centre of the preheated oven for 2 hours.

Remove from the oven and prick all over with a skewer or knitting needle, then slowly pour 2–3 tablespoons of whiskey over the cake, allowing it to soak in. Leave to cool completely in the tin, then turn out, peel off the baking paper and wrap the cake in foil. Repeat the whiskey feeding procedure every 2 weeks, allowing the cake to dry out for a week before icing it.

INGREDIENTS

200 g/7 oz plain flour, plus extra for dusting

100 g/3½ oz chilled butter

25 g/1 oz icing sugar, plus extra for dusting

1 egg yolk, beaten

2–3 tbsp milk

300 g/10½ oz ready-made mincemeat

1 egg, beaten, for glazing

Mince Pies

Nothing says Christmas quite like a mince pie. It was once traditional to make your own mincemeat, but there are now some very good ready-made ones available.

METHOD

Preheat the oven to 180°C/350°F/Gas Mark 4. Dust a 12-hole tartlet tin with flour, shaking out any excess.

Sift the flour into a mixing bowl and rub in the butter until fine crumbs form. Add the sugar and egg yolk and stir in enough milk to mix to a soft dough. Turn out onto a work surface lightly dusted with flour and knead until smooth.

Shape the dough into a ball and roll out to a thickness of 1 cm/½ inch. Cut out 12 rounds with a 7-cm/2¾-inch cutter and use to line the prepared tin.

Prick the bases with a fork and add a heaped tablespoon of mincemeat to each pie. Roll out the pastry trimmings, cut out large stars or Christmas trees and use to decorate the pies.

Brush the pastry with beaten egg and bake in the preheated oven for 15 minutes. Leave to cool in the tin for 10 minutes, then transfer to a wire rack and leave to cool completely. Dust with icing sugar just before serving.

MAKES 12

Baked Christmas Pudding

This method of cooking the Christmas pudding means you can happily leave it in the oven without worrying about topping up the cooking water on the hob.

INGREDIENTS

- butter, for greasing
- 100 g/3½ oz plain flour
- 2 tsp ground cinnamon
- 2 tsp mixed spice
- 2 tsp ground nutmeg
- 350 g/12 oz fresh breadcrumbs
- 55 g/2 oz ground almonds
- 675 g/1 lb 8 oz mixed sultanas, raisins and currants
- 100 g/3½ oz glacé cherries, chopped
- 175 g/6 oz chopped mixed peel
- juice and grated zest of 1 lemon
- juice and grated zest of 1 orange
- 25 g/8 oz grated suet
- 5 eggs, beaten
- 300 ml/10 fl oz Guinness
- 4 tbsp dark rum

METHOD

Preheat the oven to 150°C/300°F/Gas Mark 2. Grease two 1.2-litre/2-pint pudding basins.

Put the flour, cinnamon, mixed spice, nutmeg, breadcrumbs, almonds, mixed dried fruit, glacé cherries and mixed peel into a large mixing bowl and mix to combine. Make a well in the centre and add the lemon juice and zest, orange juice and zest and suet and mix well.

Add the eggs and mix well, then pour in the Guinness and rum and mix thoroughly. Divide the batter between the prepared basins and cover with a double layer of greaseproof paper and a layer of foil, securing with kitchen string.

Put the puddings into a roasting tin and add hot water until the tin is three-quarters full. Bake in the preheated oven for 6 hours.

MAKES 2

INGREDIENTS

butter, for greasing
3 eggs
85 g/3 oz caster sugar
80 g/2¾ oz plain flour
½ tsp baking powder
2 tbsp cocoa powder
holly sprig, to decorate

Frosting
55 g/2 oz butter
150 g/5½ oz plain chocolate
1 tbsp golden syrup
75 ml/2½ fl oz double cream
200 g/7 oz icing sugar, sifted, plus extra for dusting

Filling
225 ml/8 fl oz double cream

SERVES 8

Yule Log

This luscious chocolate cake is a big Christmas favourite with children.

METHOD

Preheat the oven to 200°C/400°F/Gas Mark 6. Grease a Swiss roll tin and line with baking paper. Put the eggs and caster sugar into a bowl and whisk for 10 minutes, or until thick and creamy.

Mix the flour, baking powder and cocoa powder together in a bowl, then sift into the egg and sugar mixture. Fold in very gently, then pour the mixture into the prepared tin, tipping it slightly so that the mixture goes right into the corners. Bake in the preheated oven for 10 minutes. Leave to cool in the tin for 10 minutes, then invert onto a sheet of baking paper. Peel off the lining paper and roll up the cake from a long edge, using the paper to help – the paper will be inside the rolled-up cake. Leave to cool.

To make the frosting, put the butter and chocolate into a heatproof bowl set over a saucepan of gently simmering water and heat until melted. Remove from the heat, stir in the golden syrup and cream, then beat in the icing sugar until smooth.

To make the filling, whip the cream until it holds soft peaks, then unroll the cake, remove the paper and spread with the cream before rolling it up again.

Spread the frosting over the cake and score lines in it with a fork so that it looks like tree bark. Decorate with a holly sprig and serve.

INGREDIENTS

100 g/3½ oz butter, plus extra for greasing
100 g/3½ oz caster sugar
1 egg yolk
½ tsp vanilla extract
150 g/5 oz plain flour, plus extra for dusting
55 g/2 oz ground almonds
½ tsp mixed spice

Christmas Stars

These pretty little biscuits can be decorated however you like. You can hang them from the Christmas tree on ribbons if you pierce a hole in one point of each star with a skewer before baking.

METHOD

Preheat the oven to 180°C/350°F/Gas Mark 4. Grease two large baking sheets.

Put the butter and sugar into a mixing bowl and cream together until pale and fluffy. Beat in the egg yolk and the vanilla extract. Add the flour, almonds and mixed spice and mix to a stiff dough.

Turn out the dough onto a work surface lightly dusted with flour and knead lightly. Roll out to a thickness of 5 mm/¼ inch and use a star-shaped cutter to cut out biscuits.

Carefully transfer the biscuits to the prepared baking sheets and bake in the preheated oven for 12–15 minutes until golden. Leave to cool on the baking sheets for 1–2 minutes, then transfer to a wire rack and leave to cool completely.

MAKES 15–20

Ingredients

- 250 g/9 oz ready-made shortcrust pastry
- 100 g/3½ oz butter, softened, plus extra for greasing
- 100 g/3½ oz caster sugar
- 3 eggs
- 100 g/3½ oz ground almonds
- 55 g/2 oz plain flour, plus extra for dusting
- ½ tsp almond extract
- 250 g/9 oz mincemeat
- 30 g/1 oz flaked almonds

SERVES 8

Mincemeat Bakewell Tart

An adaptation of a popular recipe for the busy cook at Christmas, this can be frozen prior to baking, then baked from frozen.

Method

Preheat the oven to 180°C/350°F/Gas Mark 4. Grease a 20-cm/8-inch loose-based fluted tart tin.

Roll out the pastry on a work surface lightly dusted with flour and use to line the tart tin. Chill in the refrigerator until needed.

Put the butter and sugar into a bowl and cream together until light and fluffy, then add the eggs, one at a time, beating well after each addition. Add the ground almonds, flour and almond extract and stir to combine.

Spread the mincemeat over the base of the pastry case, then cover with the batter, levelling it with the back of a spoon. Sprinkle over the flaked almonds and bake in the preheated oven for 35 minutes, or until golden. Leave to cool in the tin for 15 minutes, then transfer to a serving plate and serve warm.

If freezing the tart, wrap the uncooked tart in its tin in clingfilm and freeze for up to 2 months. To bake, remove the tart from the freezer, unwrap and bake for 45 minutes.

Barmbrack with Whiskey-soaked Raisins

Made with yeast, this traditional Halloween treat is a sweet bread rather than a cake. For a non-alcoholic version, replace the whiskey with cold tea.

INGREDIENTS

- 450 g/1 lb plain flour
- ½ tsp freshly grated nutmeg
- pinch of salt
- 15 g/½ oz fresh yeast
- 55 g/2 oz soft light brown sugar
- 300 ml/10 fl oz lukewarm milk
- 2 eggs, beaten
- 55 g/2 oz butter, plus extra for greasing
- 115 g/4 oz mixed peel
- 225 g/8 oz currants
- 225 g/8 oz raisins, soaked in 150 ml/5 fl oz whiskey overnight
- 1 egg yolk, beaten, for glazing

METHOD

Grease a 20-cm/8-inch round cake tin. Sift the flour, nutmeg and salt into a large mixing bowl.

In a separate bowl, blend the yeast with 1 teaspoon of the sugar and a little of the milk until it froths.

Add the remaining sugar to the flour mixture. Add the remaining milk to the yeast mixture, then add to the flour with the eggs and butter. Mix with a wooden spoon for about 10 minutes until stiff.

Fold in the mixed peel, currants and raisins (with their soaking liquid), then transfer the batter to the prepared tin. Cover with a damp tea towel and leave to rise for about 1 hour until doubled in size.

Meanwhile, preheat the oven to 200°C/400°F/Gas Mark 6. Bake the brack in the preheated oven for 1 hour, then glaze with the beaten egg yolk and bake for a further 5 minutes. Leave to cool in the tin for 10 minutes, then turn out onto a wire rack and leave to cool completely.

SERVES 10–12

Barmbrack & Butter Pudding

This is a lovely way to use up any stale barmbrack. It's quicker to make than traditional bread and butter pudding, as the fruit has already been incorporated in the brack.

INGREDIENTS

225 g/8 oz barm brack (see p. 486)
55 g/2 oz butter, plus extra for greasing
4 eggs
3 egg yolks
750 ml/1¼ pints milk
55 g/2 oz soft light brown sugar
2 tsp vanilla extract

METHOD

Grease a large baking dish.

Cut the brack into 1-cm/½-inch thick slices and spread with butter. Cut each slice in half, then arrange the slices in the prepared dish, buttered side facing upwards.

Put the remaining ingredients into a jug, whisk to combine, then pour over the brack slices. Leave to stand for 30 minutes.

Meanwhile, preheat the oven to 160°C/325°F/Gas Mark 3. Place the baking dish in a roasting tin half filled with hot water. Put the roasting tin in the oven and bake the pudding for 1 hour, or until the custard is set. Serve hot.

SERVES 6

Hot Cross Buns

Traditionally eaten on Good Friday, these sticky spiced buns are now a favourite throughout Lent. The crosses are optional.

INGREDIENTS

oil, for brushing
500 g/1 lb 2 oz strong white bread flour, plus extra for dusting
½ tsp salt
2 tsp mixed spice
1 tsp ground nutmeg
1 tsp ground cinnamon
2 tsp easy-blend yeast
55 g/2 oz golden caster sugar, plus extra for glazing
grated zest of 1 lemon
175 g/6 oz currants
85 g/3 oz chopped mixed peel
85 g/3 oz butter, melted
1 egg, beaten
225 ml/8 fl oz lukewarm milk, plus extra cold milk for glazing

Pastry crosses
55 g/2 oz plain flour
25 g/1 oz chilled butter, diced
1 tbsp cold water

MAKES 12

METHOD

Brush a baking sheet and a bowl with oil. Sift the flour, salt and spices into a mixing bowl. Stir in the yeast, sugar, lemon zest, currants and mixed peel. Make a well in the centre. Put the butter, egg and milk into a separate bowl and mix to combine. Pour into the dry ingredients and mix to a soft dough. Turn out onto a work surface lightly dusted with flour and knead for 10 minutes until smooth. Place in the oiled bowl, cover with clingfilm and set aside in a warm place for up to 2 hours, or until doubled in volume.

Turn out the dough and knead for 2 minutes. Shape into 12 balls and place on the prepared baking sheet. Cover with oiled clingfilm and set aside in a warm place for 45 minutes. Meanwhile, preheat the oven to 220°C/425°F/Gas Mark 7.

To make the pastry crosses, sift the flour into a bowl, rub in the butter and stir in the water to mix to a dough. Roll it into 24 strips, each 18 cm/7 inches. Put 3 tablespoons of milk and 3 tablespoons of sugar into a saucepan and heat until the sugar is dissolved. Brush the glaze over the buns and lay two pastry strips on each of them in a cross shape. Bake in the preheated oven for 15–20 minutes until golden. Transfer to a wire rack and leave to cool.

INGREDIENTS

175 g/6 oz butter, plus extra for greasing
175 g/6 oz caster sugar
3 large eggs, beaten
350 g/12 oz mixed currants and sultanas
55 g/2 oz chopped mixed peel
grated zest of 1 orange
grated zest of 1 lemon
225 g/8 oz self-raising flour
1 tsp mixed spice
3 tbsp brandy

Topping
450 g/1 lb marzipan
2 tsp apricot jam
1 egg, beaten

Simple Simnel Cake

Simnel cakes were made by young women in domestic service and given to their mothers on Mothering Sunday. The cakes were usually kept until Easter (Mothering Sunday often fell during Lent) and they have become a modern Easter tradition.

METHOD

Preheat the oven to 150°C/300°F/Gas Mark 2. Grease a 20-cm/8-inch round cake tin.

Put the butter and sugar into a mixing bowl and cream together until pale and fluffy. Gradually add the eggs, beating well after each addition. Fold in the mixed dried fruit, mixed peel, orange zest and lemon zest.

Sift in the flour and mixed spice and, using a metal spoon, fold in very carefully with the brandy. Spoon the batter into the prepared tin and level the top. Bake in the preheated oven for 2½–3 hours. Leave to cool in the tin for 15 minutes, then turn out onto a wire rack and leave to cool completely.

Meanwhile, make the topping. Roll out the marzipan and cut into a 20-cm/8-inch round. Brush the top of the cake with the jam and place the marzipan round on top. Using the marzipan trimmings, roll out 11 balls and place these around the edge of the topping. Brush with beaten egg and place under a medium grill until toasted.

SERVES 10

INGREDIENTS

200 g/7 oz butter, plus extra for greasing
200 g/7 oz caster sugar
3 eggs, beaten
grated zest of 2 large lemons
200 g/7 oz self-raising flour, plus extra for dusting
candied lemon slices and mini chocolate eggs, to decorate

Filling and frosting
150 g/5½ oz icing sugar, plus extra for dusting
85 g/3 oz butter, softened
½ tsp lemon extract

Easter Lemon Sponge

This light-textured, zesty cake will help offset all that Easter chocolate!

METHOD

Preheat the oven to 180°C/350°F/Gas Mark 4. Grease a 20-cm/8-inch round cake tin and dust with flour, shaking out any excess.

Put the butter and sugar into a mixing bowl and cream together until pale and fluffy. Gradually add the eggs, beating well after each addition. Add the lemon zest, stirring to incorporate.

Sift in the flour and, using a metal spoon, fold in until combined. Spoon the batter into the prepared tin and level the top. Bake in the preheated oven for 30–40 minutes until golden and a skewer inserted into the centre of he cake comes out clean. Leave to cool in the tin for 15 minutes, then turn out onto a wire rack and leave to cool completely.

Meanwhile, make the filling and frosting. Put the icing sugar and butter into a bowl and cream together until pale and fluffy. Add the lemon extract, then chill in the fridge until the cake is completely cooled.

Cut the cake in half horizontally. Spread two-thirds of the filling mixture on one half, then place the other half on top. Spread the remaining mixture on top, then dust with icing sugar and decorate with candied lemon slices and mini chocolate eggs.

SERVES 10

INGREDIENTS

175 g/6 oz butter, softened, plus extra for greasing

175 g/6 oz caster sugar, plus extra for sprinkling

1 egg, beaten

1 tbsp milk

55 g/2 oz chopped mixed peel

115 g/4 oz currants or dried cherries

350 g/12 oz plain flour, plus extra for dusting

1 tsp mixed spice

1 egg white, beaten

Easter Biscuits

A traditional Easter biscuit, this recipe makes the most of all the ingredients that were forbidden during the Lenten season.

METHOD

Preheat the oven to 180°C/350°F/Gas Mark 4. Grease two large baking sheets. Put the butter and sugar into a mixing bowl and cream together until pale and fluffy. Gradually beat in the egg and milk, then stir in the mixed peel and currants.

Sift in the flour and mixed spice and mix to a firm dough. Knead until smooth, then turn out onto a work surface lightly dusted with flour and roll out to a thickness of 5 mm/¼ inch. Cut out 24 rounds with a 5-cm/2-inch round fluted cutter, rerolling and using the trimmings. Place the biscuits on the prepared baking sheets and bake in the preheated oven for 10 minutes until golden.

Remove from the oven – do not switch off the oven – and brush with the egg white. Sprinkle with sugar and return to the oven for 5 minutes. Leave to cool on the baking sheets for 2 minutes, then transfer to wire racks and leave to cool completely.

MAKES 24

Index

A

alcohol (baking with), 180–1
allspice
   Porter Cake, 92
   Upside-down Pear Cake, 174
almonds
   Almond & Coconut Cake, 178
   Almond Fingers, 382
   Almond Macaroons, 326
   Almond Shortbread, 336
   Apple & Almond Tart, 248
   Apple & Cider Cake, 122
   Baked Christmas Pudding, 478
   Bakewell Flapjacks, 390
   Bakewell Tart, 254
   Banoffee Pie, 224
   Blueberry & Almond Tart, 218
   Cherry Bakewell Squares, 424
   Cherry Loaf, 108
   Christmas Cake, 474
   Christmas Stars, 482
   Coconut Shortbread, 338
   Coffee Walnut Macaroons, 328
   Dried Fruit Loaf, 156
   Lemon & Raspberry Drizzle Cake, 176
   Lemon Curd & Almond Tart, 216
   Mincemeat Bakewell Tart, 484
   Oaty Almond Biscuits, 318
   Orange & Almond Muffins, 368
   Pear & Almond Tart, 238
   Slab Cake, 166
   Sunken Chocolate Cake, 458
   Upside-down Plum Cake, 104
   Very Easy Walnut Loaf, 164
   Yogurt & Honey Cake, 148
Antrim, 24
apples, 231
   Apple & Almond Tart, 248
   Apple & Blackberry Cake, 120
   Apple & Blackberry Crumble Squares, 418
   Apple & Cider Cake, 122
   Apple & Walnut Squares, 422
   Apple Amber, 252
   Apple Charlotte, 208
   Apple Cinnamon Cake, 162
   Apple Crumble, 210
   Apple Fingers, 386
   Apple Flan with Baileys, 212
   Apple Pie, 206
   Autumn Crumble, 232
   Blackberry & Apple Muffins, 374
   Currant Squares, 410
   Kerry Apple Cake, 102
   Open Apple Tart, 200
   Spiced Apple & Oat Muffins, 378
apricots
   Apricot Oat Fingers, 394
   Apricot Tart, 222
   Fruit Slices, 392
Autumn Crumble, 232

B

bacon
   Bacon & Egg Flan, 264
   Chicken Pie with Potato Pastry, 268
   Donegal Pie, 260
   Steak & Stout Pie, 270
Baileys Cream liqueur
   Apple Flan with Baileys, 212
   Baileys Chocolate Cheese cake, 460
Baked Christmas Pudding, 478
bakestone, 25
Bakewell Flapjacks, 390
Bakewell Tart, 254
   Mincemeat Bakewell Tart, 484
baking techniques, 24–5
bananas
   Banana & Walnut Loaf, 94
   Banana Fruit Loaf, 188
   Banoffee Pie, 224
   Carrot Cake, 138
   Chocolate Banana Cake, 468
   Dried Fruit Loaf, 156
   Wholemeal Banana Muffins, 376
Banoffee Pie, 224
barley (baking with), 348–9
Barmbrack & Butter Pudding, 488
Barmbrack with Whiskey-soaked Raisins, 486
bastible (pot oven), 12, 24–5
Beef & Oyster Pie, 280
Belfast Baps, 88

berries. *see also* blueberries; raspberries; strawberries
  Buttermilk Berry Muffins, 370
  Fruit Meringue Pie, 226
  Lemon & Raspberry Drizzle Cake, 176
biscuits. *see also* macaroons; shortbread
  Almond Shortbread, 336
  Chocolate Biscuits, 298
  Christmas Stars, 482
  Coconut Biscuits, 312, 342
  Coconut Shortbread, 338
  Crunchy Oat Biscuits, 302
  Crunchy Savoury Oatcakes, 294
  Dark Chocolate Oaties, 300
  Easter Biscuits, 496
  Ginger Nuts, 296
  Hunting Nuts, 316
  Iced Coffee Oat Biscuits, 320
  Lemon Biscuits, 314
  Oat & Honey Crunch Biscuits, 306
  Oat Shortbread, 340
  Oaty Almond Biscuits, 318
  Oaty Fruit & Nut Biscuits, 304
  Orange Creams, 322
  Portarlington Golden Biscuits, 308
  Porter Hope Biscuits, 310
  Shah Biscuits, 324
  Shortbread Fingers, 334
  Sweet Oatcakes, 344
  Vanilla Biscuits, 332
  Walnut Biscuits, 330
blackberries, 231
  Apple & Blackberry Cake, 120
  Apple & Blackberry Crumble Squares, 418
  Autumn Crumble, 232
  Blackberry & Apple Muffins, 374
blueberries, 231
  Blueberry & Almond Tart, 218
Boiled Fruit Cake, 136
Boxty (bread), 36, 126
bran
  Wholemeal Walnut Bread, 48
brandy, 180
  Chocolate Tart, 440
  Seed Cake, 100
  Simple Simnel Cake, 492
bread. *see also* buns & rolls; soda bread
  Apple Charlotte, 208
  Barmbrack with Whiskey-soaked Raisins, 486
  Brown Bread, 22
  Cheese & Onion Bread, 40
  Cheese & Tomato Bread, 40
  Chocolate & Marmalade Bread Pudding, 456
  Guinness Bread, 34
  Hazelnut Bread, 46
  Oatmeal Bread, 28
  Oven Boxty Bread, 36
  Rye Bread, 42
  Seed Bread, 30
  Treacle Loaf, 26
  Wheaten Bread, 52
breadcrumbs
  Golden Syrup Tart, 202
  Nutty Treacle Tart, 214
  Brown Bread, 22
  Brown Soda Bread, 18
buns & rolls
  Belfast Baps, 88
  Cherry Buns, 366
  Hot Cross Buns, 490
  Marmalade Buns, 364
  Rock Buns, 360
  Spiced Buns, 358
  Vanilla Buns, 362
  Waterford Blaa Buns, 86
  Butter Cakes, 82
buttercream
  Coffee Walnut Macaroons, 328
  Easter Lemon Sponge, 494
  Orange Chocolate Layer Cake, 428
  Vanilla Buns, 362
Butterfly Cakes, 350
buttermilk
  baking with, 72
  Blackberry & Apple Muffins, 374
  Brown Soda Bread, 18
  Butter Cakes, 82
  Buttermilk Berry Muffins, 370
  Buttermilk Cake, 144
  Buttermilk Scones, 64
  Cornmeal Scones, 78
  Guinness Seaweed Soda Bread, 56

INDEX

Kerry Treacle Bread, 54
Oat Scones, 68
Oatmeal Soda Bread, 50
Oaty Gingerbread, 152
Orange Chocolate Layer Cake, 428
Oven-baked Fadge, 84
Rhubarb Cake, 112
Seed Bread, 30
Spotted Dog, 20
substitutes, 73
White Soda Bread, 16
Wholemeal Scones, 62
Wholemeal Walnut Bread, 48

C

cake crumbs
   Apricot Tart, 222
cakes (large). *see also* loaves
   Almond & Coconut Cake, 178
   Apple & Blackberry Cake, 120
   Apple & Cider Cake, 122
   Apple Cinnamon Cake, 162
   Boiled Fruit Cake, 136
   Buttermilk Cake, 144
   Carrot Cake, 138
   Cherry Cake, 132
   Chocolate & Raspberry Sandwich Cake, 450
   Chocolate Banana Cake, 468
   Chocolate Meringue Layer Cake, 430
   Chocolate Potato Cake, 452
   Chocolate Spice Cake, 434
   Christmas Cake, 474
   Coffee & Walnut Cake, 134
   Easter Lemon Sponge, 494
   Fresh Plum Cake, 106
   Guinness Chocolate Cake, 470
   Honey Cake, 190
   Irish Mist Ring Cake, 130
   Kerry Apple Cake, 102
   Lemon & Raspberry Drizzle Cake, 176
   Lemon Cake, 98
   Light Cherry Cake, 154
   Magic Vanilla Custard Cake, 172
   Marble Cake, 184
   Marmalade Cake, 142
   Orange Cake, 146
   Orange Chocolate Layer Cake, 428
   Pineapple Upside-down Cake, 140
   Porter Cake, 92
   Rhubarb Cake, 112
   Rhubarb Streusel Cake, 124
   Seed Cake, 100
   Simple Simnel Cake, 492
   Spiced Potato Cake, 128
   Sunken Chocolate Cake, 458
   Upside-down Pear Cake, 174
   Upside-down Plum Cake, 104
   Victoria Sponge, 96
   Whiskey Cake, 116
   Yogurt & Honey Cake, 148
cakes (small). *see also* buns & rolls; muffins
   Butterfly Cakes, 350
   Chocolate Butterfly Cakes, 352
   Queen Cakes, 346
candied peel
   Honey Cake, 190
   Slab Cake, 166
Caramelised Cherry Tomato & Goat's Cheese Tart, 272
caraway seeds
   Seed Cake, 100
carrots
   Carrot Cake, 138
   Individual Dingle Pies, 284
   Shepherd's Pie, 274
celebration bakes
   Baked Christmas Pudding, 478
   Barmbrack & Butter Pudding, 488
   Barmbrack with Whiskey-soaked Raisins, 486
   Christmas Cake, 474
   Easter Biscuits, 496
   Easter Lemon Sponge, 494
   Mince Pies, 476
   Mincemeat Bakewell Tart, 484
   Simple Simnel Cake, 492
   Yule Log, 480
celery
   Individual Dingle Pies, 284
cheese
   Bacon & Egg Flan, 264
   Caramelised Cherry Tomato & Goat's Cheese Tart, 272
   Cheddar Cheese Scones, 66
   Cheese & Onion Bread, 40
   Cheese & Spinach Pie, 286

Cheese & Tomato Bread, 38
Cheesy Soda Bread, 44
Roasted Vegetable Quiche, 288
Seaweed Flan, 282
cheesecakes
  Baileys Chocolate Cheesecake, 460
  Chocolate Cheesecake, 432
  Ginger & Honey Cheesecake, 228
  Irish Cream Cheesecake, 242
cherries, 231
  Baked Christmas Pudding, 478
  Cherry Bakewell Squares, 424
  Cherry Buns, 366
  Cherry Cake, 132
  Cherry Loaf, 108
  Cherry Scones, 76
  Chocolate Cherry Loaf, 448
  Easter Biscuits, 496
  Light Cherry Cake, 154
  Nutty Fruit Slices, 414
  Pineapple Upside-down Cake, 140
  Porter Cake, 92
  Slab Cake, 166
cherry tomatoes. *see* tomatoes
Chicken Pie with Potato Pastry, 268
chocolate
  Baileys Chocolate Cheesecake, 460
  Banoffee Pie, 224
  Chocolate & Marmalade Bread Pudding, 456
  Chocolate & Pear Tart, 454
  Chocolate & Raspberry Sandwich Cake, 450
  Chocolate Banana Cake, 468
  Chocolate Biscuits, 298
  Chocolate Butterfly Cakes, 352
  Chocolate Cheesecake, 432
  Chocolate Cherry Loaf, 448
  Chocolate Chiffon Pie, 438
  Chocolate Marmalade Tart, 464
  Chocolate Meringue Layer Cake, 430
  Chocolate Meringues, 444
  Chocolate Potato Cake, 452
  Chocolate Pound Cake, 466
  Chocolate Rum Pie, 462
  Chocolate Spice Cake, 434
  Chocolate Swiss Roll, 442
  Chocolate Tart, 440
  Chocolate Walnut Loaf, 446
  Chocolate Whiskey Mousse Tart, 436
  Dark Chocolate Oaties, 300
  Guinness Chocolate Cake, 470
  Irish Mist Ring Cake, 130
  Meringues, 356
  Orange Chocolate Layer Cake, 428
  Sunken Chocolate Cake, 458
  Yule Log, 480
chocolate chips
  Chocolate & Marmalade Bread Pudding, 456
  Chocolate Banana Cake, 468
  Chocolate Chip Flapjacks, 402
  Chocolate Walnut Loaf, 446
  Oat & Honey Crunch Biscuits, 306
chocolate glaze, 130
Christmas
  Baked Christmas Pudding, 478
  Christmas Cake, 474
  Christmas Stars, 482
  Yule Log, 480
cider
  Apple & Cider Cake, 122
cider vinegar
  Oaty Fruit & Nut Biscuits, 304
cinnamon
  Apple & Blackberry Cake, 120
  Apple & Cider Cake, 122
  Apple & Walnut Squares, 422
  Apple Cinnamon Cake, 162
  Apple Crumble, 210
  Apple Fingers, 386
  Apple Flan with Baileys, 212
  Apple Pie, 206
  Baked Christmas Pudding, 478
  Carrot Cake, 138
  Chocolate Spice Cake, 434
  Christmas Cake, 474
  Cinnamon Fruit Scones, 74
  Dried Fruit Loaf, 156
  Easy Fruit Loaf, 186
  Fresh Plum Cake, 106
  Fruit Slices, 392
  Honey Cake, 190
  Hot Cross Buns, 490
  Irish Tea Cake, 114
cloves

Chocolate Spice Cake, 434
Christmas Cake, 474
Dried Fruit Loaf, 156
Honey Cake, 190
Shah biscuits, 324
cocoa powder
Chocolate Biscuits, 298
Chocolate Butterfly Cakes, 352
Chocolate Meringue Layer Cake, 430
Chocolate Meringues, 444
Chocolate Walnut Loaf, 446
Marble Cake, 184
coconut
Almond & Coconut Cake, 178
Coconut & Walnut Bars, 408
Coconut Biscuits, 312, 342
Coconut Fingers, 384
Coconut Flapjacks, 416
Coconut Shortbread, 338
Iced Coffee Oat Biscuits, 320
Raspberry & Coconut Squares, 420
cod
Luxury Fish Pie, 278
coffee
Chocolate Chiffon Pie, 438
Coffee & Walnut Cake, 134
Coffee Walnut Macaroons, 328
Iced Coffee Oat Biscuits, 320
condensed milk
Banoffee Pie, 224
coriander
Apple Cinnamon Cake, 162

Cork
Blackrock Castle Observatory, 258
Clonakilty, 379
Cobh, 192-3
Old Head of Kinsale, 90
corn (baking with), 349
cornflour, 349
Cornmeal Scones, 78
courgettes
Roasted Vegetable Quiche, 288
cream cheese
Baileys Chocolate Cheesecake, 460
Carrot Cake, 138
Ginger & Honey Cheesecake, 228
Guinness Chocolate Cake, 470
Irish Cream Cheesecake, 242
Salmon & Cream Cheese Tart, 290
crumbles, 210
Apple & Blackberry Crumble Squares, 418
Apple Crumble, 210
Autumn Crumble, 232
Gooseberry & Hazelnut Crumble, 246
Mincemeat Crumble Bars, 396
Rhubarb & Ginger Crumble, 234
Crunchy Oat Biscuits, 302
Crunchy Savoury Oatcakes, 294
curd cheese
Curd Tart, 194

currants. *see also* dried fruit
Barmbrack with Whiskey-soaked Raisins, 486
Boiled Fruit Cake, 136
Buttermilk Cake, 144
Currant Squares, 410
Easter Biscuits, 496
Hot Cross Buns, 490
custard
Strawberry Tart, 240

D

Dark Chocolate Oaties, 300
dates
Date & Guinness Cake, 158
Date & Walnut Loaf, 160
Date Fingers, 412
Date Loaf, 118
Dried Fruit Loaf, 156
desserts. *see* cheesecakes; crumbles; tarts
digestive biscuits
Baileys Chocolate Cheesecake, 460
Banoffee Pie, 224
Irish Cream Cheesecake, 242
dillisk flakes
Guinness Seaweed Soda Bread, 56
Dingle Pie, 262
Individual Dingle Pies, 284
Donegal Pie, 260
double cream
Apricot Tart, 222

Banoffee Pie, 224
Cheese & Spinach Pie, 286
Chocolate & Raspberry Sandwich Cake, 450
Chocolate Cheesecake, 432
Chocolate Chiffon Pie, 438
Chocolate Meringue Layer Cake, 430
Chocolate Meringues, 444
Chocolate Rum Pie, 462
Chocolate Swiss Roll, 442
Chocolate Tart, 440
Chocolate Whiskey Mousse Tart, 436
Easy Lemon Tart, 198
Ginger & Honey Cheesecake, 228
Gooseberry Tart, 244
Lemon Swiss Roll, 168
Meringues, 356
Orange & Lemon Star Tart, 220
Roasted Vegetable Quiche, 288
Salmon & Cream Cheese Tart, 290
Victoria Sponge, 96
Walnut & Honey Tart, 204
Yule Log, 480
dried fruit
Baked Christmas Pudding, 478
baking with, 230
Banana Fruit Loaf, 188
Christmas Cake, 474
Cinnamon Fruit Scones, 74
Dried Fruit Loaf, 156
Easy Fruit Loaf, 186
Fruit Slices, 392
Fruity Flapjacks, 400
Irish Tea Cake, 114
Nutty Fruit Slices, 414
Oaty Fruit & Nut Biscuits, 304
Porter Cake, 92
Rock Buns, 360
Simple Simnel Cake, 492
Spotted Dog, 20
Dublin
Ha'penny Bridge, 472
dulse (seaweed), 282

E

Easter
Easter Biscuits, 496
Easter Lemon Sponge, 494
Simple Simnel Cake, 492
Easy Fruit Loaf, 186
Easy Lemon Tart, 198
eggs
Bacon & Egg Flan, 264
Cheese & Spinach Pie, 286
Donegal Pie, 260
Roasted Vegetable Quiche, 288
equipment, 13

F

fish
Luxury Fish Pie, 278
Smoked Salmon Tart, 276
flans
Apple Flan with Baileys, 212
Bacon & Egg Flan, 264
Fruit Flan, 256
Seaweed Flan, 282
Flapjacks, 388
Bakewell Flapjacks, 390
Chocolate Chip Flapjacks, 402
Coconut Flapjacks, 416
Fruity Flapjacks, 400
Fresh Plum Cake, 106
Fresh Strawberry Swiss Roll, 170
fromage frais
Fresh Strawberry Swiss Roll, 170
frosting
Carrot Cake, 138
Easter Lemon Sponge, 494
Guinness Chocolate Cake, 470
Yule Log, 480
fruit. *see also* dried fruit
baking with, 230
Fruit Flan, 256
Fruit Meringue Pie, 226
fruit cakes
Boiled Fruit Cake, 136
Christmas Cake, 474
Dried Fruit Loaf, 156
Easy Fruit Loaf, 186
Porter Cake, 92
Slab Cake, 166
Fruit Slices, 392
Fruity Flapjacks, 400

G

Galway
The Claddagh, 425
garlic
Cheese & Onion Bread, 40
Cheese & Spinach Pie, 286

INDEX

Cheese & Tomato Bread, 38
ginger
   Dried Fruit Loaf, 156
   Ginger & Honey Cheesecake, 228
   Ginger Cake, 110
   Ginger Nuts, 296
   Honey Cake, 190
   Hunting Nuts, 316
   Rhubarb & Ginger Crumble, 234
   Shah Biscuits, 324
   Spiced Buns, 358
   Upside-down Pear Cake, 174
Gingerbread, 150
Oaty Gingerbread, 152
glazes
   Apricot Tart, 222
   Irish Mist Ring Cake, 130
   Open Apple Tart, 200
   Strawberry Tart, 240
goat's cheese
   Caramelised Cherry Tomato & Goat's Cheese Tart, 272
golden syrup
   Crunchy Oat Biscuits, 302
   Easy Fruit Loaf, 186
   Fresh Plum Cake, 106
   Ginger Cake, 110
   Ginger Nuts, 296
   Golden Syrup Tart, 202
   Nutty Treacle Tart, 214
   Oat & Syrup Scones, 80
   Oaty Fruit & Nut Biscuits, 304
   Oaty Gingerbread, 152
   Orange Creams, 322
   Portarlington Golden Biscuits, 308
   Shah Biscuits, 324
   Vanilla Biscuits, 332
gooseberries, 231
   Gooseberry & Hazelnut Crumble, 246
   Gooseberry Tart, 244
grains (baking with), 348-9
Guinness
   Baked Christmas Pudding, 478
   Chicken Pie with Potato Pastry, 268
   Date & Guinness Cake, 158
   Guinness Bread, 34
   Guinness Chocolate Cake, 470
   Guinness Seaweed Soda Bread, 56
   Steak & Kidney Pie with Guinness, 266
Gur Cake, 406

H

hazelnuts. *see also* nuts
   Gooseberry & Hazelnut Crumble, 246
   Hazelnut Bread, 46
   Hazelnut Squares, 404
   Rhubarb & Ginger Crumble, 234
honey
   Ginger & Honey Cheesecake, 228
   Guinness Seaweed Soda Bread, 56
   Honey Cake, 190
   Irish Mist Ring Cake, 130
   Oat & Honey Crunch Biscuits, 306
   Walnut & Honey Tart, 204
   Wheaten Bread with Nuts, Seeds & Honey, 58
   Yogurt & Honey Cake, 148
Hot Cross Buns, 490
Hunting Nuts, 316

I

Iced Coffee Oat Biscuits, 320
icing
   Cherry Bakewell Squares, 424
   Honey Cake, 190
   Iced Coffee Oat Biscuits, 320
   Orange Cake, 146
   Queen Cakes, 346
Irish Cream liqueur, 181. *see also* Baileys Cream liqueur
   Irish Cream Cheesecake, 242
Irish Mist Ring Cake, 130
Irish Tea Cake, 114

J

jam
   Apricot Oat Fingers, 394
   Apricot Tart, 222
   Bakewell Flapjacks, 390
   Bakewell Tart, 254
   Butterfly Cakes, 350
   Cherry Bakewell Squares, 424
   Chocolate & Raspberry Sandwich Cake, 450
   Fruit Flan, 256
   Jam Tart, 196
   Jam Tarts (small), 354
   Open Apple Tart, 200
   Simple Simnel Cake, 492
   Strawberry Tart, 240
   Victoria Sponge, 96

K

Kerry
　Dingle seaport, 14
　Kerry Apple Cake, 102
　Kerry Treacle Bread, 54
kidney
　Steak & Kidney Pie with Guinness, 266
Kildare, 11

L

lamb
　Dingle Pie, 262
　Individual Dingle Pies, 284
　Shepherd's Pie, 274
Lemon Curd & Almond Tart, 216
lemons
　Apple Amber, 252
　Banoffee Pie, 224
　Curd Tart, 194
　Easter Lemon Sponge, 494
　Easy Lemon Tart, 198
　Lemon & Poppy Seed Muffins, 372
　Lemon & Raspberry Drizzle Cake, 176
　Lemon Biscuits, 314
　Lemon Cake, 98
　Lemon Meringue Pie, 250
　Lemon Swiss Roll, 168
　Nutty Treacle Tart, 214
　Orange & Lemon Star Tart, 220
　Yogurt & Honey Cake, 148
Light Cherry Cake, 154
liqueurs (baking with), 181
loaves
　Banana & Walnut Loaf, 94
　Banana Fruit Loaf, 188
　Cheese & Onion Bread, 40
　Cheese & Tomato Bread, 40
　Cherry Loaf, 108
　Chocolate Cherry Loaf, 448
　Chocolate Pound Cake, 466
　Chocolate Walnut Loaf, 446
　Date & Guinness Cake, 158
　Date & Walnut Loaf, 160
　Date Loaf, 118
　Dried Fruit Loaf, 156
　Easy Fruit Loaf, 186
　Ginger Cake, 110
　Gingerbread, 150
　Guinness Seaweed Soda Bread, 56
　Irish Tea Cake, 114
　Madeira Cake, 182
　Oaty Gingerbread, 152
　Rye Bread, 42
　Treacle Loaf, 26
　Very Easy Walnut Loaf, 164
loganberries, 231

M

macaroons
　Almond Macaroons, 326
　Coffee Walnut Macaroons, 328
mace
　Seed Cake, 100
Madeira Cake, 182
Magic Vanilla Custard Cake, 172
Marble Cake, 184
marmalade
　Chocolate & Marmalade Bread Pudding, 456
　Chocolate Marmalade Tart, 464
　Marmalade Buns, 364
　Marmalade Cake, 142
marzipan
　Simple Simnel Cake, 492
Meringues, 356
　Apple Amber, 252
　Chocolate Meringue Layer Cake, 430
　Chocolate Meringues, 444
　Fruit Meringue Pie, 226
　Lemon Meringue Pie, 250
mincemeat
　Mince Pies, 476
　Mincemeat Bakewell Tart, 484
　Mincemeat Crumble Bars, 396
mixed peel
　Apple Cinnamon Cake, 162
　Baked Christmas Pudding, 478
　Barmbrack with Whiskey-soaked Raisins, 486
　Currant Squares, 410
　Dried Fruit Loaf, 156
　Easter Biscuits, 496
　Hot Cross Buns, 490
　Hunting Nuts, 316
　Porter Cake, 92
mixed spice
　Baked Christmas Pudding, 478
　Banana & Walnut Loaf, 94
　Boiled Fruit Cake, 136
　Christmas Cake, 474
　Christmas Stars, 482
　Date Loaf, 118
　Easter Biscuits, 496

Easy Fruit Loaf, 186
Ginger Cake, 110
Gur Cake, 406
Hot Cross Buns, 490
Hunting Nuts, 316
Shah Biscuits, 324
Simple Simnel Cake, 492
Spiced Buns, 358
Spiced Potato Cake, 128
muffins
  Blackberry & Apple Muffins, 374
  Buttermilk Berry Muffins, 370
  Lemon & Poppy Seed Muffins, 372
  Orange & Almond Muffins, 368
  Spiced Apple & Oat Muffins, 378
  Wholemeal Banana Muffins, 376

N

natural yogurt. *see* yogurt
nutmeg
  Apple & Walnut Squares, 422
  Baked Christmas Pudding, 478
  Barmbrack with Whiskey-soaked Raisins, 486
  Chocolate Spice Cake, 434
  Dried Fruit Loaf, 156
  Hot Cross Buns, 490
  Porter Cake, 92
  Seed Cake, 100
  Whiskey Cake, 116
nuts. *see also* hazelnuts; walnuts
  Nutty Fruit Slices, 414
  Nutty Treacle Tart, 214
  Oaty Fruit & Nut Biscuits, 304

O

Oat Scones, 68
Oat Shortbread, 340
oatmeal
  Hunting Nuts, 316
  Oatmeal Bread, 28
  Oatmeal Soda Bread, 50
  Oaty Almond Biscuits, 318
  Oaty Gingerbread, 152
  Wholemeal Walnut Bread, 48
oats. *see also* porridge oats
  baking with, 348
  Chocolate Chip Flapjacks, 402
  Coconut Biscuits, 312
  Coconut Flapjacks, 416
  Crunchy Oat Biscuits, 302
  Flapjacks, 388
  Fruity Flapjacks, 400
  Oat & Honey Crunch Biscuits, 306
  Oat & Syrup Scones, 80
  Wheaten Bread with Nuts, Seeds & Honey, 58
  Wholemeal Walnut Bread, 48
Oaty Fruit & Nut Biscuits, 304
Oaty Gingerbread, 152
olives
  Cheese & Tomato Bread, 38
onions
  Bacon & Egg Flan, 264
  Beef & Oyster Pie, 280
  Cheese & Onion Bread, 40
  Individual Dingle Pies, 284
  Steak & Stout Pie, 270
Open Apple Tart, 200
orange syrup, 146
oranges
  Orange & Almond Muffins, 368
  Orange & Lemon Star Tart, 220
  Orange Cake, 146
  Orange Chocolate Layer Cake, 428
  Orange Creams, 322
  Wholemeal Banana Muffins, 376
  Yogurt & Honey Cake, 148
Oven Boxty Bread, 36
Oven-baked Fadge, 84
oysters
  Beef & Oyster Pie, 280

P

pastry. *see also* puff pastry; shortcrust pastry
  Apple & Almond Tart, 248
  Bakewell Tart, 254
  Chicken Pie with Potato Pastry, 268
  Dingle Pie, 262
  Donegal Pie, 260
  Hot Cross Buns, 490
  Pear & Almond Tart, 238
  Steak & Kidney Pie with Guinness, 266
Peanut Butter Bars, 398
pears, 231

Chocolate & Pear Tart, 454
Pear & Almond Tart, 238
Upside-down Pear Cake, 174
pies (savoury)
   Beef & Oyster Pie, 280
   Cheese & Spinach Pie, 286
   Chicken Pie with Potato Pastry, 268
   Dingle Pie, 262
   Donegal Pie, 260
   Individual Dingle Pies, 284
   Luxury Fish Pie, 278
   Shepherd's Pie, 274
   Steak & Kidney Pie with Guinness, 266
   Steak & Stout Pie, 270
pies (sweet)
   Apple Pie, 206
   Banoffee Pie, 224
   Chocolate Chiffon Pie, 438
   Chocolate Rum Pie, 462
   Fruit Meringue Pie, 226
   Lemon Meringue Pie, 250
   Mince Pies, 476
   Vanilla Rhubarb Pie, 236
Pineapple Upside-down Cake, 140
Plain White Scones, 60
plums
   Fresh Plum Cake, 106
   Upside-down Plum Cake, 104
polenta
   Cornmeal Scones, 78
poppy seeds
   Lemon & Poppy Seed Muffins, 372

porridge oats. *see also* oats
   Apricot Oat Fingers, 394
   Autumn Crumble, 232
   Bakewell Flapjacks, 390
   Crunchy Savoury Oatcakes, 294
   Dark Chocolate Oaties, 300
   Date & Guinness Cake, 158
   Date Fingers, 412
   Gooseberry & Hazelnut Crumble, 246
   Guinness Seaweed Soda Bread, 56
   Iced Coffee Oat Biscuits, 320
   Oat Scones, 68
   Oat Shortbread, 340
   Oaty Fruit & Nut Biscuits, 304
   Raspberry & Coconut Squares, 420
   Spiced Apple & Oat Muffins, 378
   Sweet Oatcakes, 344
   Vanilla Biscuits, 332
Portarlington Golden Biscuits, 308
Porter Cake, 92
Porter Hope Biscuits, 310
pot ovens (bastible), 24–5
potatoes
   baking with, 126–7
   Chicken Pie with Potato Pastry, 268
   Chocolate Potato Cake, 452
   Donegal Pie, 260
   Individual Dingle Pies, 284
   Luxury Fish Pie, 278
   Oven Boxty Bread, 36
   Oven-baked Fadge, 84
   Potato Scones, 70
   Shepherd's Pie, 274
   Spiced Potato Cake, 128
prawns
   Luxury Fish Pie, 278
puff pastry
   Open Apple Tart, 200

Q

Queen Cakes, 346
quiche
   Roasted Vegetable Quiche, 288

R

raisins. *see also* dried fruit
   Barm brack with Whiskey-soaked Raisins, 486
   Boiled Fruit Cake, 136
   Buttermilk Cake, 144
   Chocolate Chip Flapjacks, 402
   Gur Cake, 406
   Irish Tea Cake, 114
   Porter Cake, 92
   Spiced Potato Cake, 128
   Steak & Stout Pie, 270
raspberries, 231
   Chocolate & Raspberry Sandwich Cake, 450
   Lemon & Raspberry Drizzle Cake, 176
   Raspberry & Coconut Squares, 420
redcurrant jelly
   Blueberry & Almond Tart, 218
rhubarb, 230–1
   Rhubarb & Ginger Crumble, 234

Rhubarb Cake, 112
Rhubarb Streusel Cake, 124
Vanilla Rhubarb Pie, 236
rice (baking with), 349
Roasted Vegetable Quiche, 288
Rock Buns, 360
rum
Chocolate Rum Pie, 462
Rye Bread, 42

S
salmon
Salmon & Cream Cheese Tart, 290
Smoked Salmon Tart, 276
scones
Butter Cakes, 82
Buttermilk Scones, 64
Cheddar Cheese Scones, 66
Cherry Scones, 76
Cinnamon Fruit Scones, 74
Cornmeal Scones, 78
Oat & Syrup Scones, 80
Oat Scones, 68
Plain White Scones, 60
Potato Scones, 70
Wholemeal Scones, 62
seaweed
Guinness Seaweed Soda Bread, 56
Seaweed Flan, 282
seeds. *see also* poppy seeds; sunflower seeds
Seed Bread, 30
Seed Cake, 100
semolina
Fruit Slices, 392
Lemon Curd & Almond Tart, 216
sesame seeds
Seed Bread, 30
Shah Biscuits, 324
Shepherd's Pie, 274
shortbread
Almond Shortbread, 336
Coconut Shortbread, 338
Oat Shortbread, 340
Shortbread Fingers, 334
shortcrust pastry
Almond Fingers, 382
Apple Pie, 206
Bacon & Egg Flan, 264
Beef & Oyster Pie, 280
Blueberry & Almond Tart, 218
Caramelised Cherry Tomato & Goat's Cheese Tart, 272
Cheese & Spinach Pie, 286
Chocolate & Pear Tart, 454
Chocolate Chiffon Pie, 438
Chocolate Marmalade Tart, 464
Chocolate Rum Pie, 462
Chocolate Whiskey Mousse Tart, 436
Coconut Fingers, 384
Curd Tart, 194
Currant Squares, 410
Easy Lemon Tart, 198
Fruit Meringue Pie, 226
Golden Syrup Tart, 202
Gooseberry Tart, 244
Gur Cake, 406
Individual Dingle Pies, 284
Jam Tart, 196
Lemon Curd & Almond Tart, 216
Nutty Treacle Tart, 214
Orange & Lemon Star Tart, 220
Roasted Vegetable Quiche, 288
Salmon & Cream Cheese Tart, 290
Seaweed Flan, 282
Smoked Salmon Tart, 276
Steak & Stout Pie, 270
Strawberry Tart, 240
Vanilla Rhubarb Pie, 236
Walnut & Honey Tart, 204
Simple Simnel Cake, 492
Slab Cake, 166
Smoked Salmon Tart, 276
soda bread, 72, 73
Brown Soda Bread, 18
Cheesy Soda Bread, 44
Guinness Seaweed Soda Bread, 56
Kerry Treacle Bread, 54
Oatmeal Soda Bread, 50
Spotted Dog, 20
White Soda Bread, 16
Wholemeal Walnut Bread, 48
Yogurt Soda Bread, 32
soft cheese
Chocolate Cheesecake, 432
soured cream
Guinness Chocolate Cake, 470
Spiced Apple & Oat Muffins, 378
Spiced Buns, 358
Spiced Potato Cake, 128
spinach

Cheese & Spinach Pie, 286
Luxury Fish Pie, 278
Roasted Vegetable Quiche, 288
Smoked Salmon Tart, 276
sponge cakes
  Easter Lemon Sponge, 494
  Victoria Sponge, 96
Spotted Dog, 20
steak
  Steak & Kidney Pie with Guinness, 266
  Steak & Stout Pie, 270
stout. see also Guinness
  baking with, 180
  Porter Cake, 92
  Steak & Stout Pie, 270
strawberries, 231
  Fresh Strawberry Swiss Roll, 170
  Strawberry Tart, 240
streusel
  Ginger & Honey Cheesecake, 228
  Rhubarb Streusel Cake, 124
sultanas. see also dried fruit
  Apple & Cider Cake, 122
  Fresh Plum Cake, 106
  Irish Tea Cake, 114
  Nutty Fruit Slices, 414
  Porter Cake, 92
  Slab Cake, 166
  Spiced Potato Cake, 128
  Whiskey Cake, 116
summer fruit, 230
sunflower seeds
  Rye Bread, 42
  Seed Bread, 30
  Wheaten Bread with Nuts, Seeds & Honey, 58
Sunken Chocolate Cake, 458
Sweet Oatcakes, 344
Swiss rolls
  Chocolate Swiss Roll, 442
  Fresh Strawberry Swiss Roll, 170
  Lemon Swiss Roll, 168

T

tarts
  Apple & Almond Tart, 248
  Apple Charlotte, 208
  Apricot Tart, 222
  Bakewell Tart, 254
  Blueberry & Almond Tart, 218
  Caramelised Cherry Tomato & Goat's Cheese Tart, 272
  Chocolate & Pear Tart, 454
  Chocolate Marmalade Tart, 464
  Chocolate Tart, 440
  Chocolate Whiskey Mousse Tart, 436
  Curd Tart, 194
  Easy Lemon Tart, 198
  Golden Syrup Tart, 202
  Gooseberry Tart, 244
  Jam Tart, 196
  Jam Tarts (small), 354
  Lemon Curd & Almond Tart, 216
  Mincemeat Bakewell Tart, 484
  Nutty Treacle Tart, 214
  Open Apple Tart, 200
  Orange & Lemon Star Tart, 220
  Pear & Almond Tart, 238
  Salmon & Cream Cheese Tart, 290
  Smoked Salmon Tart, 276
  Walnut & Honey Tart, 204
tea
  Irish Tea Cake, 114
tins (baking), 13
tomatoes
  Caramelised Cherry Tomato & Goat's Cheese Tart, 272
  Cheese & Tomato Bread, 38
  Chicken Pie with Potato Pastry, 268
traybakes
  Almond Fingers, 382
  Apple & Blackberry Crumble Squares, 418
  Apple & Walnut Squares, 422
  Apple Fingers, 386
  Apricot Oat Fingers, 394
  Cherry Bakewell Squares, 424
  Chocolate Chip Flapjacks, 402
  Coconut & Walnut Bars, 408
  Coconut Fingers, 384
  Coconut Flapjacks, 416
  Currant Squares, 410
  Date Fingers, 412
  Flapjacks, 388
  Fruit Slices, 392
  Hazelnut Squares, 404
  Mincemeat Crumble Bars, 396
  Nutty Fruit Slices, 414
  Peanut Butter Bars, 398

INDEX

Raspberry & Coconut Squares, 420
treacle
Ginger Cake, 110
Gingerbread, 150
Guinness Seaweed Soda Bread, 56
Hunting Nuts, 316
Kerry Treacle Bread, 54
Oatmeal Bread, 28
Oaty Gingerbread, 152
Rye Bread, 42
Treacle Loaf, 26
Wholemeal Walnut Bread, 48

U

Upside-down Pear Cake, 174
Upside-down Plum Cake, 104

V

vanilla
Magic Vanilla Custard Cake, 172
Vanilla Biscuits, 332
Vanilla Buns, 362
Vanilla Rhubarb Pie, 236
vegetables
Roasted Vegetable Quiche, 288
Very Easy Walnut Loaf, 164
Victoria Sponge, 96

W

walnuts. see also nuts
Apple & Walnut Squares, 422
Banana & Walnut Loaf, 94
Carrot Cake, 138
Chocolate Walnut Loaf, 446
Coconut & Walnut Bars, 408
Coffee & Walnut Cake, 134
Coffee Walnut Macaroons, 328
Date & Walnut Loaf, 160
Iced Coffee Oat Biscuits, 320
Nutty Fruit Slices, 414
Very Easy Walnut Loaf, 164
Walnut & Honey Tart, 204
Walnut Biscuits, 330
Wheaten Bread with Nuts, Seeds & Honey, 58
Wholemeal Walnut Bread, 48
Waterford Blaa Buns, 86
wheat germ
Wholemeal Walnut Bread, 48
Wheaten Bread, 52
Wheaten Bread with Nuts, Seeds & Honey, 58
whiskey
baking with, 180
Barmbrack with Whiskey-soaked Raisins, 486
Chocolate Whiskey Mousse Tart, 436
Christmas Cake, 474
Whiskey Cake, 116
White Soda Bread, 16
wholemeal flour
Brown Bread, 22
Brown Soda Bread, 18
Crunchy Savoury Oatcakes, 294
Fruit Slices, 392
Gooseberry & Hazelnut Crumble, 246
Guinness Seaweed Soda Bread, 56
Nutty Fruit Slices, 414
Oat Scones, 68
Oatmeal Bread, 28
Seed Bread, 30
Treacle Loaf, 26
Wheaten Bread, 52
Wheaten Bread with Nuts, Seeds & Honey, 58
Wholemeal Banana Muffins, 376
Wholemeal Scones, 62
Wholemeal Walnut Bread, 48
Yogurt Soda Bread, 32
Wholemeal Walnut Bread, 48

Y

yogurt
Rye Bread, 42
Wheaten Bread with Nuts, Seeds & Honey, 58
Yogurt & Honey Cake, 148
Yogurt Soda Bread, 32
Yule Log, 480

Conversion charts

See recipes for ingredients weights and measures and for cooking times. Always remember to check that frozen meat and fish are thoroughly defrosted before cooking. Cooking times given may produce different results according to oven type.

Imperial	Metric
1/2 oz	15 g
1 oz	29 g
2 oz	57 g
3 oz	85 g
4 oz	113 g
5 oz	141 g
6 oz	170 g
8 oz	227 g
10 oz	283 g
12 oz	340 g
13 oz	369 g
14 oz	397 g
15 oz	425 g
1 lb	453 g

Fahrenheit	Centigrade
100 °F	37 °C
150 °F	65 °C
200 °F	93 °C
250 °F	121 °C
300 °F	150 °C
325 °F	160 °C
350 °F	180 °C
375 °F	190 °C
400 °F	200 °C
425 °F	220 °C
450 °F	230 °C
500 °F	260 °C
525 °F	274 °C
550 °F	288 °C

Cups	Ounces	Millilitres	Tbsp
8 cup	64 oz	1895 ml	128
6 cup	48 oz	1420 ml	96
5 cup	40 oz	1180 ml	80
4 cup	32 oz	960 ml	64
2 cup	16 oz	500 ml	32
1 cup	8 oz	250 ml	16
3/4 cup	6 oz	177 ml	12
2/3 cup	5 oz	158 ml	11
1/2 cup	4 oz	118 ml	8
3/8 cup	3 oz	90 ml	6
1/3 cup	2.5 oz	79 ml	5.5
1/4 cup	2 oz	59 ml	4
1/8 cup	1 oz	30 ml	3
1/16 cup	1/2 oz	15 ml	1

PICTURE CREDITS

For permission to reproduce copyright photographs, the publisher gratefully acknowledges the following:

1 S/S: Lysenko Andrii
3 S/S: Laura Ken
11 S/S: Jessie EB
12 S/S: Joy Brown
14 S/S: Patryk Kosmider
17 S/S: Janet Moore
19 S/S: Leigh Boardman
21 S/S: Axel Bueckert
23 S/S: Tatuasha
24 Creative Commons
25 National Museum of Ireland
25 National Museum of Ireland
27 Ben Potter
29 S/S: AnjelikaGr
31 S/S: Lucie Peclova
33 S/S: Laura Adamache
35 Ben Potter
37 Ben Potter
39 S/S: Timolina V
41 S/S: Sergii Koval
43 S/S: Svetlana Shashkina
45 Ben Potter
47 S/S: Lokuttara
49 S/S: Alexander Sviridov
51 S/S: Brent Hofacker
53 S/S: Abimages
55 Ben Potter
57 S/S: Bartosz Luczak
59 S/S: Remistudio
61 Ben Potter
63 Ben Potter
65 Ben Potter
67 S/S: Olepeshkina
69 Ben Potter
71 Ben Potter
72 S/S:
75 Ben Potter
77 S/S: David Guyler
79 Ben Potter
81 Ben Potter
83 Ben Potter
85 Ben Potter
87 S/S: Spass
89 S/S: Joerg Beuge
90 S/S: Hugh O'Connor
93 S/S: Joerg Beuge
95 S/S: Thomas M Perkins
97 S/S: Monkey Business Images
99 S/S: Giordano Aita
101 Ben Potter
103 S/S: M Shev
105 S/S: 18042011
107 S/S: Rimma Bondarenko
109 S/S: Larik Malasha
111 S/S: Pitamaha
113 S/S: Kostrez
115 S/S: A rarn
117 S/S: D Pimborough
119 S/S: AG Creations
121 S/S: Bartosz Luczak
123 S/S: SherSor
125 S/S: Sham Clicks
126 S/S: New Africa
129 Ben Potter
131 S/S: Istetiana
133 Ben Potter
135 S/S: SmudgeChris
137 S/S: Joerg Beuge
139 S/S: Ann Shepulova
141 S/S: Lesya Dolyuk
143 Ben Potter
145 S/S: locrifa
147 S/S: CookieNim
149 S/S: Sergii Koval
151 S/S: Donna Gibbs-Williams
153 S/S: Ffolas
155 S/S: Angelika Heine
157 S/S: Zygonema
159 S/S: Trending Now
161 S/S: Richard Johnson
163 S/S: M Shev
165 S/S: Creativeye
167 S/S: Jamie Rogers
169 S/S: Shaiith
171 S/S: Istetiana
173 S/S: Barth Fotografie
175 S/S: Michael C Gray
177 S/S: Debra Anderson
179 S/S: VM
180 S/S: New Africa
183 S/S: AG Creations
185 S/S: IngridHS
187 S/S: Anna Ustynnikova
189 S/S: Fiery Phoenix
191 S/S: Enrique Madge
192 S/S: Michalakis Palis
195 S/S: Anna Shepulova
197 S/S: Alexey Borodin
199 S/S: HL Photo
201 S/S: Tetiana Shumbasova
203 S/S: Monkey Business Images
205 S/S: Natkinzu
207 S/S: Charles Brutlag
209 S/S: MikroKon
211 S/S: Viennetta
213 S/S: Claire Fraser Photography
215 Ben Potter
217 S/S: Maria Kovaleva
219 Ben Potter
221 Ben Potter
223 S/S: Bonchan
225 S/S: Jantanee Boonkhaw
227 S/S: Fotologija
229 Ben Potter
230 S/S: Amelia NF
233 Ben Potter
235 Ben Potter
237 S/S: Amy Kerkemeyer
239 S/S: MSPhotographic
241 S/S: Gresei
243 S/S: YukikaeB
245 S/S: Shmeliova Natalia
247 S/S: M Shev
249 Ben Potter
251 S/S: Foodio
253 S/S: Yulia-Bogdanova
255 S/S: Monkey Business Images
257 Ben Potter
258 S/S: Mikemike
261 Ben Potter
263 Ben Potter
265 S/S: Margouillat Photo
267 S/S: Elzbieta Sekowska
269 Ben Potter
271 S/S: Beef Ie
273 S/S: Nataliia Doroshenko
275 S/S: Farbled
277 S/S: Olaf Speier
279 S/S: Inkru
281 Ben Potter
283 Ben Potter
285 S/S: Rawpixel
287 S/S: Esin Deniz
289 S/S: Jacek Chabraszewski
291 S/S: Torri Photo
292 S/S: Martin Hesketh
295 S/S: Kiian Oksana
297 S/S: Marie C Fields
299 S/S: AS Food Studio
301 S/S: P-fotography
303 S/S: M Shev
305 S/S: CookieNim
307 S/S: Dream
309 S/S: Moving Moment
311 S/S: CatchaSnap
313 S/S: BBA Photography
315 S/S: Viktory Panchenko
317 Ben Potter
319 S/S: Dina Photo Stories
321 Ben Potter
323 Ben Potter
325 S/S: Brent Hofacker
327 S/S: Tobik
329 S/S: Elena Veselova V
331 Shutterstock
333 Ben Potter
335 Ben Potter
337 S/S: Everydayplus
339 S/S: StockphotoVideo
341 S/S: Photogal
343 Ben Potter
345 S/S: Shtukicrew
347 S/S: Kitch Bain
348 S/S: B113
351 S/S: M Shev
353 Ben Potter
355 Ben Potter
357 S/S: Denis Film
359 Ben Potter
361 S/S: D Pimborough
363 S/S: Olga Kapitula
365 S/S: Nungning
367 S/S: Dream
369 S/S: Zoyas
371 S/S: Sergii Koval
373 S/S: Irina Goleva
375 S/S: Comaniciu Dan
377 S/S: M Shev
379 S/S: Allison McAdams
380 S/S: Marcela Mul
383 S/S: Richard M Lee
385 Ben Potter
387 Ben Potter
389 S/S: Merc
391 Ben Potter
393 Ben Potter
395 Ben Potter
397 Ben Potter
399 Ben Potter
401 S/S: Adam Edwards
403 S/S: M Shev
405 Ben Potter
407 Ben Potter
409 Ben Potter
411 Ben Potter
413 Ben Potter
415 Ben Potter
417 S/S: CKP
419 S/S: Ira Pavlina
421 Ben Potter
423 S/S: Sergii Koval
425 S/S: Go My Media
426 S/S: STLJB
429 Ben Potter
431 Ben Potter
433 S/S: Anastasia Sitnikova
435 S/S: Pavel Ivashechkin
437 Ben Potter
439 S/S: Maxwell Photography
441 S/S: Sergii Koval
443 S/S: Lesya Dolyuk
445 Shutterstock
447 S/S: Oksana Mizina
449 S/S: Saprunova Marina
451 Ben Potter
453 Ben Potter
455 S/S: Studiogi
457 S/S: Zigzag Mountain Art
459 S/S: Irina Meliukh
461 Ben Potter
463 S/S: Nest 557
465 S/S: V Nelea
467 S/S: AL Talya
469 S/S: UAphoto
471 S/S: XDP
472 S/S: Marti B Stock
475 S/S: Joerg Beuge
477 S/S: Magdanatka
479 S/S: Bitt
481 S/S: Lilyana Vynogradova
483 S/S: Kati Molin
485 S/S: Nelea
487 S/S: Monkey Business Images
489 Ben Potter
491 S/S: MS Photographic
493 S/S: Zoryanchik
495 Ben Potter
497 S/S: Sarah Marchant

S/S: Shutterstock
Some recipes in this book were previously published in *The Irish Granny's Pocket Bread and Baking Book*, *The Pocket Irish Pub Cookbook*, *Essential Farmhouse Recipes* and *Granny's Farmhouse Kitchen*.
T161/12-25/01/PRC-ZT